普通高等教育"十一五"国家级规划教材

总主编 胡壮麟

北京市高等教育精品教材立项项目

英语综合教程

（修订版）

第 2 册

（学生用书）

主　编　刘世铸　程幼强
副主编　李正鸿　常子霞
编　者　（以姓氏笔画排序）
　　　　王　申　王　祎　任　悦　刘世铸　张　丽　李媛霞
　　　　李　强　李　霞　陈　琛　周　薇　庞双子　祝　然
　　　　夏　谨　徐荣娟　程洪梅　靳　锁

北京大学出版社
PEKING UNIVERSITY PRESS

图书在版编目(CIP)数据

英语综合教程. 第 2 册(学生用书)/刘世铸，程幼强主编. —2 版. —北京：北京大学出版社，2012.8
(21 世纪英语专业系列教材)
ISBN 978-7-301-21114-4

Ⅰ. 英… Ⅱ. ①刘…②程… Ⅲ. 英语-高等学校-教材 Ⅳ. H31

中国版本图书馆 CIP 数据核字(2012)第 189549 号

书　　　名：英语综合教程(修订版)第 2 册(学生用书)
著作责任者：刘世铸　程幼强　主编
总　策　划：张　冰
责　任　编　辑：孙　莹
标　准　书　号：ISBN 978-7-301-21114-4/H·3114
出　版　发　行：北京大学出版社
地　　　址：北京市海淀区成府路 205 号　100871
网　　　址：http://www.pup.cn
电　　　话：邮购部 62752015　发行部 62750672　编辑部 62754382　出版部 62754962
电子邮箱：编辑部 pupwaiwen@pup.cn　总编室 zpup@pup.cn
印　刷　者：北京虎彩文化传播有限公司
经　销　者：新华书店
　　　　　　787 毫米×1092 毫米　16 开本　13.5 印张　365 千字
　　　　　　2007 年 9 月第 1 版
　　　　　　2012 年 8 月第 2 版　2023 年 12 月第 4 次印刷
定　　　价：35.00 元

未经许可，不得以任何方式复制或抄袭本书之部分或全部内容。
版权所有，侵权必究　　举报电话：010-62752024
　　　　　　　　　　　　电子邮箱：fd@pup.cn

《21世纪英语专业系列教材》编写委员会

（以姓氏笔画排序）

王立非	王守仁	王克非
王俊菊	文秋芳	石　坚
申　丹	朱　刚	仲伟合
刘世生	刘意青	殷企平
孙有中	李　力	李正栓
张旭春	张庆宗	张绍杰
杨俊峰	陈法春	金　莉
封一函	胡壮麟	查明建
袁洪庚	桂诗春	黄国文
梅德明	董洪川	蒋洪新
程幼强	程朝翔	虞建华

总 序

  北京大学出版社自2005年以来已出版"语言与应用语言学知识系列读本"多种，为了配合第十一个五年计划，现又策划陆续出版"21世纪英语专业系列教材"。这个重大举措势必受到英语专业广大教师和学生的欢迎。

  作为英语教师，最让人揪心的莫过于听人说英语不是一个专业，只是一个工具。说这些话的领导和教师的用心是好的，为英语专业的毕业生将来找工作着想，因此要为英语专业的学生多多开设诸如新闻、法律、国际、经济、旅游等其他专业的课程。但事与愿违，英语专业的教师们很快发现，学生投入英语学习的时间少了，掌握英语专业课程知识甚微，即使对四个技能的掌握并不比大学英语学生高明多少，而那个所谓的第二专业在有关专家的眼中只是学到些皮毛而已。

  英语专业的路在何方？有没有其他路可走？这是需要我们英语专业教师思索的问题。中央领导关于创新是一个民族的灵魂和要培养创新人才等的指示精神，让我们在层层迷雾中找到了航向。显然，培养学生具有自主学习能力和能进行创造性思维是我们更为重要的战略目标，使英语专业的人才更能适应21世纪的需要，迎接21世纪的挑战。

  如今，北京大学出版社外语编辑部的领导和编辑同志们，也从教材出版的视角探索英语专业的教材问题，从而为贯彻英语专业教学大纲做些有益的工作，为教师们开设大纲中所规定的必修、选修课程提供各种教材。他们把英语专业教材的出版看作是第十一个五年计划期间组织出版"十一五"国家重点出版规划项目——《面向新世纪的立体化网络化英语学科建设丛书》的重要组成部分。这套系列教材要体现新世纪英语教学的自主化、协作化、模块化和超文本化，结合外语教材的具体情况，既要解决语言、教学内容、教学方法和教育技术的时代化，也要坚持弘扬以爱国主义为核心的民族精神。因此，今天北京大学出版社在大力提倡专业英语教学改革的基础上，编辑出版各种语言、文学、文化课程的教材，以培养具有创新性思维、具有实际工作能力的学生，充分体现了时代精神。

  北京大学出版社的远见卓识，也反映了英语专业广大师生盼望已久的心愿。由北京大学等全国几十所院校具体组织力量，积极编写相关教材。这就是说，这套教材是由一些高等院校有水平、有经验的第一线教师们制定编写大纲，反复讨论，特别是考虑到在不同层次、不同背景学校之间取得平衡，避免了先前的教材或偏难或偏易的弊病。与此同时，一批知名专家教授参与策划和教材审定工作，保证了教材质量。

  当然，这套系列教材出版只是初步实现了出版社和编者们的预期目标。为了获得更大效果，希望使用本系列教材的教师和同学不吝指教，及时将意见反馈给我们，使教材更加完善。

  航道已经开通，我们有决心乘风破浪，奋勇前进！

胡壮麟

北京大学蓝旗营

2007年2月

再版前言

《英语综合教程》是根据《高等学校英语专业英语教学大纲》编写,致力于培养学生具有扎实的语言基本功、宽广的知识面、一定的相关专业知识、较强的能力和较高的人文素质。本套教材为基础英语课程教材,共四册,可供高等院校英语专业一二年级学生使用。本册为第二册,适用于一年级第二学期。

本册教材共分12个单元,每个单元由Text A和Text B两篇课文、辅学资料及相关的练习构成。全书24篇课文均选自英语原文文本,根据学生现阶段的语言能力和水平,编者对其中语言难度过大的部分进行了必要的删改。

本册教材的选题旨在帮助学生树立正直的人生态度。注意由浅入深、难易结合。全书24篇课文分别涉及家庭亲情、生活准则、道德伦理、民生关爱、文化教育、哲学宗教、古典艺术等多个主题,在夯实学生语言基本功,拓展其知识面的同时,提高英语专业学生的人文素养,健康、向上,具有代表性。课文收录了有关乔达摩·悉达多、苏格拉底和米开朗基罗等历史巨人的生平,旨在为学生树立高尚、坚韧的人生楷模,有助于唤起学生对正义、良知的深入思索。

本册教材的每一单元由Unit Goals, Before Reading, Text A, Better Know More, Check Your Understanding, A Sip of Word Formation, You'd Like to Be, Text B, Comprehension Questions, Writing Practice, Further Study共十一个部分组成:

☞ 每个单元以Unit Goals开篇,明确指出该单元的学习重点和难点,让教与学均做到目的清晰,增强学生的学习意识。

☞ 每个单元设有特色的预热练习,引导学生进入单元学习。Hands-on Activities and Brainstorming以文化补充为目的使学生在学习本单元前对背景知识等有一个初步了解,并培养学生的动手能力和表达能力。A Glimpse at Words and Expressions展示Text A课文中的部分重点词语,让学生在学习课文之前能够了解课文的语言特色,并培养学生的语感。

☞ Better Know More就Text A涉及的人物、文化背景和专有名词进行必要的解释和说明。

☞ Check Your Understanding 以口头形式考查学生对 Text A 内容的理解。这一部分练习旨在鼓励学生开口,强化其语用能力和对语法的感知能力。

☞ A Sip of Phonetics 分阶段向学生介绍语音知识,训练学生正确发音。

☞ You'd Like to Be 为 Text A 的练习,共分六个部分,着重操练课文中的语言点,培养学生在语篇和语境中学习语言的能力。其中 A Skilled Text Weaver 侧重词汇练习;A Sharp Interpreter 检验学生对课文关键句和难句的理解;A Solid Sentence Constructor 训练学生对课文中重点句型和新词语的运用能力;A Superb Bilingualist 是汉译英的练习。练习的标题一气呵成,正是培养英语专业学生的目的所在。

☞ Comprehension Questions 鼓励学生对课文深入思考并展开讨论。

☞ Writing Practice 围绕 Text B 以撰写课文梗概的方式,训练学生的短文写作能力。这一部分在不同的单元,设计有所不同。1—5 单元的练习较简单,先向学生提供一系列有关课文内容的引导性问题,同时提供关键词,然后要求学生将问题答案连接起来,稍作处理即成为 Text B 的梗概。在 6—9 单元,编者有意取消了关键词,仅保留引导性问题,要求学生通过熟读课文独立找到答案,进而形成课文梗概。在 11—12 单元,编者要求学生就 Text B 的内容自主提问,然后自行回答,并独立形成撰写课文梗概的思路。该写作练习由易到难,逐步培养学生的阅读能力和逻辑思维能力。

☞ Further Study 对学有余力的学生进行宽泛知识的推介,例如相关电影及网站,使学生可以深入学习。

本教材由天津外国语学院和南开大学共同编写。程幼强负责教材的设计和创意,并与李正鸿、王世庆、魏巍、李四清分担各个单元的选材和编写。在编写过程中,总主编胡壮麟教授给予了专业指导,提出了很多宝贵的建议。在此全体编者向胡壮麟教授表示衷心的感谢!外籍专家 Michael DeRabo, Joshua Parker 审读了本书稿,我们也一并在此表示谢意。

本教材同时配有教师用书(电子版),为教师提供讲解教材所需的教学思路、必要的补充材料和练习参考答案。本册教材如有疏漏和不完善之处,恳请广大读者批评指正。

编者

2011 年 1 月

Content

目录

Unit 1	Fairy Tale 1
	Text A Beauty and the Beast / 2
	Text B Beauty and the Beast / 12

Unit 2	Friendship 17
	Text A The Value of Friendship / 18
	Text B All Un-Alone in the City / 26

Unit 3	Money and Happiness 32
	Text A The Real Truth of Money / 33
	Text B Happiness / 42

Unit 4	Education 48
	Text A National Wealth Tax to Fund Education? / 49
	Text B Are Single-Sex Classrooms Legal? / 58

Unit 5	Biography 64
	Text A Ernest Hemingway / 65
	Text B Joseph Heller / 76

Unit 6	Reflections on Life 83
	Text A Think inside the Square to Keep Those Love Fires Burning / 84
	Text B Learn How to Face Difficulty / 91

Unit 7	Renowned Universities 95
	Text A Oxford University / 96
	Text B What Is the Wisconsin Idea? / 105

Unit 8 Poverty 110

Text A   Child Labour Rooted in Africa's Poverty / 111
Text B   Understanding Poverty / 118

Unit 9 Tragedy 122

Text A   Sophocles and *Oedipus Rex* / 123
Text B   *Oedipus Rex* / 135

Unit 10 Reflections on Wars 142

Text A   The Terrorist in the Mirror / 143
Text B   I Express My Shame / 152

Unit 11 Honesty 159

Text A   Honesty Is the Best Policy / 160
Text B   To Lie or Not to Lie? / 171

Unit 12 Ambition 177

Text A   Ambition: Why Some People Are Most Likely to Succeed / 178
Text B   The Roots of My Ambition / 190

生词总表 Vocabulary 197

Unit 1

Fairy Tale

Unit Goals

Upon completing the texts in this unit, students should be able to:
- identify some of the typical characteristics of a fairy tale, such as character, setting and plot;
- develop the ability to read narratives critically;
- use negative prefixes correctly to form new words.

Before Reading

Hands-on Activities and Brainstorming

1. Go to your university library and read fairy tale and folktale collections or visit Dr. A.L. Ashiliman's website of Folklore and Mythology Electronic Texts at http://www.pitt.edu/~dash/type0510a.html to find out the differences between fairy tales and folktales. The following questions may help you get a better understanding of the fairy tale:
   (1) What is a fairy tale?
   (2) What are the special features of fairy tales?
   (3) What kind of character, setting and plot is expected in fairy tales?
   (4) Why is fairy tale a preferred form of storytelling for people everywhere?
   (5) What are the common themes of fairy tales?
2. Beauty falls into two kinds: physical beauty and inner beauty. Societies differ in their judgments on beauty. Beauty standards tend to change with time. What do you say to these statements? Do you think there is a universal beauty standard that every culture can agree on? You are encouraged to make a presentation on it.

A Glimpse at Words and Expressions

Please read the following sentences. Pay attention to the underlined part in each sentence and to how it is used in the sentence and then decide on its meaning. Write down the meaning in the brackets.

1. They gave themselves ridiculous airs, and would not   (   )
   keep company with any but persons of quality.
2. This news had liked to have turned the heads of the two   (   )
   eldest daughters, who immediately flattered themselves
   with the hopes of returning to town.
3. ...they went to law with him about the merchandise, ...   (   )
4. If your daughter should refuse to die in your stead, you   (   )
   will return within three months.
5. Will you give me leave to see you sup?   (   )
6. "...I shall always esteem you as a friend, endeavor to be   (   )
   satisfied with this."
7. ...and I was so afflicted for having lost you, that I resolved   (   )
   to starve myself...
8. A wicked fairy had condemned him to remain under that   (   )
   shape until a beautiful virgin should consent to marry him.

Text A

Beauty and the Beast

By Jeanne-Marie Le Prince de Beaumont
(Abridged and Edited)

There was once a very rich merchant, who had six children, three sons, and three daughters. His daughters were extremely handsome, especially the youngest. When she was little everybody admired her, and called her "The little Beauty."

The two eldest had a great deal of pride, because they were rich. They gave themselves
5 ridiculous airs, and would not keep company with any but persons of quality. They went out every day to parties of pleasure, plays, concerts, and so forth, and they laughed at their youngest sister, because she spent the greatest part of her time in reading good books.

All at once the merchant lost his whole fortune, excepting a small country house at a great distance from town, and told his children with tears in his eyes, they must go there and
10 work for their living.

The family had lived about a year in retirement, when the merchant received a letter with an account that a vessel, on board of which he had effects, was safely arrived. This news had liked to have turned the heads
15 of the two eldest daughters, who immediately flattered themselves with the hopes of returning to town, for they were quite weary of a country life; and when they saw their father ready to set out, they begged

---

handsome /ˈhænsəm/ *adj.* [of women] attractive, with large strong features rather than small delicate ones
effects /əˈfekts/ *n.* movable belongings; goods
flatter (oneself) *v.* to choose to believe sth. good about oneself and one's abilities, especially when other people do not share this opinion
weary /ˈwɪəri/ *adj.* no longer interested in or enthusiastic about sth.

20 of him to buy them new gowns, headdresses, ribbons, and all manner of trifles; but Beauty asked for nothing but a rose. The good man went on his journey, but when he came there, they went to law with him about the merchandise, and after a great deal of trouble and pains to no purpose, he came back as poor as before.

25 He was within thirty miles of his own house, thinking on the pleasure he should have in seeing his children again, when going through a large forest he lost himself. He began to apprehend being either starved to death with cold and hunger, or else devoured by the wolves. All of a sudden, he saw a light at some distance. The
30 merchant returned God thanks for this happy discovery, and hastened to the place, but was greatly surprised at not meeting with anyone in the outer courts of a castle.

He waited a considerable time, until it struck eleven, and still nobody came. At last he was so hungry that he could stay no longer, but took a chicken, and ate it in two mouthfuls. As he was very much fatigued, and it was past midnight, he concluded it was best to shut the
35 door, and go to bed.

It was 10 the next morning before the merchant waked, and as he was going to rise he was astonished to see a good suit of clothes in the room of his own. He looked through a window, but instead of snow saw the most delightful arbors, interwoven with the most beautiful flowers that were ever beheld.

40 The good man drank his chocolate, and then went to look for his horse, but passing through an arbor of roses he remembered Beauty's request to him, and gathered a branch on which were several; immediately he heard a great noise, and saw such a frightful Beast coming towards him, that he was ready to faint away.

"You are very ungrateful," said the Beast to him, in a terrible voice; "I have saved your
45 life by receiving you into my castle, and, in return, you steal my roses, which I value beyond anything in the universe, but you shall die for it; I give you but a quarter of an hour to prepare yourself, and say your prayers."

The merchant fell on his knees, and lifted up both his hands, "My lord," said he, "I beseech you to forgive me, indeed I had no intention to offend in gathering a rose for one of
50 my daughters, who desired me to bring her one."

"My name is not My Lord," replied the monster, "but Beast; I don't love compliments. But you say you have got daughters. I will forgive you, on condition that one of them
55 come willingly, and suffer for you. If your daughter should refuse to die in your stead, you will return within three months."

The merchant had no mind to sacrifice his daughters to the ugly monster, but he
60 thought, in obtaining this respite, he should have the satisfaction of seeing them once more, so he promised he would return, and the Beast told him he might set out when he

gown /gaʊn/ n. a woman's dress, especially a long one for special occasions
apprehend /ˌæprɪˈhend/ v. [old-fashioned] to understand or recognize sth.
devour /dɪˈvaʊr/ v. to eat all of sth. quickly
hasten /ˈheɪsən/ v. to go or move somewhere quickly
interweave /ˌɪntəˈwiːv/ v. to twist together two or more pieces of thread, wool, etc.
behold /bɪˈhəʊld/ v. [old use or literary] to look at or see sb./sth.
beseech /bɪˈsiːtʃ/ v. [formal] to ask sb. for sth. in an anxious way because one wants or needs it very much
respite /ˈrespɪt/ n. a short delay allowed before sth. difficult or unpleasant must be done

pleased, "but," added he, "you shall not depart empty
handed; go back to the room where you lay, and you will
see a great empty chest; fill it with whatever you like best,
and I will send it to your home."

"Well," said the good man to himself, "if I must die,
I shall have the comfort, at least, of leaving something to
my poor children." He returned to the bedchamber, and
finding a great quantity of broad pieces of gold, he filled
the great chest, and in a few hours the good man was at
home.

His children came round him, but instead of
receiving their embraces with pleasure, he looked on them,
and holding up the branch he had in his hands, he burst into
tears.

On giving Beauty the rose, her father could not help but
tell her what had happened. The brothers offered to slay the
Beast but the father knew that they would die in the process.
Beauty insisted on taking her father's place, and so she
returned with him to the Beast's palace where he reluctantly
left her.

As soon as her father was gone, Beauty sat down in the
great hall, and fell a crying likewise; but as she was mistress
of a great deal of resolution, she recommended herself to
God, and resolved not to be uneasy the little time she had to
live; for she firmly believed Beast would eat her up that night.

But at night, as she was going to sit down to supper, she heard the noise Beast made, and could not help being sadly terrified. "Beauty," said the monster, "will you give me leave to see you sup?"

"That is as you please," answered Beauty trembling.

"No," replied the Beast, "you alone are mistress here; you need only bid me gone, if my presence is troublesome, and I will immediately withdraw. But, tell me, do not you think me very ugly?"

"That is true," said Beauty, "for I cannot tell a lie, but I believe you are very good natured."

"Yes, yes," said the Beast, "my heart is good, but still I am a monster."

"Among mankind," said Beauty, "there are many that deserve that name more than you, and I prefer you, just as you are, to those, who, under a human form, hide a treacherous, corrupt, and ungrateful heart."

Beauty spent three months very contentedly in the palace. Every evening Beast paid her a visit, and talked to her, during supper, very rationally, with plain

bedchamber /ˈbedˌtʃembə/ *n.* [old use] a bedroom
slay /sleɪ/ *v.* [old-fashioned or literary] to kill sb./sth. in a war or a fight
mistress /ˈmɪstrɪs/ *n.* [formal] a woman who is in a position of authority or control, or who is highly skilled in sth.; (in the past) the female head of a house
bid /bɪd/ *v.* [old use or literary] to tell sb. to do sth.
treacherous /ˈtretʃərəs/ *adj.* that cannot be trusted; intending to harm sb.

good common sense, but never with what the world calls wit; and Beauty daily
110 discovered some valuable qualifications in the monster, and seeing him often had so accustomed her to his deformity, that, far from dreading the time of his visit, she would often look on her watch to see when
115 it would be nine, for the Beast never missed coming at that hour. There was but one thing that gave Beauty any concern, which was, that every night, before she went to bed, the monster always asked her, if she
120 would be his wife. One day she said to him, "Beast, you make me very uneasy, I wish I could consent to marry you, but I am too sincere to make you believe that will ever happen; I shall always esteem you as a friend, endeavor to be satisfied with this."
125 "I must," said the Beast, "for, alas! I know too well my own misfortune, but then I love you with the tenderest affection. However, I ought to think myself happy, that you will stay here; promise me never to leave me."

> deformity /dɪˈfɔːmɪti/ n. a condition in which a part of the body is not the normal shape because of injury, illness or because it has grown wrongly
> dread /drɛd/ v. to be very afraid of sth.
> consent /kənˈsɛnt/ v. to agree to sth. or give one's permission for sth.
> esteem /ɪˈstiːm/ v. [old-fashioned, formal] to think of sb./sth. in a particular way
> blush /blʌʃ/ v. to be embarrassed about sth.
> pine /paɪn/ v. to become very sad and weak because one misses sb./sth. very much
> fret /frɛt/ v. to be worried or unhappy and not able to relax
> assent /əˈsɛnt/ v. [formal] to agree to a request, an idea or a suggestion
> afflict /əˈflɪkt/ v. [formal] to affect sb./sth. in an unpleasant or harmful way

130

135

Beauty blushed at these words; she had seen in her glass, that her father had pined himself sick for the loss of her, and she longed to see him again. "I could," answered she, "indeed, promise never to leave you entirely, but I have so great a desire to see my father, that I shall fret to death, if you refuse me that satisfaction."

"I had rather die myself," said the monster, "than give you the least uneasiness. I will send you to your father, you shall remain with him, and poor Beast will die with grief."

"No," said Beauty, weeping, "I love you too well to be the cause of your death. I give
140 you my promise to return in a week. You have shown me that my sisters are married, and my brothers gone to the army; only let me stay a week with my father, as he is alone." The Beast assented on the condition that she return in seven days, lest he die.

The next morning she was at home. Her father was overjoyed to see her, but the sisters were jealous of Beauty, her newly found happiness and material comfort with the Beast.
145 They persuaded Beauty to stay longer, which she did, but on the tenth night she dreamed of the Beast who was dying. She threw herself upon him without any dread, and finding his heart beat still, she fetched some water from the canal, and poured it on his head. Beast opened his eyes, and said to Beauty, "You forgot your promise, and I was so afflicted for having lost you, that I resolved to starve myself, but since I have the happiness of seeing you
150 once more, I die satisfied."

"No, dear Beast," said Beauty, "you must not die. Live to be my husband; from this

moment I give you my hand, and swear to be none but yours. Alas! I thought I had only a friendship for you, but the grief I now feel convinces me, that I cannot live without you." Beauty scarcely had pronounced these words, when she saw the palace sparkle with light; and fireworks, instruments of music; everything seemed to give notice of some great event. But nothing could fix her attention; she turned to her dear Beast, for whom she trembled with fear; but how great was her surprise! Beast was disappeared, and she saw, at her feet, one of the loveliest princes that eye ever beheld; who returned her thanks for having put an end to the charm, under which he had so long resembled a Beast.

charm /tʃɑrm/ *n.* an act or words believed to have magic power
resemble /rɪˈzɛmbəl/ *v.* to look like or be similar to another person or thing

A wicked fairy had condemned him to remain under that shape until a beautiful virgin should consent to marry him. Beauty, agreeably surprised, gave the charming prince her hand to rise; they went together into the castle, and Beauty was overjoyed to find, in the great hall, her father and his whole family.

Better Know More

1. Beauty and the Beast

Beauty and the Beast (French: *La Belle et la Bete*) is a traditional fairy tale across the world. The first version was published in 1740. The best-known version, published in 1756, was written by Jeanne-Marie Le Prince de Beaumont. An English translation appeared in 1757. *Beauty and the Beast* has been notably adapted for prose, stage, screen, and television over the years. It has perhaps gained recent fame with the retelling in the 1991 Disney animation.

2. Jeanne-Marie Le Prince de Beaumont (1711–1780)

Jeanne-Marie Le Prince de Beaumont was a French novelist. She was born into a large family that could not provide her with a dowry sizable enough for her to enter into an advantageous marriage. Her first marriage lasted for two years and was annulled in 1745. Three years later she moved to England and worked as a governess to the children of the Prince of Wales. It was then that she began to publish educational and moral stories and poems for children, the most famous of which is the revised *Beauty and the Beast*. Beaumont's version of the fairy tale has proven to be the most popular source for adaptations.

Check Your Understanding

Please answer the following questions based on what you have learnt in the text.

1. What was the difference between Beauty and her sisters?
2. Why did the old merchant move his family to the countryside?
3. What was the reaction of the two eldest daughters when they heard that the ship had safely arrived?
4. Why did the Beast think the old merchant was ungrateful?
5. On what conditions would the Beast forgive the old merchant?
6. Why did the Beast agree to send Beauty home?
7. Why did Beauty finally consent to marry the Beast?

A Sip of Word Formation

A great part of English words are formed through affixation. Affixation is generally defined as the formation of words by adding word forming or derivational affixes to stems. This process is also known as derivation, for new words created in this way are derived from old forms. The words formed in this way are called derivatives. According to the positions, which affixes occupy in words, affixation falls into two subclasses: prefixation and suffixation.

Prefixation is a way of forming new words by adding prefixes to stems. Usually, prefixes do not change the part of speech of a word. Their chief function is to modify its meaning, although there are exceptions. Prefixes can be divided, based on their meanings, into: negative prefixes, reversative prefixes, pejorative prefixes, prefixes of degree or size, locative prefixes, prefixes of time and order, number prefixes and miscellaneous prefixes.

Negative Prefixes

Dis-, *un-*, *in-*, and *non-* are negative prefixes.
1. The prefix *dis-* is usually added to verbs (e.g. *dislike, disband*). It means "opposite feeling" or "opposite action".
2. *Un-* is used to negate simple and derived adjectives (e.g. *uncomplicated, unhappy, unsuccessful,* and *unreadable*). Adjectival *un-* derivatives usually express contraries, especially with simple bases.
3. *In-* is often used for many adjectives of Latin origin, also those ending in *-ible* (e.g. *inedible, invisible*). The variations of *in-* are listed as follows:

Prefixes + initial consonant of the attached root	Words (adj.)	Meaning
il + l	illogical	not logical
il + l	illiberal	not liberal
im + m	immature	not mature
im + p	impartial	not partial
ir + r	irresistible	not resistible
ir + r	irresolute	not resolute

It is also important to distinguish the meaning of the prefix *il*-, *im*-, *ir*-, or *in*- from those carrying the meaning "in, into, on" which forms a verb.

Prefixes + initial consonant of the attached root	Words (v.)	Meaning
il + l	illuminate	to throw light on
im + m	immigrate	to enter and settle in a country to which one is not native
im + p	import	to bring or carry in from a foreign source
ir + r	irradiate	to throw rays of light on
in + other consonants	inbreathe	to breathe in; inhale

This prefix *non*- can be attached to adjectives and has the meaning of "not X" (e.g. *noncombustible*). In contrast to *un*- and *in*-, negation with *non*- does not carry evaluative force, as can be seen from the pairs unscientific vs. nonscientific. Furthermore, *non*- primarily forms contradictory and complementary opposites. Nouns prefixed with *non*- can either mean "absence of X" or "not having the character of X" (e.g. *nonprofit*, *nonstop*).

Build Your Vocabulary

For each of the following sentences, a word is provided in the brackets. Use the appropriate form of the word to fill in the blank in the sentence, so that the sentence is logical and grammatical.

1. Her insusceptibility did not at first _____ suitors; but several years later, they were

tired of their quest for love. (courage)
2. Wearing shorts and sleeveless T-shirts to church is completely _____. (appropriate)
3. In order to avoid bringing _____ to his family, he refused to collaborate with the enemy. (honor)
4. Jack London writes in *Michael, Brother of Jerry*, "Very early in my life, possibly because of the _____ curiosity that was born in me, I came to dislike the performances of trained animals." (satiate)
5. _____ communication is usually understood as the process of communication through wordless message, e.g., gesture, facial expression and eye contact, etc. (verbal)
6. If both the union and the board of directors are _____, a strike will be inevitable. (compromise)
7. _____ love means showing love to a person regardless of his qualities, beliefs or actions. (condition)
8. Gandhi is a strong advocate of _____, which is essential to a culture of peace. (violence)

You'd Like to Be

A Skilled Text Weaver

Fill in the blanks with the words you have learnt in this text, one word for each blank. You are advised to read the text carefully until you have become very familiar with it before starting to work on this task.

Shrek, a green ogre living peacefully in a swamp, finds his life disrupted when fairytale creatures are forced into the swamp by the _____ Lord Farrquaad who considers himself to be the king. With the _____ of the very loud and loquacious Donkey, Shrek leaves the swamp to ask Farrquaaad to return the privacy of the swamp.

Meanwhile, in his castle of Duloc, Magic Mirror reveals to Farrquaad that he can become a real king by marrying a princess. After some reflection Farrquaad chooses the _____ Fiona, who is imprisoned in a castle, to be his wife.

When Shrek and Donkey arrive at Farrquaad's palace and make known their request, Farrquadd _____ to it on _____ that they rescue Fiona from the castle. Though the castle is guarded by a fire-breathing dragon who somehow takes a fancy to Donkey, they succeed in rescuing Fiona. Shrek's ogrely _____ at first disappoints Fiona who has always dreamed of being rescued by Prince Charming. However, despite their differences, Shrek and Fiona grow fond of each other on the way back. They fall in love. Still Shrek has to give Fiona back to Farrquaad to honor his promise.

Shrek returns to the now-vacated swamp alone. He is so _____ by the thought of losing Fiona that he _____ to get her back. Shrek and Donkey _____ to the castle and interrupt the ongoing wedding. Surprisingly, Fiona turns into an ogre in front of everybody. Disgusted at her ugliness, Farrquaad _____ her imprisoned. Dragon bursts in and _____ him. Though Fiona is a total ogre now, Shrek believes she is still the most beautiful princess he has ever _____. Back to the swamp, they get married and live happily ever since.

A Sharp Interpreter

Please paraphrase the following sentences. Change the sentence structure wherever necessary.

1. They gave themselves ridiculous airs, and would not keep company with any but persons of quality.
2. This news had liked to have turned the heads of the two eldest daughters, who immediately flattered themselves with the hopes of returning to town.
3. ... but as she was mistress of a great deal of resolution, she recommended herself to God, and resolved not to be uneasy the little time she had to live; ...
4. "Among mankind," says Beauty, "there are many that deserve that name more than you, and I prefer you, just as you are, to those, who, under a human form, hide a treacherous, corrupt, and ungrateful heart."
5. I wish I could consent to marry you, but I am too sincere to make you believe that will ever happen; ...
6. But nothing could fix her attention; she turned to her dear Beast, for whom she trembled with fear; ...

A Solid Sentence Constructor

The following is a list of words and expressions you have learnt in the text. Please make a sentence with each of them.

1. to interweave
2. to beseech
3. to esteem
4. on condition that
5. to resemble
6. to sacrifice
7. to condemn

A Careful Writer

The following are three groups of words. You are required to study the words in each group carefully and then use them to write a paragraph of your own. Make sure that the paragraphs you have written are grammatical and coherent.

1. blush compliment flatter mistress

2. air fatigue weep weary deserve

3. trifle starve ungrateful merchandise

A Superb Bilingualist

Please translate the following sentences into English using words or expressions provided in the brackets.

1. 你刚才的一番话终于让我明白了完成这个项目的意义。(convince)
2. 大学毕业之后,伊丽莎白来到了一座陌生的城市。面对各种各样的困难,她努力使自己适应了新生活。(accustom ... to ...)
3. 小镇上的居民渴望在那片空地上建起一座公园,那样孩子们就可以不在街道上玩耍了。(pine for)
4. 乔治对日复一日的工作感到厌烦,便辞去工作,开始了环球旅行。(weary)
5. 最新的研究表明,糖尿病以及高血压会加速老年痴呆症(Alzheimer)患者的死亡。(hasten)
6. 由于可能会被弹劾,尼克松于1974年8月9日辞去总统职务,受命接替他的是福特。(in one's stead)
7. 告别了昔日的烦恼,雅各布满腔热忱地迎接新生活。(embrace)
8. 让我们携手并肩,为实现中非发展,推动建设持久和平、共同繁荣的和谐世界而努力奋斗。(endeavor)

Text B

Beauty and the Beast

By A. J. Jacobs
(Abridged and Edited)

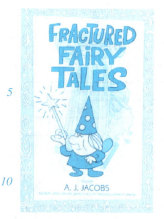

Once upon a time there was a magnificent golden castle on a silver cloud high up in the sky, which has nothing to do with anything because our story is about an old woodchopper who lived in a shack, but that's a good way to start a fairy tale. The old man was very happy, but he had a daughter, who was very unhappy because... well, she was rather plain. Actually, she was really plain. In fact, she had a face like five miles of bad road.

Anyway, it was time for her to marry, but because she was so fat and ugly, none of the young men of the kingdom ever came to ask for her hand, or any other part of her body, for that matter. Then one day, the old man decided to cheer her up.

"Child, it is your birthday and I've brought you something to keep you from being so lonely."

"A man?" she asked, wide-eyed.

"Nope. A mule."

He pointed to a brown, furry, four-legged, grunting beast. Well, a mule wasn't exactly the kind of companion she had in mind, but at least it was somebody to talk to.

"Hi there, silly beast," said the girl to the mule. "I wonder if you were once a handsome prince changed into a mule by a wicked witch. If so, I could break the spell with a kiss." She smacked the mule right on it's lips. It was no use. The mule was a mule and had always been a mule.

The next day the old man instructed his daughter to take a bundle of sticks to the village.

"A bundle of sticks?" she asked him. "What for?"

"How should I know," said the old man. "But somebody is always carrying a bundle of sticks around in fairy tales. You know that."

So the young girl took the bundle of sticks and decided to ride her trusty mule into the village. But something very strange happened. Unknown to her, the moment she climbed onto the mule's back, she turned into a beautiful maiden. You know the type: blond hair, blue eyes, a figure like she spends days doing Jazzercise.

Anyway, when she reached the village, she could hardly believe her eyes, for all the young men, instead of laughing and throwing mud at her, bowed, tipped their hats and made catcalls. She was still trying to figure it out

---

shack /ʃæk/ *n.* a small building, usually made of wood or metal, that has not been built well
furry /ˈfɜːri/ *adj.* covered with fur
grunt /grʌnt/ *v.* [of animals] to make a short low sound in the throat
smack /smæk/ *v.* to kiss with loud noise
catcall /ˈkætˌkɔːl/ *n.* a noise or shout expressing anger at or disapproval of sb. who is speaking or performing in public

when a handsome young prince rode up to her on a snow-white horse.

"Ah, fair lady!" he exclaimed. "You are truly the most lovely beauty in the land."

"Why, my young prince," she replied, batting her eyes. "Are you nuts or sumpthin?"

"With your permission," said the prince, "I should like to call upon you tonight. How about when the clock strikes the hour of eightish?"

Flushed with excitement, the girl raced home, but when she arrived and stepped off her mule — she immediately returned to her fat, little ugly self. That night, promptly at eightish o'clock, the prince, sitting astride his white charger, knocked on the door.

The girl opened the door and smiled her crooked-toothed smile — one that made chopped yak liver seem appealing — and chirped, "Helloooo."

"Um," said the prince, who at that moment was desiring a bit of Pepto-Bismol, or the medieval equivalent, "Is your sister at home?"

"I don't have a sister," the girl said.

"Your aunt then," the prince said.

"I don't have an aunt."

"Your cousin? Your best friend? Your babysitter?"

"What are you talking about?" asked the girl. "I live here alone with my father."

The prince, figuring he had found the wrong house, galloped quickly off on his white steed. The poor girl was left standing at the door, broken-hearted and trying to understand what had gone wrong. The following day, her father again asked her to go into the village. This time to pick up a bundle of sticks.

"It'll take your mind off your ugliness," the old man said patting her kindly on her head.

No sooner had the girl climbed on the mule's back than—once again she changed into a beautiful maiden. On the way to the village she chanced to pass a clear, still pool of water. Looking into it, she saw her reflection and was shocked to see she was now very beautiful. She hopped off her mule for a close look and instantly she changed back into her former ugly self. And then, she suddenly realized what had happened.

"I get it now," she said out loud to no one in particular, as people in fairy tales sometimes do. "This is a magic mule. As long as I sit on this beast, I'm a beauty!"

The girl climbed back onto the mule, and beautiful again. And the beauty and the beast dashed to find the prince. When he saw her coming, he rode up to her on his gallant steed.

"Ah, lovely beauty," he said. "I have found you again. Please say you will be mine so that we may be married."

---

nut /nʌt/ n. [informal] a strange or crazy person
flushed /flʌʃt/ adj. [of a person] red; with a red face
astride /əˈstraɪd/ prep. with one leg on each side of sth.
crooked /ˈkrʊkɪd/ adj. not in a straight line; bent or twisted
yak /jæk/ n. an animal of the cow family, with long horns and long hair, that lives in central Asia
chirp /tʃɜːp/ v. to make short high sounds like small birds and some insects
equivalent /ɪˈkwɪvələnt/ n. something that has the same value, purpose etc. as sth. else
gallop /ˈɡæləp/ v. to ride a horse very fast
steed /stid/ n. [literary or humorous] a horse to ride on
hop /hɑp/ v. [of a person] to move by jumping on one foot
gallant /ˈɡælənt/ adj. brave, especially in a very difficult situation

"Yes, but on one condition," she said, "that I remain on my mule at all times."

Of course, this seemed like a strange request, but the prince agreed.

85 "So be it, my love," he said. "And so that we start off on the right foot—or on the right hoof—I shall stay on my horse as long as you stay on your mule."

And thus they were married by a priest,
90 who delivered the sermon on a donkey. As the years went by, the young girl was very happy, although the poor mule did get a bit of a backache. And true to his word, the prince also stayed on his horse.

And as any good husband would, he took her dancing every Saturday night at the
95 palace, where they were the most striking couple on the dance floor. Or actually, the most striking quadruple on the dance floor.

One day, as the girl rode in the garden—the wind blew off her bonnet. Not stopping to think, she hopped off her mule to get the hat and—she immediately turned into an ugly, disgusting hag again. Realizing her mistake, she scrambled to get back in the saddle again.
100 But it was too late, for just then the prince rode up.

"Pardon me, old hag," said the prince. "Have you seen my wife? Wait a minute, this is her mule?"

"Yes," blushed the hag, gulping. "And I am your wife."

She began to sadly confess the whole story to her husband, but instead of being angry,
105 he did an amazing thing. He clapped his hands and laughed for joy.

This is what he said: "Ha, ha, ha, ha. Yahoo! Yipee!"

"I don't get it," said the girl. "Are you happy to find out that I'm really ugly?"

"No!" said the prince. "I'm happy to know that I can finally get off this blasted horse. You see, I'm only a handsome prince when I
110 stay on him."

And with that, the prince hopped off his horse and he changed into one of the ugliest men ever to walk the earth. He was fat and short and bald and full of warts. His face
115 looked like ten miles of bad road.

"Ugh! You're uglier than me!" said the girl, with glee.

"We were meant for each other!" said the man, as they embraced.

120 "Just think—no more saddle sores!"

And so, the ugly man and the ugly girl were able to live happily ever after, which only goes to prove that "A mule and his honey are soon parted."

hoof /hʊf/ n. the hard part of the foot of some animals, e.g. horses
quadruple /kwɑˈdrʌpəl/ n. a set of four similar things as a unit
bonnet /ˈbɒnɪt/ n. a hat tied with strings under the chin, worn by women in the past
hag /hæg/ n. [offensive] an ugly and/or unpleasant old woman
gulp /gʌlp/ v. to swallow, but without eating or drinking anything, especially because of a strong emotion such as fear or surprise
blasted /ˈblæstɪd/ adj. [informal] used when one is very annoyed about sth.
wart /wɔrt/ n. a small hard lump that grows on the skin
sore /sɔr/ n. a painful, often red, place on one's body

Notes

For some of the terms in the following, no explanation is provided. You are required to explain them by making use of the library, the Internet or whatever sources accessible.

1. Beauty and the Beast

_____
_____
_____
_____
_____
_____

2. Jazzercise

A fitness program that combines elements of jazz dance into aerobic exercise. The name also refers to the company that develops and markets the program. The Jazzercise program was first created in 1969 by Judi Sheppard Missett, who is now CEO of Jazzercise, Inc. Missett first thought of the program while teaching traditional jazz dance classes in Evanston, Illinois. Missett moved to Carlsbad, California to start Jazzercise, Inc. and began training instructors.

3. Pepto-Bismol

Pepto-Bismol is an over-the-counter drug that relieves problems of an upset stomach. Its active ingredient is bismuth salicylate. Pepto-Bismol was developed more than 100 years ago in the U.S., which was originally sold as a remedy for infant diarrhea. The primary symptoms aided by Pepto-Bismol are diarrhea, indigestion, heartburn and other temporary discomforts of the stomach. Now it has been nicknamed "the pink stuff" for its colorant in various advertising campaigns.

Comprehension Questions

Please answer the following questions based on what you have learnt in the text.

1. Why was the old man's daughter unhappy?

2. What did the father give his daughter as a birthday present? How did she like it?
3. What magic things occurred the moment the girl got onto the mule?
4. Was the prince a really handsome guy? Why/Why not?

Writing Practice

Sometimes a person's appearance alone could be deceitful. A very attractive outer appearance may turn out to be an elaborate façade hiding a cruel and nasty personality. Have you ever experienced this? Has a "beautiful" person ever tried to make you feel ugly? If yes, jot down the details of your experience. If not, use your imagination to make up a fictional experience in which you've met someone beautiful but proven in the end ugly inside. Then, consider whether you would prefer to meet someone who is beautiful but shallow, or someone who radiates inner beauty. Explain your reasoning in one paragraph.

Further Study

This is the end of Unit 1; but you can also gain more knowledge by accessing the following resources.

Once upon a time there was a dwarf who got into the fairy tale by mistake. For there were already seven other dwarfs who did their work. He himself was only the eighth, and nothing was actually prepared for him. So the eighth dwarf trotted about the pages in a bad mood and did not know what to do with himself. He came to that spot where the giant was killed, and he found it completely senseless as he always had each time he had come across it. He peevishly sauntered further on until he came to the spot where the handsome prince, who was usually on his knees before the princess, was missing. The dwarf felt so embarrassed that his hair stood on its end, and he fled away. When he did not encounter any of the other dwarfs along the way, he finally ran to the end of the fairy tale. There, however, the dwarf saw that they lived happily ever after. So he really became furious and trampled on the terrible words with his feet.

Is this a fairy tale? Why or Why not? You'll need to explain the generic criteria on which you base your argument. In what ways does the tale conform to the criteria? For more details on the elements of a fairy tale, please visit: http://library.usask.ca/education/files/Guides/fairy.pdf. If you are interested in reading fairy tales, please visit http://ivyjoy.com/fables/index.shtml to find more.

Unit 2

Friendship

Unit Goals

Upon completing the texts in this unit, students should be able to:
- ☞ understand the significance of friendship and what it means to be a friend;
- ☞ apply what they have learned in their own lives and develop some ways of keeping friendship alive;
- ☞ use prefixes of attitude correctly to form new words.

Before Reading

Hands-on Activities and Brainstorming

1. Humans are social beings. In one way or another we are all connected to each other. When we are in trouble, we hope there is someone out there whom we can trust and count on for help. This "someone" is what we call "friends." They are always ready to listen and lend a helping hand to us. Try to make a presentation on friendship by answering the following questions:
   (1) How do you define friendship?
   (2) What do you think are good ways of maintaining friendship?
   (3) Do adult friendship and childhood friendship differ in any way?
   (4) What does friendship mean to you?
2. Go to the library or surf the Internet for friendship stories to really appreciate its importance.

A Glimpse at Words and Expressions

Please read the following sentences. Pay attention to the underlined part in each sentence and to how it is used in the sentence and then decide on its meaning. Write down the meaning in the brackets.

1. It seems to me that for most people, the very mention of a certain name will bring back a rush of childhood memories. (   )

2. I think the best estimate we have for the stability of friendships is that they last—on the average—a few months. (   )

3. We conducted a solemn wedding ceremony for two of her teddy bears and spied on the neighborhood boys as they played outside. (   )

4. I was always a bit tall and lanky for my age, and called a "show-off" on more than one occasion. (   )

5. But clearly it goes beyond that if you're dealing with friendships that have last a while. (   )

6. Some nights after the sun had long since retired. (   )

7. As we grew, we stayed close and served as role models for each other. (   )

8. While I realize that my parents had the most important role in molding the person I was to eventually become, my childhood friend was a close second. (   )

Text A

The Value of Friendship

By Tara Swords
(Abridged and Edited)

It seems to me that for most people, the very mention of a certain name will bring back a rush of childhood memories—memories of summer days spent together barefoot and of deep secrets passed from behind a guarding hand cupped to the mouth. Memories that turn up the corners of your lips in a slight smile and make you squint your eyes as though doing so will give a clearer view of the past. For me, that name is Joelle.

I met her when I was just 6. Joelle was 5, and we both made our way to the same baby-sitter's house every school morning at 7:00 a.m. She always wore her school jacket with the sleeves stylishly pushed up to her elbows. For no particular reason, we didn't like each other.

But two years later, when my parents bought a house on the other side of our small, central Illinois town, we found ourselves next-door neighbors. One cool spring night,

cup /kʌp/ v. to place one's curved hand or hands around sth.
stylishly /ˈstaɪlɪʃli/ adv. fashionably

shortly after my family had moved in, I saw her playing in her driveway, the sleeves of her St. Mary's school jacket pushed confidently up to her elbows. I nervously approached her
20 with a pair of shoes that no longer fit me. She accepted the peace offering, and agreed to a bike ride around the block.

Our first conversation: "Do you like fish?" she asked me as we neared the end of
25 our street.

"Yes," I said. "Do you?"

"No!"

But we agreed that bike rides were fun, cats were cute and acrobats were the coolest.
30 So on that spring evening as we rode toward the cornfield bordering the southeast side of tiny Metamora, Illinois, and chatted about inane subjects, a friendship was born.

Psychologists often disagree about the
35 impact childhood friendships like this one have on the development of kids' personalities. But quite often, the truth of the matter is that friends come and go while children are young, and that is perfectly healthy.

Thomas Berndt, professor of psychology at Purdue University, says what forms childhood friendships is a similarity in social circumstances: living in the same
40 neighborhood, riding the same bus. If those circumstances change, so do the friendships. From the ages of 5 through 10, I think the best estimate we have for the stability of friendships is that they last—on the average—a few months.

> driveway /ˈdraɪˌweɪ/ n. a short private road leading to a house
> inane /ɪnˈeɪn/ adj. extremely foolish; irrational
> perfect /ˈpɜːfɪkt/ v. to make sth. perfect or as good as one can
> cartwheel /ˈkɑːtˌhwiːl/ n. a fast physical movement in which one turns in a circle sideways by putting one's hands on the ground and bringing one's legs, one at a time, over one's head 侧手翻
> backflip /ˈbækˌflɪp/ n. a backward somersault 后空翻
> choreograph /ˈkɒriəˌɡræf/ n. to compose the sequence of steps and moves for (a dance performance)
> swingset /ˈswɪŋset/ n. a frame for children to play on, including one or more swings
> exasperate /ɪɡˈzæspəˌreɪt/ v. to irritate intensely
> rambunctious /ræmˈbʌŋkʃəs/ adj. difficult to control or handle
> petite /pəˈtiːt/ adj. [of a woman] attractively small and dainty
> freckle /ˈfrɛkəl/ n. a small light brown spot on the skin, caused and made more pronounced by exposure to the sun 雀斑

45

50

55

So Joelle and I weren't typical. In fact, after that first ride around the block, almost every part of my childhood involved Joelle. We played outside every night after school, attempting to perfect cartwheels and backflips until our mothers called us in at dark. We choreographed dances to all the best wham songs and became masters of the swingset in her backyard. We conducted a solemn wedding ceremony for two of her teddy bears and spied on the neighborhood boys as they played outside.

Yet we were different—at least in the ways that might keep some children from becoming friends. We attended different elementary schools; Joelle, a St. Mary's Falcon, and I, a Metamora Redbird, were cross-town rivals by day. She was quiet and shy; I often talked too much and, according to my exasperated grandmother, "was too rambunctious." Joelle was small and petite and a bit serious, with freckles that made adults coo over her cuteness. I was always a bit tall and lanky for my age, and called a "show-off" on more than one occasion.

We had some ferocious fights. Joelle's mother watched out for me during the summer when school was out and both my parents were at work, and if we got into an argument, I would run into my empty house and lock the door. Joelle and her little brother would gleefully ring our doorbell until the battery died or the circuit shorted—whichever happened first. Yet there was always an unstated understanding between us that we were friends, and that was unchangeable.

"Kids care more about friendship at a young age than they are able to say," says Berndt. "If you ask them, they say a friend is someone you play with, who you give your toys to, and who doesn't fight with you. But clearly it goes beyond that if you're dealing with friendships that have lasted a while." That was true for us. I think we understood the value of our friendship, but rarely talked about it.

Some evenings after dark, when we were assumed to be taking baths or doing homework in our own homes, I would sneak over to her house and enter through the garage door that led to the basement—just so we could talk a while longer. I now know that there is something ferocious and innocent in that time when young girls will steal away into the night just to spend time with a best friend, something that—when later replaced with late-night phone calls to boys—can never be reclaimed.

Some nights after the sun had long since retired, we would march a mile or two into the cornfields that stretched out behind our subdivision as far as the eye could see. After about 45 minutes of walking huddled together with the flashlight beam jumping nervously, we would reach a tiny, century-old graveyard tucked away and forgotten in the middle of the field. Half amazed and half scared to death, we would shine the beam on the crumbling tombstones to read the names and dates, wondering what sort of people had lived there before us. We always felt most sad when the dates on the stones were too close together. Though we were but children ourselves, it must have made us confront our own mortality, and there was comfort in not doing that alone. I remember feeling horror at the idea that of all the important events in our lives, only the dates of two would serve as evidence that we had existed.

As we grew, we stayed close and served as role models for each other. Both of us always got high grades, and probably motivated each other to excel in school as a result. While today I delight in some of the harmless mischief we instigated, we were good kids that listened to our parents on the big issues, and never did anything that could get us into real trouble. In a way, we were our own support system for doing the right thing when parents weren't physically there to guide us.

And now, my memories of her are too

---

coo /kuː/ *v.* to speak in a soft gentle voice
lanky /ˈlæŋki/ *adj.* [lankier, lankiest] awkwardly thin and tall
ferocious /fəˈrəʊʃəs/ *adj.* savagely fierce, cruel, or violent
gleefully /ˈɡliːfəli/ *adv.* joyfully
circuit /ˈsɜːkɪt/ *n.* a system of conductors and components forming a complete path for an electric current
reclaim /rɪˈkleɪm/ *v.* to retrieve or recover
subdivision /ˌsʌbdɪˈvɪʒən/ *n.* an area of land divided into plots
tuck /tʌk/ *v.* [often tuck away] to store in a secure or secret place
crumble /ˈkrʌmbəl/ *v.* to break or fall apart into small fragments
motivate /ˈməʊtəˌveɪt/ *v.* to stimulate the interest of
excel /ɪkˈsel/ *v.* to be exceptionally good at an activity or subject
instigate /ˈɪnstɪˌɡeɪt/ *v.* to bring about or initiate

many to count—a kind of animated collage: The day her house caught on fire, she grabbed her cat and ran to the safety of my bedroom; She taught me to shave my legs; I was the one driving her mother's car with Joelle sitting beside me when we crashed into a truck that had run a stop sign; We cried together as we rode in the ambulance to the hospital, and I was glad that I hadn't gotten blood on the shirt that she had let me borrow that day; We double-dated to prom, just as we'd always planned.

Now, college degrees later and miles away, we are still close. We live in different cities and work different jobs. And while I realize that my parents had the most important role in molding the person I was to eventually become, my childhood friend was a close second. It makes me wonder about the future, about my "someday" children and the people who will have an unforgettable impact on their lives, regardless of me. I will help nurture those friendships, knowing that their quality of life will be so enriched. The effects of a good, true friendship never fade: As children, Joelle and I explored and exploited the freedoms of being young and carefree; and as adults, the mere remembrance of that fact is enough to make me cherish the good in my life.

> animated /ˈænəˌmeɪtɪd/ adj. lively
> collage /kəˈlɑʒ/ n. a combination or collection of various things
> prom /prɑm/ n. a formal dance party, especially at a high school or college typically at or near the end of an academic year 班级舞会
> remembrance /rɪˈmɛmbrəns/ n. a memory

Better Know More

1. Tara Swords

Tara Swords is a full-time freelance writer and editor based in Chicago, United States. She has written about business, technology, lifestyle, health, community affairs, and women's issues. After gaining a master's degree in journalism, she has worked in multiple media, including radio, television, newspaper, magazine, and the web. For more information, visit her website http://www.taraswords.com.

2. Purdue University

Purdue University, located in Indiana, U.S., is the flagship university of the six-campus Purdue University System. It was founded in 1869, in the name of its benefactor John Purdue, as a college of science, technology, and agriculture. The university has been enormously influential in America's history of aviation, and its aviation technology and aeronautical engineering programs remain among the most competitive in the world.

3. **Wham!**

"Wham!" was a top British duo formed in 1981 by George Michael and Andrew Ridgeley. The Wham songs, like Young Guns and Wham Rap, have great influence on the public, especially on teenage girls.

Check Your Understanding

Please answer the following questions based on what you have learnt in the text.

1. Do psychologists agree on the impact that childhood friendship has on the development of kids' personalities?
2. Why does the author say "after that first ride around the block, almost every part of my childhood involved Joelle"?
3. How did Joelle and the author serve as role models for each other?
4. Why does the author say "my memories of her are too many to count—a kind of animated collage"?
5. According to the author, what role does a true friendship play in our life?

A Sip of Word Formation

Prefixes of Attitude

Co-, *pro-*, *counter-*, and *anti-* are prefixes of attitude.

1. *Co-* is usually added to nouns, verbs and adjectives with the meaning of together with (e.g. *co-author, co-exist, co-operative*);
2. *Pro-* is usually added to adjectives and nouns, with the meaning of in favor of, supporting (e.g. *pro-active, pro-democracy*).
3. The prefix *counter-* is usually added to nouns, verbs, adjectives and adverbs with the meaning of:
   (1) against or opposite (e.g. *counter-revolution, counter-attack, counter-offensive, counter-productively*);
   (2) corresponding (e.g. *counter-point*)
4. *Anti-* is usually added to nouns, adjectives with the meaning of:
   (1) opposed to or against (e.g. *anti-body, anti-biotic*);
   (2) the opposite of (e.g. *anti-climax, anti-social*);
   (3) preventing (e.g. *anti-freeze, anti-aircraft*).

Build Your Vocabulary

For each of the following sentences, a word is provided in the brackets. Use the appropriate form of the word to fill in the blank in the sentence, so that the sentence is logical and grammatical.

1. _____ Brits produce a video campaign: "A World without America," to combat anti-Americanism in the U.K. (America)
2. The foreign minister held talks with his American _____. (part)
3. Last June, the Chinese People's Institute of Foreign Affairs sponsored the International Seminar on the Five Principles of Peaceful _____. (exist)
4. We are seeking for _____ partners to bring benefit from the scientific and technical achievements to society as early as possible. (operate)
5. The _____ movement was started by a woman whose son was killed in the war. (war)
6. _____ behavior is an activity that impacts on other people in a negative way. (society)
7. The board members of the company discussed real difficulty brought by new policies and came up with _____. (measure)

You'd Like to Be

A Skilled Text Weaver

Fill in the blanks with the words you have learnt in this text, one word for each blank. You are advised to read the text carefully until you have become very familiar with it before starting to work on this task.

The boys, _____ by Professor Keating, their new teacher of English literature, secretly revived a literary club, to which Keating once belonged. Every midnight when they were _____ to be sleeping, they would _____ out of the dorms to meet in a cave in the school grounds. What they had done in the cave was regarded by others as utterly _____ and unorthodox—a _____ of many things, from _____ together to recite poems to playing _____ to tease girls. They also called Keating "O Captain! My Captain!" in _____ of a Walt Whitman poem. Their purpose of restoring the club, though _____, was well understood by the teacher as challenging the authority and developing independent thinking. Obviously such a club was against the ethos of the school which was defined as "tradition, honor, discipline and excellence." The head master was so _____ that he fired Keating for _____ the students to restart the club and failing in _____ them in a positive way.

A Sharp Interpreter

Please paraphrase the following sentences. Change the sentence structure wherever necessary.

1. I think the best estimate we have for the stability of friendships is that they last—on the average—a few months.
2. Joelle and her little brother would gleefully ring our doorbell until the battery died or the circuit shorted—whichever happened first.
3. "Kids care more about friendship at a young age than they are able to say."
4. I now know that there is something ferocious and innocent in that time when young girls will steal away into the night just to spend time with a best friend, something that—when later replaced with late-night phone calls to boys—can never be reclaimed.
5. After about 45 minutes of walking huddled together with the flashlight beam jumping nervously, we would reach a tiny, century-old graveyard tucked away and forgotten in the middle of the field.
6. I remember feeling horror at the idea that of all the important events in our lives, only the dates of two would serve as evidence that we had existed.
7. And while I realize that my parents had the most important role in molding the person I was to eventually become, my childhood friend was a close second.

A Solid Sentence Constructor

The following is a list of words and expressions you have learnt in the text. Please make a sentence with each of them.

1. to delight in
2. to excel in
3. whichever
4. regardless of
5. to perfect
6. to reclaim
7. to be assumed to
8. remembrance

A Careful Writer

The following are three groups of words. You are required to study the words in each group carefully and then use them to write a paragraph of your own. Make sure that the paragraphs you have written are grammatical and coherent.

1. neighborhood   swingset   rival   squint

2. lanky   freckle   stylish   crumble

3. acrobat   petite   barefoot   coo

📖 A Superb Bilingualist

Please translate the following sentences into English using words or expressions provided in the brackets.

1. 她对残疾运动员的敬佩之情油然而生。(a rush of)
2. 她虽然家境贫寒,却志存高远。(nurture)
3. 爸爸送给妈妈的定情信物一直被妈妈珍藏在衣橱的抽屉里。(tuck away)
4. 谁也不会想到,竟然是他的父亲教唆他去犯罪。(instigate)
5. 他无论怎样努力,也无法与对方达成协议,最后愤然离开了会场。(exasperate)
6. 该国的排外情绪异常高涨,其他国家对此都十分关注。(ferocious)
7. 好的管理者不是严格地管理员工,而是善于有效地激励员工。(motivate)

Text B

All Un-Alone in the City

Why the lastest chatter about friendship doesn't feel very relevant to New York?

By Liesl Schilliner
(Abridged and Edited)

It's not polite to talk about numbers: But how many men and/or women have you added to your list since you've lived in New York? Are we talking single digits? Double digits? Triple digits? How many of them were long-term, how many short-term, and how many turned out to be one-week (or one-night) wonders? Do you still keep in touch with them, and do you remember their names? Do they remember yours?

We're talking, of course, about friends—a topic of joy, anxiety, and competition in the city that invented *Friends*, *Seinfeld*, and *Sex and the City*; a city in which invidious comparison is available with the flick of the remote, or with a glance into any restaurant window. A city in which, at the moment, it is August, and many of the people we count as friends are away for weekends, or weeks at a time, leading to a sudden slip-off phone calls and e-mails that produces the existential question: Do I exist when the hulk of my friends are absent? It's like a dip in the Force.

In June, sociologists at Duke and the University of Arizona released a study that showed that, over the past twenty years, the number of people that the average American has heart-to-heart talks with (or, in shorthand, "friends") has dropped by one-third, from about three people in 1985 to about two in 2004. For many people, the only confidant left is a spouse. Then, last month, Joseph Lipstein, the Chicagoan taxouomist of American social mores, released a book called *Friendship: An Exposé* in which he addressed the broad topic of friends much as an exterminator might address the broad spectrum of pests, suggesting it was high time that Hallmark came out with a card that read on the cover: "We've been friends for a very long time," and continued on the inside, "What do you say we stop?"

Assuming (which may not be entirely fair) that people have the friends they deserve, and that, given human nature, if they really wanted more, they'd make an effort to socialize beyond their lawns. New Yorkers are once

> **invidious** /ɪnˈvɪdiəs/ *adj.* unpleasant and unfair, likely to offend sb. or make others jealous
> **flick** /flɪk/ *n.* a quick look through the pages of a book, magazine, etc.
> **hulk** /hʌlk/ *n.* a very large person, especially one who moves in an awkward way
> **dip** /dɪp/ *n.* a decrease in the amount or success of sth., usually for only a short period
> **confidant** /ˈkɒnfɪˌdænt/ *n.* one to whom secrets or private matters are disclosed
> **spouse** /spaʊs/ *n.* a husband or a wife
> **taxonomist** /tækˈsɒnəmɪst/ *n.* one who studies or is skilled in taxonomy
> **exterminator** /ɪkˈstɜːməˌneɪtə/ *n.* one who destroys completely (a race or group of people or animals)
> **spectrum** /ˈspɛktrəm/ *n.* a complete or wide range of related qualities, ideas, etc.

again faced with evidence that the priorities of the average American may have little to do with our own. For us, not having a spouse is acceptable; not having friends is anathema—a sign that your neuroses are so beyond—Woody Allen that only a shrink would take your calls. And when we marry, the comfort and reassurance of family life are constantly weighed against the stimulation and temptations of urban life and the preexisting bonds of longtime friendships. A hundred years ago (and earlier), before modern transportation made it easy for people to carom across the continent(s) at will, people largely stayed where they were dropped, leading to the invention of such strategies as "etiquette," which is, essentially, the art of not alienating the people you are constrained to live among. But New Yorkers are unusual in that they still stay put (except in August), though not so much through constraint as through choice. The result of staying put is that the old-fashioned art of cultivating and maintaining your circle is as necessary here as it was in a small town in Indiana in 1875 or 1975.

I remember, arriving alone in Manhattan at the tail end of the eighties, being alarmed that I lacked the built-in friend base that my New York-born contemporaries had. Having grown up in Indiana, I had witnessed the efforts that adults went to in low-population zones to whip up a social whirl: gourmet clubs, canoeing expeditions, picnics, car races. Activities changed—my mother would joke about going to a "dog shoot in Fowler" (a nearby hamlet) to pad the schedule—but friends remained the same.

In New York, there was no need to resort to dog shoots, but how did an absolute beginner go about finding a plus-one, much less a plus-posse, when everyone seemed so dazzlingly unavailable? At work, in those early days, I furtively filled out a Rolodex card with the names and numbers of nearly everyone I spoke to for more than ten minutes, wondering it they would mystically morph into Friends. I labeled the card "Amici" and filed it under A, so that if the Rolodex flapped open, nobody would guess the meaning of my hopeful jottings. Over time, thankfully, I was able to shred the card. There is no idiot's guide to how to make friends in New York, but if there were

---

priority /praɪˈɒrɪti/ *n.* sth. that one thinks is more important than other things and should be dealt with first

anathema /əˈnæθəmə/ *n.* a thing or an idea which one hates because it is the opposite of what one believes

neurosis /nʊˈrəʊsɪs/ *n.* a mental illness in which one suffers strong feelings of fear and worry (pl. neuroses)

shrink /ʃrɪŋk/ *n.* [slang, humorous] a psychologist or a psychiatrist

reassurance /ˌriːəˈʃʊərəns/ *n.* the fact of giving advice or help that takes away one's fears or doubts

constantly /ˈkɒnstəntli/ *adv.* repeatedly; all the time

stimulation /ˌstɪmjuˈleɪʃən/ *n.* the effect of a stimulus on nerves or organs

temptation /tɛmpˈteʃən/ *n.* the desire to do or have sth. that one knows is bad or wrong

preexisting /ˌpriːɪɡˈzɪstɪŋ/ *adj.* existing from an earlier time

carom /ˈkærəm/ *v.* to strike and rebound

etiquette /ˈɛtɪˌkɛt/ *n.* the formal rules of correct or polite behavior in society or among members of a particular profession

alienate /ˈeɪljəˌneɪt/ *v.* to make one feel that he does not belong in a particular group

constrain /kənˈstreɪn/ *v.* to force sb. to do sth. or behave in a particular way

whip sb./sth. up to deliberately try and make people excited or feel strongly about sth.

whirl /hwɜːrl/ *n.* a number of activities or events happening successively

gourmet /ɡʊrˈmeɪ/ *n.* one who knows a lot about good food and wines and who enjoys choosing, eating and drinking them

pad /pæd/ *v.* to lengthen (sth. written or spoken) with unrelated material

dazzlingly /ˈdæzlɪŋli/ *adv.* to impress sb. a lot with one's beauty, skill, knowledge, etc.

furtively /ˈfɜːtɪvli/ *adv.* behaving in a way that shows one wants to keep sth. secret and does not want to be noticed

morph /mɒf/ *v.* to alter or animate by transformation

flap /flæp/ *v.* to strike with a sudden blow

one, it would have to include a thorough classification chart of the indigenous friend varieties.

There are the friends-from-the-office, whom you see most often, because of the workaholism of this town , but don't necessarily hang with outside of work (a subset of this is the office "marriage"); there are the "tribe" friends, the essential, familially claustrophobic pack everybody depends on; the drop-of-a-hat friends, tireless explorers of the city's delights whom you ring up when your tribe members are King low; activity-friends, whom you round up for poker games or bike rides; too-busy friends (which can include married friends), who E you and phone you and suggest meetings that they generally, sheepishly, cancel; friends you only see at parties; old lovers (popular among the breezy, the thick-skinned, and masochists); old friends, who include schoolmates, college roommates, family, and anyone who knew you before you were employed; new friends, who come and go like junior-high crushes; and friends-of-the-heart (who can be drawn from any of the above groups, and who can change).

In five boroughs, holding some 8 million people, the risk of being crossed off someone's mental "friends" list, or supplanted by a fascinating interloper, is an ever-present spur to comradely effort. Proust wrote that the threat of infidelity hovers over successful marriages; in the same way, the expendability of local friendships keeps players on their toes. Andwhen a friendship dies, its casualties cannot easily avoid each other, given the persistence of social circuits-leading to confrontations out of Choderlos de Laclos—men flinging drinks and fists at one another, women cutting each other dead. To escape the awkwardness, you'd have to leave town for good ... another kind of death.

To Epstein, friendship seems to be no big whoop. "Friendship does not arise out of necessity, but out of preference," he chin-strokingly opines. Yes and no. I have never come across a New Yorker who does not regard friends as a necessity; and while making friends may happen out of choice, keeping them over time requires the same tact and harmonizing of egos that occur in family life. How New Yorkers pull off this delicate balancing act, while holding down their jobs, is one of the city's enduring mysteries. In fact, in seventeen years of socializing in this town, at thousands of social occasions (breakfast, lunch, brunch, dinner, book party,

---

workaholism /ˈwɔːkəˌhɒlɪzəm/ *n.* compulsiveness about working
claustrophobic /ˌklɔstrəˈfobɪk/ *adj.* abnormally afraid of closed-in places 患幽闭恐怖症的
breezy /ˈbrizi/ *adj.* having or showing a cheerful and relaxed manner
masochist /ˈmæsəukist/ *n.* someone who obtains pleasure from receiving punishment 受虐狂
borough /ˈbʌro/ *n.* a town or part of a city that has its own local government
supplant /səˈplænt/ *v.* to take the place of sb./sth. (especially sb./sth. older or less modern)
interloper /ˈɪntəˌlopə/ *n.* one who is present in a place or a situation where he does not belong
spur /spə/ *n.* a fact or an event that makes one want to do sth. better or more quickly
infidelity /ˌɪnfɪˈdelɪti/ *n.* the act of not being faithful to one's wife, husband or partner, by having sex with sb. else
expendability /əkˌseptəˈbɪlɪti/ *n.* the quality of being expendable and not worth preserving
confrontation /ˌkɒnfrʌnˈteʃən/ *n.* a situation in which there is an angry disagreement between people or groups who have different opinions
fling /flɪŋ/ *v.* to throw sb./sth. somewhere with force, especially because one is angry

party party), I have found only one rule of friendship etiquette that remains constant: Maximum number of times you can meet somebody on second introduction, forget their name, yet still become friends. Maximum number of times you can meet somebody on second introduction, forget their face, yet still become friends.

Notes

For some of the terms in the following, no explanation is provided. You are required to explain them by making use of the library, the Internet or whatever sources accessible.

1. Liesl Schillinger

Liesl Schillinger is a New York-based arts writer. Born and raised in college towns across the Midwestern United States, chiefly Indiana and Oklahoma, she attended Yale University, where she studied Comparative Literature. From 1988 to 2005, she worked at The New Yorker as editor for the magazine's Goings on About Town section. She now writes full time and is a regular contributor to *The New York Review of Books* and is pursuing the goal of living like an expatriate in her own city.

2. Friends

Friends is one of the most watched television shows of the 1990s and 2000s. Set in Manhattan, it is a comedy series about six young people. It offers a vivid portrayal of modern life, where people try to ease the pressure by seeking companionship, comfort and support from each other.

3. Seinfeld

4. Sex and the City

5. Duke

6. The University of Arizona

The University of Arizona, founded in 1885, is the first university in the state of Arizona. Its mission is "to discover, educate, serve, and inspire". It is one of the elected members of the Association of American Universities (an organization of North America's premier research institutions).

7. Choderlos de Laclos (1741–1803)

Choderlos de Laclos was a French novelist, official and army general, known for writing the epistolary novel *Dangerous Liaisons*. The novel explores the amorous intrigues of the aristocracy and has inspired a large number of critical commentaries, plays and films.

Comprehension Questions

Please answer the following questions based on what you have learnt in the text.

1. What did the study conducted by the sociologists at Duke and the University of Arizona show about friendship?
2. According to the author, how was "etiquette" invented and what is its function?
3. In Indiana, how did adults socialize?
4. How many kinds of friends are mentioned in the text?

5. According to Epstein, how does friendship arise? What do you think?

Writing Practice

Friends are the signposts along our roads. "Friendship is about looking into the eyes of another and seeing myself." Friendship is about giving and receiving. Please write a brief commentary on the following poem of friendship.

Love and Friendship
by Emily Bronte

Love is like the wild rose–briar,
Friendship like the holly–tree?
The holly is dark when the rose–briar blooms
But which will bloom most constantly?

The wild–rose briar is sweet in the spring,
Its summer blossoms scent the air;
Yet wait till winter comes again
And who will call the wild–briar fair?

Then scorn the silly rose–wreath now
And deck thee with the holly's sheen,
That when December blights thy brow
He may still leave thy garland green.

Further Study

This is the end of Unit 2; but you can also gain more knowledge by accessing the following resources.

Recommended film: *The Dead Poets' Society*—The Welton Academy is a well-respected prep school where education is an entirely pragmatic and dry affair. When John Keating, a new teacher of English literature, comes to the school, he introduces his students to poetry and the liberal philosophies. Inspired by his unconventional teaching, the students revive *The Dead Poets' Society*, which Keating used to belong to. The purpose of restarting this literary club is to challenge the authority and develop independent thinking. The head master is so infuriated by their "unorthodoxy" that he fires Keating. Students rise in defense of their beloved teacher.

Unit 3

Money and Happiness

Unit Goals

Upon completing the texts in this unit, students should be able to:
- ☞ understand what true happiness is and how to achieve and maintain it;
- ☞ develop the ability to convince others through presenting major and minor details in a logical manner;
- ☞ use pejorative prefixes correctly to form new words.

Before Reading

Hands-on Activities and Brainstorming

1. Visit the website http://www.authentichappiness.sas.upenn.edu/newsletter.aspx?id=49 to get acquainted with what is considered the three traditional theories on happiness.
"The wealthier a person is, the happier he/she would be." That means that happiness grows with accumulation of material possessions. What is your evaluation on Money and Happiness? What do you think gives people the greatest happiness? It is highly recommended that you make it into a presentation.
2. There are many words and expressions that can be used to describe how happy a person is. Make a list of them and share it with the other students. Can you think of some words that are used to describe how unhappy a person is?

A Glimpse at Words and Expressions

Please read the following sentences. Pay attention to the underlined part in each sentence and to how it is used in the sentence and then decide on its meaning. Write down the meaning in the brackets.

1. A depression so <u>debilitating</u> that it's hard to get out of bed. (   )

2. Too many Americans view expensive purchases as "short-cuts" to well-being. (   )
3. The poor are rendered unhappy by the relentless frustration and stress of poverty. (   )
4. The study, which has been replicated in the U.S., shows that Grandma had a point. (   )
5. That seems true because of a phenomenon that sociologists call reference anxiety—or more popularly, keeping up with the Joneses. (   )
6. Most people know relatively little about those who were living higher on the hog. (   )
7. Income growth has almost come to a halt for the middle class. (   )
8. But we are all conditioned to think there's something wrong if we don't make more money each year. (   )

Text A

The Real Truth of Money

By Gregg Easterbrook
(Abridged and Edited)

If you made a graph of American life since the end of World War II, every line concerning money and the things that money can buy would soar upward, a statistical monument to materialism. Inflation-adjusted income per American has almost tripled. The size of the typical new house has more than doubled. A two-car garage was once a goal; now we're nearly a three-car nation. Designer everything, personal electronics and other items that didn't even exist a half-century ago are now affordable. No matter how you chart the trends in earning and spending, everything is up, up, up. But if you made a chart of American happiness since the end of World War II, the lines would be as flat as a marble tabletop. In polls taken by the National Opinion Research Center in the 1950s, about one-third of Americans described themselves as "very happy." The center has conducted essentially the same poll periodically since

statistical /stəˈtɪstɪkəl/ *adj.* relating to, or employing statistics or the principles of statistics
inflation /ɪnˈfleɪʃən/ *n.* a general rise in the prices of services and goods in a particular country, resulting in a fall in the value of money
designer /dɪˈzaɪnə/ *n.* [only before noun] made by a well-known and fashionable designer
chart /tʃɑːt/ *v.* to record or follow the progress or development of sb./sth.

then, and the percentage remains almost exactly the same today.

Yet if you charted the incidence of depression since 1950, the lines suggested a growing epidemic. Depending on what assumptions are used, clinical depression is 3 to 10 times as common today as two generations ago. A recent study by Ronald Kessler of Harvard Medical School estimated that each year, one in fifteen Americans experience an episode of major depression—meaning not just a bad day but a depression so debilitating that it's hard to get out of bed. Money jangles in our wallets and purses as never before, but we are basically no happier for it, and for many, more money leads to depression. How can that be?

Of course, our grandmothers, many of whom lived through the Depression and the war, told us that money can't buy happiness. We don't act as though we listened. Millions of us spend more time and energy pursuing the things money can buy than engaging in activities that create real fulfillment in life, like cultivating friendships, helping others and developing a spiritual sense.

We say we know that money can't buy happiness. In the *TIME* poll, when people were asked about their major source of happiness, money ranked 14th. Still, we behave as though happiness is one wave of a credit card away. Too many Americans view expensive purchases as "shortcuts to well-being," says Martin Seligman, a psychologist at the University of Pennsylvania. But people are poor predictors of where those shortcuts will take them.

To be sure, there is ample evidence that being poor causes unhappiness. Studies by Ruut Veenhoven, a sociologist at Erasmus University in Rotterdam, show that the poor—those in Europe earning less than about $10,000 a year—are rendered unhappy by the relentless frustration and stress of poverty. But you knew that.

The surprise is that after a person's annual income exceeds $10,000 or so, Veenhoven found, money and happiness decouple and cease to have much to do with each other. The study, which has been replicated in the U.S., shows that Grandma had a point. Over the past two decades, in fact, an increasing body of social-science and psychological research has shown that there is no significant relationship between how much money a person earns and whether he or she feels good about life. TIME's poll found that happiness tended to increase as income rose to $50,000 a year. (The median annual U.S. household income is around $43,000.) After that,

---

incidence /ˈɪnsɪdəns/ *n.* ~ of sth. (written) the extent to which sth. happens or has an effect
debilitating /dɪˈbɪlɪˌteɪtɪŋ/ *adj.* making sb.'s mind or body weak
jangle /ˈdʒæŋɡəl/ *v.* to make a harsh sound, like two pieces of metal hitting each other
live through to experience difficult or dangerous conditions
predictor /prɪˈdɪktə/ *n.* [formal] sth. that can show what will happen in the future
render /ˈrɛndə/ *v.* to cause sb./sth. to be in a particular state or condition
relentless /rɪˈlɛntlɪs/ *adj.* not stopping or getting less strong
decouple /diˈkʌpəl/ *v.* to end the connection or relationship between two things
replicate /ˈrɛplɪˌkeɪt/ *v.* to copy sth. exactly
have a point to have an opinion that is right
median /ˈmiːdiən/ *n.* [only being noun] [technical] having a value in the middle of a series of values

more income did not have a dramatic effect. Edward Diener, a psychologist at the University of Illinois, interviewed members of the Forbes 400, the richest Americans. He found the
65 Forbes 400 were only a tiny bit happier than the public as a whole. Because those with wealth often continue to feel jealousy about the possessions or prestige of other wealthy people, even large sums of money may fail to confer well-being.

That seems true because of a phenomenon that sociologists call reference anxiety — or, more popularly,
70 keeping up with the Joneses. According to that thinking, most people judge their possessions in comparison with others'. People tend not to ask themselves, does my house meet my needs? Instead they ask, is my house nicer than my neighbor's? If you
75 own a two-bedroom house and everyone around you owns a two-bedroom house, your reference anxiety will be low, and your two-bedroom house may seem fine. But if your two-bedroom house is surrounded by three-and four-bedroom houses, with someone around the corner doing a tear-down to
80 build a McMansion, your reference anxiety may rise. Suddenly that two-bedroom house—one that your grandparents might have considered quite nice, even luxurious—doesn't seem enough. And so the money you spent on it stops providing you with a sense of well-being.

Our soaring reference anxiety is a product of the widening gap in income distribution. In other words, the rich are getting richer and faster, and the rest of us are none too happy
85 about it. During much of U.S. history, the majority lived in small towns or urban areas where conditions for most people were approximately the same—hence low reference anxiety. Also, most people knew relatively little about those who were living higher on the hog.

But in the past few decades, new economic forces have changed all that. Rapid growth in income for the top 5% of households has brought about a substantial cohort of people who
90 live notably better than the middle class does, amplifying our reference anxiety. That wealthier minority is occupying ever larger homes and spending more on each change of clothes than others spend on a month's rent. It all feeds middle-class anxiety, even when the middle is doing O.K. In nations with high levels of income equality like the Scandinavian countries, well-being tends to be higher than in nations with unequal wealth distribution
95 such as the U.S. Meanwhile, television and the Web make it easier to know how the very well off live. (Never mind whether they're happy.) Want a peek inside Donald Trump's gold-plated world? Just click on the TV, and he'll show you. Wonder what Bill Gates' 66,000 square
100 feet mega mansion is like? Just download the floor plan from the Internet!

Paradoxically, it is the very increase in money—which creates the wealth so visible in today's society—that triggers dissatisfaction. As
105 material expectations keep rising, more money may engender only more desires. "What people

---

prestige /prɛˈstiʒ/ n. the respect or admiration that sb./sth. has because of their special position, or what they have done
confer /kənˈfə/ v. to give sb. an award, a university degree or particular honor or right
live high on the hog to live luxuriously
cohort /ˈkoˌhɔrt/ n. a group of people who share the common feature or aspect of behavior
amplify /ˈæmpləˌfaɪ/ v. to increase sth. in strength, especially sound
mega /ˈmegə/ adj. very large or impressive

want in terms of material things and life experiences has increased almost exactly in lockstep with the postwar earnings curve," Diener notes. As men and women move up the economic ladder, most almost immediately stop feeling grateful for their elevated circumstances and focus on what they still don't have. Suppose you lived in a two-bedroom house for years and dreamed of three bedrooms. You finally get that three-bedroom house. Will it bring you happiness? Not necessarily. Three bedrooms will become your new norm, and you'll begin to long for a four-bedroom abode.

That money never satisfies is suggested by this telling fact: polls show that Americans believe that, whatever their income level, they need more to live well. Even those making large sums said still larger sums were required. We seem conditioned to think we do not have enough, even if objectively our lives are comfortable.

lockstep /ˈlɒkstep/ *n.*	a situation where things happen at the same time or change at the same time
elevated /ˈelɪˌveɪtɪd/ *adj.*	high in rank
abode /əˈbəʊd/ *n.*	the place where sb. lives
telling /ˈtelɪŋ/ *adj.*	having a great or important effect; significant
condition /kənˈdɪʃən/ *v.*	to train sb./sth. to behave in a particular way or to become used to a particular situation
lot /lɒt/ *n.*	a person's luck or situation in life
anticipate /ænˈtɪsəˌpeɪt/ *v.*	to think with pleasure and excitement about sth. that is going to happen
decent /ˈdiːsənt/ *adj.*	[especially spoken] of a good enough standard or quality
licensed /ˈlaɪsnst/ *adj.*	having official permission to do sth.
paradoxically /ˌpærəˈdɒksɪklɪ/ *adv.*	inconsistently
impediment /ɪmˈpedɪmənt/ *n.*	something that delays or stops the progress of sth. else
fixated /ˈfɪkseɪtɪd/ *adj.*	unable to stop thinking about something
scheme /skiːm/ *n.*	a plan or system for doing or organizing sth.

Then again, if we think our lot is improving, happiness follows. Carol Graham, an economist at the Brookings Institution in Washington, found that people's expectations about the future may have more influence on their sense of well-being than their current state does. People living modestly but anticipating better days to come, Graham thinks, are likely to be happier than people living well but not looking forward to improvements in their living standards. Consider two people: one earns $50,000 a year and foresees a 10% raise, and the other makes $150,000 but does not expect any salary increase. The second person is much better off in financial terms, but the first is more likely to feel good about life.

And guess what? The U.S. hasn't had a decent raise in two decades. Income growth has almost come to a halt for the middle class. In real terms, although median household income is higher than ever, median household income has increased only around 15% since 1984. That means most people have never had it better but do not expect any improvement in the near future. People tend to focus on the negative part and ignore the positive.

Living standards, education levels and other basic measures of U.S. social well-being have improved so much so quickly in the postwar era that another big leap seems improbable. If the typical new house is more than 2,300 sq. ft., if more than half of high school graduates advance to college, if there are more cars and trucks in the U.S. than there are licensed drivers—all current statistics—then the country may need stability and equality more than it needs more money. But because we are all conditioned to think there's something wrong if we don't make more money each year, high standards of living in the U.S. may, paradoxically, have become an impediment to happiness. Fixated on always getting more, we fail to appreciate how much we have. Of course, in the grand scheme it's better that there are large numbers of Americans who are materially comfortable, if a bit whiny about it, than who are destitute. And never forget: one in eight Americans are poor. Poverty remains a stark reality amid American affluence.

> destitute /ˈdestɪˌtut/ *adj.* without money, food and the other things necessary for life
> stark /stɑrk/ *adj.* looking severe and without any color or decoration

155 Psychology and sociology aside, there is a final reason money can't buy happiness: the things that really matter in life are not sold in  stores. Love, friendship, family, respect, a place in the community, the belief that your life has purpose—those are the essential of human fulfillment, and they cannot be 160 purchased with cash. Everyone needs a certain amount of money, but chasing money rather than meaning is a formula for discontent. Too many Americans have made materialism and the cycle of work and spend their principal goals. Then they wonder why they don't feel happy.

Better Know More

1. Inflation-adjusted income

Inflation-adjusted income refers to the income after inflation adjustment. Inflation adjustment is the process of adjusting economic indicators and the prices of goods and services from different time periods to the same price level. To adjust for inflation, an indicator is divided by the inflation index. This adjustment process takes prices—generally for a given year (e.g., "1942 dollars")—in the original "nominal dollars" (or "current dollars")（现值美元）and renders them into "constant dollars"（定值美元）.

2. Forbes 400

The Forbes 400, also known as 400 Richest Americans, is a list published by *Forbes Magazine* of the richest 400 Americans, ranked by net worth. It is published in September each year, and 2010 marks the 29th year. The Forbes 400 records who dominates the wealth in America, which exhibits the shape of American economy. The magazine displays the story of someone's rise to fame, their company, age, industrial residence, and education.

3. Reference anxiety

In psychology, anxiety is a feeling of dread, fear, or apprehension, often with no clear justification. Anxiety differs from true fear in that it is typically the product of subjective, internal emotional states rather than a response to a clear and actual danger. It is marked by physiological signs such as sweating, tension, and increased pulse, by doubt concerning the reality and nature of the perceived threat, and by self-doubt about one's capacity to cope with it. Some anxiety inevitably arises in the course of daily life and is normal, but persistent, intense, chronic, or recurring anxiety not justified by real-life stresses is usually regarded as a sign of an emotional disorder. In this text, reference anxiety refers to the anxiety people feel by comparing with others.

4. **Keeping up with the Joneses**

It is an idiom in many parts of the English-speaking world which refers to the comparison to one's neighbor as a standard for social caste or the accumulation of material goods; in Chinese, "攀比". To fail to "keep up with the Joneses" is regarded as demonstrating socio-economic or cultural inferiority.

5. **Donald Trump**

Donald Trump is an American business magnate, socialite, author and television personality. He is the Chairman and CEO of the Trump Organization, a US-based real-estate developer. Trump is also the founder of Trump Entertainment Resorts, which operates numerous casinos and hotels across the world. Trump's extravagant lifestyle and outspoken manner have made him a celebrity for years, a status amplified by the success of his NBC reality show, *The Apprentice*.

Check Your Understanding

Please answer the following questions based on what you have learnt in the text.

1. What were the social conditions in the U.S. after World War II?
2. How do you understand "more money leads to depression"?
3. Why was Grandma referred to in the text?
4. How does wealth affect people's choices and attitudes towards life?
5. According to the author, what is the best therapy for unhappiness?
6. What is the relationship between money and happiness according to the author's viewpoint?

A Sip of Word Formation

📖 Pejorative Prefixes

Mis-, *mal-*, and *pseudo-* are the pejorative prefixes.
1. The prefix *mis-* can be traced back to Old English. The basic meaning of the prefix *mis-* is "bad, badly; wrong, wrongly" (e.g. *misfortune, misbehavior*). Besides, *mis-* also frequently forms compounds by attaching to nouns that come from verbs (e.g. *miscalculation, mismanagement, mispronunciation*).

2. The prefix *mal*- denotes total opposite to the stem, which means "not correct or correctly" (e.g. *malpractice*) or "bad or badly" (e.g. *maltreat*).
3. *Pseudo*- means "fake, false" (e.g. *pseudoscience*), or "not genuine or pretended" (e.g. *pseudointellectual*).

Build Your Vocabulary

For each of the following sentences, a word is provided in the brackets. Use the appropriate form of the word to fill in the blank in the sentence, so that the sentence is logical and grammatical.

1. The failure of the whole project can be attributed partially to the newly-promoted manager's _____ of the market. (judge)
2. The real reason for the current crisis is that the economic leaders allowed Fannie Mae and Freddie Mac to _____ mortgage rates. (management)
3. The police identified a handful of _____ as the prime suspects for the frequent vandalism at the City Hall. (content)
4. The student was banned from using the university's facilities for two weeks due to gross _____ online. (conduct)
5. Mary Ann Evans wrote under the _____ of George Eliot. (name)
6. The abnormal termination of a computer program usually results from an unrecoverable error or _____. (function)
7. _____ is a must to a hunter under the potential attack of the game. He can skillfully turn the game to a more friendly target. (direct)
8. _____ are perhaps the single greatest source of our arguments and fights with each other. (understand)

You'd Like to Be

A Skilled Text Weaver

Fill in the blanks with the words you have learnt in this text, one word for each blank. You are advised to read the text carefully until you have become very familiar with it before starting to work on this task.

To succeed and prosper in a global economy and interconnected world, Chinese college students have realized the importance of international knowledge, intercultural communication skills, and global perspectives. The past decade has witnessed a increase of Chinese students studying in universities of _____ all over the world. A of students have become part of this wave and the number is still on the rise.

Among all the factors that _____ such a wave, the recent _____, or the

_____ living conditions, has been identified as the major driving force, thanks largely to the economic growth in China. It is _____ that students, therefore, should have had unprecedented opportunities to fully immerse themselves in global learning and _____ their understandings of diversified disciplines. _____, _____ results of recent surveys tell another story. A _____ amount of these students report to have encountered many _____: language barrier, cultural shock, maladjustments, academic failure, etc. It is highly recommended that more research should be _____ on how international students should better adjust to learning in exotic cultures.

A Sharp Interpreter

Please paraphrase the following sentences. Change the sentence structure wherever necessary.

1. If you made a graph of American life since the end of World War II, every line concerning money and the things that money can buy would soar upward, a statistical monument to materialism.
2. Yet if you charted the incidence of depression since 1950, the lines suggested a growing epidemic.
3. The study, which has been replicated in the U.S., shows that Grandma had a point.
4. But because we are all conditioned to think there's something wrong if we don't make more money each year, high standards of living in the U.S. may, paradoxically, have become an impediment to happiness.
5. Paradoxically, it is the very increase in money—which creates the wealth so visible in today's society—that triggers dissatisfaction.
6. Our soaring reference anxiety is a product of the widening gap in income distribution.

A Solid Sentence Constructor

The following is a list of words and expressions you have learnt in the text. Please make a sentence with each of them.

1. to live through
2. episode
3. a cohort of
4. to have a point
5. to cease to
6. none too
7. to render
8. to tend to

A Careful Writer

The following are two groups of words. You are required to study the words in each group carefully and then use them to write a paragraph of your own. Make sure that the paragraphs you have written are grammatical and coherent.

1. designer   debilitating   soaring   confer

2. conditioned   foresee   scheme   destitute   stark

A Superb Bilingualist

Please translate the following sentences into English using words or expressions provided in the brackets.

1. 商业大亨唐纳德·特朗普出任电视真人秀节目《飞黄腾达》(The Apprentice)的总制片人后,知名度大增。(make ... of ...)
2. 别再为你的野蛮行为找借口了！还说什么举止行为与情绪有很大关系！荒谬！(have much to do with)
3. 随着苹果公司相继推出iPad和MacBook Air,一场电子产品的创新革命一触即发。(around the corner)
4. 在这个国家,贪官污吏日食万钱；而他们的同胞却在忍饥挨饿。(live high on the hog)
5. 我听过最无稽的论调是:通货膨胀随着人口的增加而增长。(in lockstep with)
6. 经济危机两年以来,各国政府采用了各种方法恢复经济并取得了明显的效果:通货膨胀得以抑制,失业率保持平稳。(come to a halt)
7. 辩方律师强有力的论辩使陪审团为之信服。(telling)

Text B

Happiness

By Jenny McPhee
(Abridged and Edited)

For centuries, scientists and academics have studied what is wrong with us, paying scant attention to exploring what already works. The new happiness movement, which involves psychologists, neurologists, sociologists, and even economists, investigates not what is wrong but what is right, and seeks to discover how we can use our positive emotions to improve our quality of life.

A harbinger of this growing field is Martin E.P. Seligman, Ph. D., former head of the American Psychological Association and author of the best-selling book *Learned Optimism*. He calls his brand of happiness "positive psychology" and promotes it as a healthy alternative to either years of exploring an unhappy childhood with a psychotherapist or drugs such as Prozac, Zoloft, and Paxil. "This relentless focus on the negative," Seligman claims, "has left psychology blind to the many instances of ... drive and insight that develop out of undesirable, painful life events."

Basically, Seligman's idea is that you can train yourself to spin the events in your life from an optimistic point of view. For example, if you're fired from your job, see it as an opportunity for a new beginning. Your relationship breaks up, so you decide to find someone who plays to your strengths, not your weaknesses. And you learn to fully appreciate the good things that happen to you—no thinking you pulled the wool over their eyes when you get a promotion. Seligman is convinced that "the positive social science of the 21st century will have as a useful side effect the possibility of prevention of the serious mental illnesses; for there are a set of human strengths that most likely buffer against mental illness: courage, optimism, interpersonal skill, work ethic, hope... But it will have as its direct effect a scientific understanding of the practice of civic virtue and of the pursuit of the best things in life."

Recent studies linking happiness—in particular laughter—and health would appear to back Seligman's theory: People who smile more frequently tend to have lower blood pressure and stronger immune systems. A current UCLA study is attempting to find clear biological evidence for laughter's therapeutic effects on cancer patients. And filmmaker Mira Nair recently made a documentary on India's

---

scant /skænt/ *adj.* hardly any, not very much and not as much as there should be

neurologist /nʊˈrɑlədʒɪst/ *n.* a doctor who studies and treats diseases of the nerves

harbinger /ˈhɑrbɪndʒə/ *n.* a sign that shows that sth. is going to happen soon, often sth. bad

psychotherapist /ˌsaɪkoˈθɛrəpɪst/ *n.* a person who studies the psychotherapy

spin /spɪn/ *v.* to present information or a situation in a particular way, especially one that makes you or your ideas seem good

buffer /ˈbʌfə/ *v.* to protect sb. from sth.

civic /ˈsɪvɪk/ *adj.* connected with the people who live in a town or city

immune /ɪˈmjoːn/ *adj.* that cannot be caught or be affected by a particular disease or illness

laughing clubs, a widespread phenomenon in which people laugh together for about 20 minutes a day with beneficial results. Employers have found that since initiating the laughing clubs in factories, there is less absenteeism and better performance among the workers.

But doesn't "the pursuit of the best things in life" cost money? How many times have we said to ourselves, If only I were rich, I would be so much happier? Economists are increasingly interested in just how money does contribute to our happiness levels. In fact, in 2000, the Woodrow Wilson School of Public and International Affairs at Princeton University opened its Center for Health and Well-being, staffed by a significant number of economists. For some time now, psychologists have been declaring that the old adage is true: Money can't buy happiness.

There is, in fact, a wide body of evidence showing that people who aspire to have money, fame, and beauty are less happy than those who engage in daily activities they find fulfilling and pleasurable.

initiate /ɪˈnɪʃiˌet/ v. [formal] to make sth. begin
absenteeism /ˌæbsənˈtiˌɪzəm/ n. the fact of being frequently away from work or school, especially without good reasons
adage /ˈædɪdʒ/ n. a well-known phrase expressing a general truth about people or the world
preliminary /prɪˈlɪməˌnɛri/ adj. happening before a more important action or event
intriguing /ɪnˈtriːgɪŋ/ adj. very interesting because of being unusual or not having an obvious answer
neurobiology /ˌnʊrobaɪˈɑlədʒi/ n. the study of cells of the nervous system and the organization of these cells into functional circuits
perceive /pəˈsiv/ v. to understand or think of sth. in a particular way
ephemeral /ɪˈfɛmərəl/ adj. lasting or used for only a short period of time
inherit /ɪnˈhɛrɪt/ v. to have qualities, physical features, etc. that are similar to those of your parents, grandparents, etc.
plasticity /plæˈstɪsəti/ n. the quality of being easily made into different shapes
hardwired /ˈhɑːdˈwaɪəd/ adj. [technical] (of computer functions) built into the permanent system and not provided by software
stroke /strok/ n. a single movement of the arm when hitting sb./sth.

Pursuing the small pleasures of life as a formula for happiness is reinforced by the preliminary findings of perhaps the most intriguing, indeed revolutionary, area in the new happiness studies: the neurobiology of happiness. Emotions—happiness, sadness, fear, anger, love, desire—have traditionally been perceived as spiritual, ephemeral things that were not of the body, belonging instead to the realm of the soul. Now, however, researchers are making connections between brain activity and emotions. As neurologist Antonio Damasio, Ph.D., M.D., best-selling author of The Feeling of What Happens, describes, "We are not thinking machines. We are feeling machines that think."

Some studies suggest that about 50 percent of a person's capacity for happiness is inherited. But others are wary of putting a fixed numerical value on the possibility for happiness, especially since one amazing neurological discovery of the past 15 years is the brain's plasticity. At one time, scientists thought that after the first years of life the brain was hardwired never to be altered. Neuroscientists are now finding that our environment not only can cause enduring changes to our DNA, it can affect the very shape of the brain, even into old age.

This discovery has led experts to prescribe brain exercises for a wide range of conditions from massive strokes to mild memory loss. "The brain is like a muscle," says behavioral neuroscientist Edward Taub, Ph.D. "And the more that you exercise it, the better it gets." Taub and others in the field recommend daily mind exercises for everyone, things like brushing your teeth with your left hand if you are right-handed, alternating the wrist on which you wear your watch, or making a mental list of all the objects you see when you walk into a room. Above all, they are recommending what Buddhists and New Agers have long been telling us: Avoid or minimize stress. Studies by Stanford University neuroscientist and biologist Robert Sapolsky, Ph.D., suggest that stress takes a large toll not only on memory but on the overall well-being of your brain.

| alternate /ˈɔltərˌneɪt/ v. (of things or people) to follow one after the other in a repeated pattern |
| minimize /ˈmɪnəˌmaɪz/ v. to reduce sth., especially sth. bad to the lowest possible level |
| cue /kju/ n. an action or event that is a signal for sb. to do sth. |
| persimmon /pəˈsɪmən/ n. a sweet tropical fruit that looks like a large orange tomato |
| geneticist /dʒəˈnɛtɪsɪst/ n. a scientist who studies genetics |
| epicure /ˈɛpɪˌkjʊrs/ n. a person who enjoys food and drink of high quality and knows a lot about it |

Which brings us back to the science of happiness, and how might we go about reshaping our brains and lives in order to maintain lower levels of stress and higher levels of contentment? Drugs are one way, but if a psychopharmacological solution is not for you (there is still the side-effects problem), there may be a more organic solution. Exercises devised to help improve your overall sense of well-being could involve determining the specific environmental cues in your life that activate neural systems that cause you to feel happy—eating a perfectly ripe persimmon, perhaps. Then, make sure you frequently do the things that fill you with a sense of joy, fun, and satisfaction. In The New York Times, behavioral geneticist David Lykken, Ph.D., gave this advice: "Be an experiential epicure... Find the small things that you know give you a little high... and sprinkle your life with them."

Forty-two years ago, Rodgers and Hammerstein, in their musical The Sound of Music, gave us the prescription in song: "I simply remember my favorite things. And then I don't feel so bad." And, as Aristotle indicated over two millennia ago, being happy is "an activity in accordance with excellence," and excellence is something one must continuously work toward, not unlike engaging in regular exercise for a healthy body. Soon, it will be perfectly normal to go to your personal neurotrainer to work out the mind in order to have a happier and healthier life. In the meantime, just what is it that makes you happy?

Notes

For some of the terms in the following, no explanation is provided. You are required to explain them by making use of the library, the Internet or whatever sources accessible.

1. American Psychological Association

2. **Prozac, Zoloft, Paxil**
Prozac 百忧解；Zoloft 舍曲林；Paxil 帕罗西汀。这三种都是治疗精神抑郁的药物。

3. **UCLA**

4. **Documentary**
In this text, documentary refers to documentary film, which is a broad category of moving pictures intended to document some aspect of reality. A "documentary film" was originally a movie shot on film stock—the only medium available—but now includes video and digital productions that can be either direct-to-video or made for a television program. "Documentary" has been described as a "filmmaking practice, a cinematic tradition, and mode of audience reception" that is continually evolving and is without clear boundaries.

5. **New Agers**
New Agers are the representatives of the New Age Movement, a wide-ranging set of beliefs and practices that are an outgrowth of the counterculture of the 1960s and 70s in the United States. New Agers believe that a spiritual era is dawning in which individuals and society will be transformed. The movement encompasses a wide range of ideas, including personal spiritual growth and self-realization, holistic medicine (including the use of crystals for healing), reincarnation, astrology, and the mystical energies said to be induced by pyramids. Many critics of the movement regard it as anti-intellectual.

6. **The New York Times**

7. **Rodgers and Hammerstein in their musical** *The Sound of Music*

The Sound of Music (1959) is a musical with music by Richard Rodgers, lyrics by Oscar Hammerstein II and a book by Howard Lindsay and Russell Crouse. It is based on the memoir of Maria von Trapp, *The Story of the Trapp Family Singers*. Many songs from the musical have become standards, including the title song *The Sound of Music, Edelweiss, My Favorite Things*, and *Do-Re-Mi*. The original Broadway production opened in November 1959, and the show has enjoyed numerous productions and revivals since then. It was adapted as a 1965 film musical starring which won Academy Awards. *The Sound of Music* was the final musical written by Rodgers and Hammerstein; Hammerstein died of cancer nine months after the Broadway premiere.

8. **Aristotle**

_____
_____
_____
_____
_____

Comprehension Questions

Please answer the following questions based on what you have learnt in the text.

1. By "The new happiness movement ... seeks to discover how we can use our positive emotions to improve our quality of life," what does the author mean?
2. Is "positive psychology" a much more effective way to promote one's happiness than the traditional medical therapy?
3. Is the idea "one's capacity for happiness is inherited" logical, according to the author? Why?
4. What is the main idea of the text?

Writing Practice

Happiness seems to be an eternal topic in our lives. A lot of scholars have made arguments about it, some seeking its origin, others exploring its means and still others wondering where it finally leads. The author of this article, on the other hand, chooses another perspective by illustrating the relationships between money and happiness. The author poses serious questions, cites surprising examples and makes telling comparisons.

Now you are supposed to express your ideas on the relationship between money and happiness. You can support or criticize the author's opinion. You can also form your own perspective.

Further Study

This is the end of Unit 3; but you can also gain more knowledge by accessing the following resources.

Recommended film: *Tuesdays with Morrie*—Mitch became caught up with his career as a sport commentator and journalist. He ignored his girlfriend and did not make time to do things in life that are of the most value to a human being. Morrie was one of Mitch's professors at college and a famous scholar. One day Mitch was watching television and saw Morrie giving an interview. In the interview, Morrie said albeit he knew he was dying of Lou Gehrig disease, he was trying to live his life to the full. All he really wanted was happiness for himself, his friends and family. After that interview, every Tuesday Mitch flew to Massachusetts to have long talks about life's greatest lessons with his professor until his death. This film was adapted from a book with the same title by Mitch Albo.

Unit 4

Education

Unit Goals

Upon completing the texts in this unit, students should be able to:
- ☞ understand the situation of public education in America and the debates that have been going on around public education and single-sex education;
- ☞ develop the ability to think critically;
- ☞ use prefixes of degree or size correctly to form new words.

Before Reading

📖 Hands-on Activities and Brainstorming

1. American education system is different from Chinese education system in many ways. Visit the website http://www.usastudyguide.com/usaeducationasystem.htm for knowledge about the development of American education system and then make a comparison between the two, highlighting their advantages and disadvantages. It is highly recommended that you develop it into a presentation.
2. Since the 1990s, the concept of quality-oriented education has gradually found its place in Chinese education. Changes have been made to curriculum goals, structure and content, as well as teaching and learning approaches with a view to cultivating students' creative spirit and ability. Do you think the changes have led to satisfactory results? Give examples to support your argument.

📖 A Glimpse at Words and Expressions

Please read the following sentences. Pay attention to the underlined part in each sentence and to how it is used in the sentence and then decide on its meaning. Write down the meaning in the brackets.

1. Academic standards have sunk <u>out of sight.</u>　　　　　　　(　　　)

2. When those poor results are recognized, the system and its defenders can be counted on to say that the problem is insufficient spending. (   )

3. Reich argues that while public school systems in affluent areas are turning out students who are college or work-ready because they have learned "to identify and solve new problems, ..." (   )

4. Therefore, we have to do something to equalize spending so that all students will have an equal shot at a good education. (   )

5. We know that because there are many nongovern mental schools in poor urban areas that produce remarkable skilled graduates, despite the fact they operate on shoestring budgets. (   )

6. He wants to do away with local property taxes to fund public education and institute a national wealth tax instead. (   )

7. People are entitled to do with what they want with their own income or wealth. (   )

8. In many states, public schools in poorer areas receive state assistance that boosts their spending to levels that rival that of the most prosperous areas. (   )

Text A

National Wealth Tax to Fund Education?

By George C. Leef
(Abridged and Edited)

"Public education" in the United States is very high in cost and very low in positive results. While some students graduate from public schools with sharp intellectual skills (often owing more to their home environment than to their school instruction), many others drift aimlessly through 12 years of classes where little is expected of them, academic standards have sunk out of sight, and discipline is a joke. The teachers are protected by union contracts with

drift /drɪft/ *v.* to move or to do sth. without a particular plan or purpose

piranha-like teeth and they have little incentive to do their best.

And what their best might be is highly questionable. Thanks to strict state licensing laws, it is almost obligatory for anyone who wants to teach in public schools to go through a lengthy course of study in a college or university "school of education," where the emphasis is on dubious pedagogical theories such as cooperative learning and multicultural sensitivity rather than on the mastery of subject matter and how best to impart that knowledge to students. School administrators seldom have the freedom to hire teachers who haven't been through the school swamp, no matter how much more competent uncertified people who happen to really know their math, chemistry, history, English, etc., maybe.

From its innumerable regulations that impede efficiency to the overarching fact that there is no penalty for failure, public education follows a socialist recipe and we get educational results that are the equivalent of Soviet-built cars.

When those poor results are recognized, the system and its defenders can be counted on to say that the problem is insufficient spending. Never mind that real spending on public education has been rising steadily for decades or that non-government schools produce better educational results with far lower per-pupil spending. The problem is always that we aren't "investing" enough in public education. In a recent National Public Radio commentary, Robert Reich (who served as Bill Clinton's secretary of labor and now teaches at Brandeis University) took exactly that approach.

Reich argues that while public school systems in affluent areas are turning out students who are college or work-ready because they have learned "to identify and solve new problems, recognize patterns, and think critically," schools in poorer areas aren't able to do that. The reason, of course, is money. Poorer school districts can't afford to hire really well-trained teachers and have small classes, Reich says. Therefore, we have to do something to equalize spending so that all students will have an equal shot at a good education.

Before we get to Reich's solution, let's stop and ask whether a shortage of money is really the problem. In many states, public schools in poorer areas receive state assistance that boosts their spending to levels that rival

---

piranha-like *adj.* having the feature of piranha which is a small American fresh water fish that attacks and eats live animals
incentive /ɪnˈsentɪv/ *n.* something that encourages one to do sth.
questionable /ˈkwestʃənəbəl/ *adj.* doubtful as regards truth or validity
obligatory /əˈblɪɡəˌtɔrɪ/ *adj.* [formal] that one must do because of the law, rules, etc.
lengthy /ˈleŋkθi/ *adj.* very long, and often too long, in time or size
dubious /ˈdubiəs/ *adj.* that one cannot be sure about; that is probably not good
pedagogical /ˌpedəˈɡɑdʒɪkl/ *adj.* concerning teaching methods
sensitivity /ˌsensɪˈtɪvɪti/ *n.* the ability to experience and understand deep feelings, especially in art and literature
impart /ɪmˈpɑrt/ *v.* [formal] to pass information, knowledge, etc. to other people
swamp /swɑmp/ *n.* an area that is very wet or covered with water and in which plants, trees, etc. are growing
competent /ˈkɑmpɪtənt/ *adj.* having enough skill or knowledge to do sth. well or to the necessary standard
uncertified /ʌnˈsɜrtəˌfaɪd/ *adj.* not officially recognized as having a certain status or meeting certain standards
innumerable /ɪˈnumərəbəl/ *adj.* too many to be counted
impede /ɪmˈpid/ *v.* [often passive][formal] to delay or stop the progress of sth.
overarching /ˌovəˈɑrtʃɪŋ/ *adj.* [usually before nouns] very important because it includes or influences many things
recipe /ˈresəˌpi/ *n.* a method or an idea that seems likely to have a particular result
equalize /ˈikwəˌlaɪz/ *v.* to make things equal in size, quantity, value, etc. in the whole of a place or group
shot /ʃɑt/ *n.* [informal] an attempt to do sth. or achieve sth., especially sth. difficult
boost /bust/ *v.* to make sth. increase, or become better or successful

that of the most prosperous areas. In Michigan, for example, per-pupil spending in Detroit in 2002 was $9,532, compared to the state average of $7,733. "Poor" Detroit was not far behind ritzy neighboring Birmingham, where per-pupil spending was $11,456. True, there is some difference, but it's not Appalachia versus Beverly Hills. Furthermore, we have already experimented with huge increases in educational spending in poor areas. In Kansas City, because of an edict from a federal judge in 1985, spending was vastly increased to build state-of-the-art schools that have been called Taj Mahals. After nearly 20 years of that policy, however, student test scores were as low as ever. High per-pupil spending is not a sufficient condition for good educational results.

Nor is it a necessary condition. We know that because there are many nongovernmental schools in poor urban areas that produce remarkably skilled graduates, despite the fact that they operate on shoestring budgets. Often, those schools use makeshift buildings, hire uncertified teachers, and have relatively large classes (something that is common in Japan, where high teacher quality is regarded as far more beneficial than low class size). There is a great deal of information on the success of non-government urban schools; one good source is Sol Stern's book *Breaking Free*. It is therefore true that high spending is not a necessary condition for educational success.

The problems that beset public education are deep and inherent, rooted in the very nature of any enterprise that obtains its revenue not from willing payers, but from taxes. Throwing more money at public education cannot solve the problems.

Still, Professor Reich wants to throw more money into public education.

He wants to do away with local property taxes to fund public education and institute a national wealth tax instead, which he recommends setting at "one tenth of one percent of everyone's total assets each year, to be distributed to school districts around the country on the basis of the number of kids they have to educate." Reich contends that his national wealth tax would be "simple and fair," a means of giving "every school a fighting chance."

How could there be any objections to that?

First it wouldn't be simple. We would need a new federal agency to determine the value of everyone's assets. The Internal Revenue Code goes on for thousands of pages in the attempt to define "income" and the effort to place a value on everyone's wealth would be hardly less difficult. A new federal bureaucracy demands reports on the value of everything

---

prosperous /ˈprɑspərəs/ *adj.* rich and successful
ritzy /ˈrɪtsi/ *adj.* expensive and fashionable
edict /ˈiːdɪkt/ *n.* an official order or statement given by sb. in authority
federal /ˈfɛdərəl/ *adj.* (within the federal system, especially the US) connected with national government rather than the local government of an individual state
shoestring /ˈʃuːˌstrɪŋ/ *adj.* using very little money
beset /bɪˈsɛt/ *v.* to affect sb./sth. in an unpleasant or harmful way
inherent /ɪnˈhɪrənt/ *adj.* that is a basic or permanent part of sth. and that cannot be removed
revenue /ˈrɛvənjuː/ *n.* (also revenues) the money that a government receives form taxes or that an organization, etc. receives from its business
distribute /dɪˈstrɪbjuːt/ *v.* to give things to a large number of people; to share sth. among a number of people
contend /kənˈtɛnd/ *v.* to say that sth. is true, especially in an argument
agency /ˈeɪdʒənsi/ *n.* (especially AmE) a government department that provides a particular service
bureaucracy /bjʊˈrɑkrəsi/ *n.* a system of government in which most of the important decisions are taken by state officials rather than by elected representatives

from houses to stamp collections, golf clubs to fishing boats. Maybe Reich isn't bothered by that prospect, but I find it most unappealing.

Second, it wouldn't be fair. There is nothing fair about confiscating any amount of wealth from people who don't want to support schools in Detroit, New York, Washington, D.C., or even their hometown. People are entitled to do what they want with their own income or wealth. Professor Reich is free to give as much money as he wants to help poor schools from his own pocket, and he's free to implore us to do likewise, but he has no moral right to compel the rest of us to do the same.

Third, it would never stop. Reich may think that his initial .001 wealth tax would be enough money, but as sure as the sun will rise tomorrow, it wouldn't be. The education establishment's appetite for money is unending, and once the camel had its nose inside the wealth-tax tent, it would continue pushing in. Just as the income tax started out small but rapidly grew, so would the wealth tax for education.

unappealing /ˌʌnəˈpiːlɪŋ/ adj.	not attractive or pleasant
confiscate /ˈkɒnfɪˌskeɪt/ v.	to officially take sth. away from sb., especially as a punishment
entitle /ɛnˈtaɪtl/ v.	[often passive] to give sb. the right to have or to do sth.
implore /ɪmˈplɔːr/ v.	to ask sb. to do sth. in an anxious way because one wants or needs it very much
appetite /ˈæpɪˌtaɪt/ n.	a strong desire for sth.
pathetic /pəˈθɛtɪk/ adj.	making one feel pity or sadness
monstrosity /mɒnˈstrɒsɪti/ n.	something that is very large and very ugly, especially a building
prop /prɒp/ v.	[often disapproving] to help sth. that is having difficulties
tyrannical /tɪˈrænɪkəl/ adj.	using power or authority over people in an unfair and cruel way
regime /reɪˈʒiːm/ n.	a method or system of government, especially one that has not been elected in a fair way
fatten /ˈfætn:/ v.	to make sb./sth. fatter, especially an animal before killing it for food; to become fatter
trough /trɒf/ n.	a long narrow open container for animals to eat or drink from
advocate /ˈædvəˌkeɪt/ v.	to support sth. publicly

And fourth, it wouldn't do any good. The reason inner-city schools do so poorly is not that they don't have enough money to spend, but that the funds they receive are sent into a bureaucratic black hole. In New York, for example, schools remain in pathetic condition, despite an enormous budget, because of such monstrosities as the School Construction Authority. The late Peter Bauer used to point out that foreign aid did far more to prop up tyrannical regimes than to help hungry people and that is exactly what would happen with increased government spending on public education. Dumping more money into public education would fatten the wallets of those who feed at the public education trough, but it wouldn't lead to better student learning.

Poor people can buy high-quality food, clothing, and other necessities because they get the benefit of a free market in those things. For good education, what they need is a free market in schools. If you really care about the education of children—and not just poor ones—you should forget about new taxes or "reforms" and advocate the separation of school and state.

Better Know More

1. Public education

Public education is schooling provided by the government, and paid for by taxes. It is generally available to all. In most countries, it is compulsory for children to attend up to a certain age. Public education can be contrasted with private schooling, in which schools are run independently and charge students tuition fees. In the U.S., schools run by the states at the expense of the taxpayers and not charging tuition are called *public schools*, but in other English-speaking countries that term may have quite a different meaning.

2. Appalachia

Appalachia is a term used to describe a region in the eastern United States that stretches from southern New York State to northern Alabama, Mississippi, and Georgia. Prior to the 20th century, the people of Appalachia were geographically isolated from the rest of the country. As a result, they have been unable to catch up to the modernization that lowlanders have achieved. Severe poverty has made the living standard comparable to that of third world countries. Rot, termite infestations, holes, cracked and broken foundations, and the like have rendered many of their homes beyond repair.

3. Beverly Hills

Beverly Hills is an enclaved city in Los Angeles County in Southern California, surrounded almost entirely by Los Angeles. Since the 1950's Beverly Hills has marketed itself as one of the most glamorous places in the world to shop. The Golden Triangle, formed by Beverly Hills and its wealthy neighbors Bel-Air and Holmby Hills, is regarded as the apex of chic shopping and fashion. Beverly Hills is home to many Hollywood celebrities, corporate executives and other wealthy individuals and families.

4. Taj Mahal

In 1631 Taj Mahal (泰姬陵) was built by a Muslim, Emperor Shah Jahan in memory of his dear wife and queen Mumtaz Mahal at Agra, India. It is regarded as one of the great wonders of the world. This extravagant Indian mausoleum is built entirely of white marble featuring Persian, Islamic and Indian architectural styles. The Indian Taj Mahal is a beautiful World Heritage site while the high school Taj Mahal referred to in the text is an embarrassment that the government cannot afford.

5. Breaking Free

Sol Stern's *Breaking Free* explores the growing demand for school choice among poor families. Stern vividly describes how cash-starved Catholic schools in the South Bronx are performing small educational miracles every day with children whom the public schools have given up on. Drawing on personal observation and intimate conversations with parents, students and educators, *Breaking Free* is the first book to transform school choice from an abstract policy issue into a question of basic personal freedom, and indeed, for minority children at the bottom of the social ladder, into a question of survival.

Check Your Understanding

Please answer the following questions based on what you have learnt in the text.

1. According to the author, what is the disadvantage of public schools?
2. What is responsible for the teachers' poor performance in U.S. public schools?
3. Is money the key factor that determines the quality of education? Why?
4. Why does the author mention Appalachia and Beverly Hills when talking about per-pupil spending?
5. Can you point out the metaphors employed in this text?
6. According to the author, what is the solution to the problems of public education?

A Sip of Word Formation

Prefixes of Degree or Size

Arch-, *super-*, *out-*, *sur-*, *sub-*, *over-*, *under-*, *hyper-*, *ultra-*, and *mini-* are prefixes of degree or size.

1. *Arch-* is usually added to nouns, which means most important, most extreme or main (e.g. *arch-enemy, arch-fascist*).
2. *Super-* can be attached to the noun, adjective, verb, and adverb. When it is added to the noun, adjective and adverb to form new nouns, adjectives and adverbs, the new words take on the meaning "extremely, more or better than normal" (e.g. *superman, superrich*). Sometimes, when added to the noun and verb, it can be explained as "above or over" (*superstructure, superintend*).
3. *Out-* can be added to verbs, nouns and adjectives. When attached to verbs, it means "greater, better, further, longer, etc." (e.g. *outwitted*). When attached to nouns and adjectives, it means "outside; away from" (e.g. *outgoing, outcast*).
4. *Over-* can be attached to nouns, verbs, adjectives and adverbs. It means (1) more than usual; too much (e.g. *overcurious, overeat*); (2) completely (e.g. *overhaul*); (3) upper; outer; extra (e.g. *overcoat*); (4) over; above (e.g. *overhang*).

5. *Under-* can be added to nouns, verbs, and adjectives. It has three kinds of meaning:
   (1) being under or below the thing (e.g. *undercover, underneath, underpass*);
   (2) below another rank or status (e.g. *undersecretary*);
   (3) something done to an insufficient amount or degree (e.g. *underfed, undercooked, underdeveloped*).
6. *Hyper-* comes from the Greek prefix *huper-*, which comes from the preposition "huper," with the meaning of "over, beyond". The basic meaning of the prefix *hyper-* is "excessive or excessively" (e.g. *hyperactive*).
7. *Ultra-* can be added to adjective and noun, with the meaning of "extremely; beyond a particular limit" (e.g. *ultraconservative*).
8. *Mini-* can be attached to nouns, meaning "small" (e.g. *miniskirt*).
9. The prefix *sub-* can be traced back to the Latin preposition sub, meaning "under". Some words beginning with *sub-* that came into English from Latin include *submerge, suburb,* and *subvert*.
   sub- can also form compounds by combining with verbs as well as with adjectives and nouns. When *sub-* is used to form words in English, it can mean:
   (1) under (e.g. *submarine, subsoil*);
   (2) subordinate (e.g. *subcommittee, subplot*);
   (3) less than completely (e.g. *subhuman, substandard*).
10. The prefix *sur-* means "over; above" (e.g. *surpass, surrealism*) or "around" (e.g. *surround*).

Build Your Vocabulary

For each of the following sentences, a word is provided in the brackets. Use the appropriate form of the word to fill in the blank in the sentence, so that the sentence is logical and grammatical.

1. Pepsi and Coke have been _____ for a long time. (rival)
2. The _____ skin of new-born babies cannot stand the fragrance added in many lotions. (sensitive)
3. We shouldn't be _____ about the differences. Let's try to look for more common ground. (critical)
4. Nowadays, _____ has become a problem we have to face. It causes problems in housing and employment. (population)
5. _____, also known as small culture, collective culture or vice culture, refers to unique beliefs, value and lifestyles that the members of particular sub-groups share. (cultural)
6. John Keats died young, but his reputation and influence _____ him. (live)
7. The span of the harbor bridge and the parabolic shells of the _____ opera house are Sydney's landmarks. (modern)
8. _____ are much smaller in size and cost, and they are often programmed to perform specific functions for a particular business activity. (computer)
9. A couple of years ago, I was working _____ on a case. (cover)

10. The 2009 Florida Legislature passed "Protecting Florida's Health Act" which levies a _____ on both cigarettes and tobacco products. (charge)

You'd Like to Be

📖 A Skilled Text Weaver

Fill in the blanks with the words you have learnt in this text, one word for each blank. You are advised to read the text carefully until you have become very familiar with it before starting to work on this task.

Though higher education is not _____ in most countries, many parents try every means to send their children to prestigious universities, for they believe that college education is a sure way to success. However, surveys show that their belief is _____. The grim reality is that quite a number of college students don't enjoy their life at college and many graduates are not _____ enough for their work. Consequently, they just _____ aimlessly from job to job. John is one of such students.

When he first entered the university, he was amazed at the _____ facilities and the _____ beauty of his campus, which was surrounded by towering mountains. Nevertheless, he soon grew bored with the monotonous college life and was fed up with the _____ and tedious lectures. He complained of a lack of _____ system to encourage teachers and students to work hard. He was even _____ of the qualification of some of his teachers who could not effectively _____ enlightening knowledge to the students. When college life came to an end, John was very happy to leave. With a college degree, he found working eight hours per day as a junior clerk extremely _____. Instead, running his own business was quite to his _____. He borrowed some money from his parents and began his business on a _____. Of course, his lack of experience and _____ unexpected difficulties _____ the progress of his business. Months later, he had to admit that his _____ business was a failure. What made it worse, he got a _____ for tax evasion and all of his assets were _____. Poor John! He had to compete with others in the job market again!

📖 A Sharp Interpreter

Please paraphrase the following sentences. Change the sentence structure wherever necessary.

1. While some students graduate from public schools with sharp intellectual skills (often owing more to their home environment than to their school instruction), many others drift aimlessly through 12 years of classes where little is expected of them, academic standards have sunk out of sight, and discipline is a joke.

2. School administrators seldom have the freedom to hire teachers who haven't been through the school swamp, no matter how much more competent uncertified people who happen to really know their math, chemistry, history, English, etc., may be.
3. Therefore, we have to do something to equalize spending so that all students will have an equal shot at a good education.
4. Reich contends that his national wealth tax would be "simple and fair," a means of giving "every school a fighting chance."
5. The reason inner-city schools do so poorly is not that they don't have enough money to spend, but that the funds they receive are sent into a bureaucratic black hole.
6. Dumping more money into public education would fatten the wallets of those who feed at the public education trough, but it wouldn't lead to better student learning.

A Solid Sentence Constructor

The following is a list of words and expressions you have learnt in the text. Please make a sentence with each of them.

1. to entitle
2. to beset
3. makeshift
4. to do away with
5. to impede
6. dubious

A Careful Writer

The following are three groups of words. You are required to study the words in each group carefully and then use them to write a paragraph of your own. Make sure that the paragraphs you have written are grammatical and coherent.

1. shot   rival   contend   shoestring   incentive

_____
_____
_____
_____
_____
_____

2. count on   impart   competent   unappealing   advocate

_____
_____
_____

3. bureaucracy obligatory penalty confiscate implore

A Superb Bilingualist

Please translate the following sentences into English using words or expressions provided in the brackets.

1. 新政策将支持房价上涨,并鼓励房主继续借款和消费。(prop up)
2. 贸易自由化对促进全球经济健康发展具有十分重要的意义。(overarching)
3. 现在我们处于被淘汰的边缘,所以我们必须打平或赢得这场比赛。(equalize)
4. 他们依靠进口来刺激经济,随后的经济复苏证明了这个做法是明智的。(count on)
5. 他白手起家,经过艰苦劳动和精心策划,才发展到今天这个样子。(shoestring)
6. 我想报名参加关于中餐烹调基本知识的课程。(impart)

Text B

Are Single-Sex Classrooms Legal?

By Elizabeth Green
(Abridged and Edited)

Two years ago, after reading a book called *Why Gender Matters*, Jo Lynne DeMary, who was then superintendent of Virginia public schools, became convinced that separating boys and girls into singlesex classrooms and schools could help both genders learn better. So she started developing a plan to help Virginia schools split up the groups, even recruiting an expert who could do training and making an instructional video. Then, in a phone call, Leonard Sax—the book's author—told her that her plan might violate federal rules.

> **gender** /ˈdʒɛndə/ *n.* the fact of being male or female
> **superintendent** /ˌsuːpərɪnˈtɛndənt/ *n.* a person who has a lot of authority and manages and controls an activity, a place, a group of workers, etc.
> **violate** /ˈvaɪəˌleɪt/ *v.* to go against or refuse to obey a law, an agreement, etc.

At the time, rule books suggested that Title IX, the 1972 law against sex discrimination in education, effectively prohibited single-sex classrooms except in a few special cases. Upon learning this, DeMary canceled the whole project. "Right there, just in the state of Virginia, we could have had hundreds of schools doing this," says Sax, an advocate of single-sex classrooms.

But on October 24, the Department of Education announced new Title IX regulations based on the guidelines of a *No Child Left Behind amendment*. Old regulations allowed for same-gender classes only in rare cases like physical education and human sexuality classes. But lawmakers in 2001 wanted to make those rules more flexible, and so the new ones expand that option to any class or school that can prove gender separation leads to improved student achievement. The change could lead to a wave of single-sex classrooms and even schools in public systems across the country. But it will also likely lead to legal challenges.

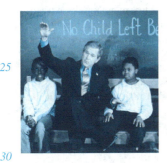

While advocates such as Sax see the new regulations as a welcome and long-overdue change, opponents like Marcia Greenberger, co-president of the National Women's Law Center, call it "an invitation to discriminate." The new regulations, they say, actually violate the original Title IX law. Therefore, schools that separate boys and girls will do so "at their peril," says Jocelyn Samuels, NWLC's vice president for education and employment. Potential legal battles will focus on how Title IX should be interpreted, but at the heart of the debate is one question: How would we rather our children learn, apart or together?

In the past 10 years, more public schools have been answering "apart." One of the first of the new groups to promote gender separation was the Young Women's Leadership School, founded in 1996 by Ann Rubenstein Tisch, then a journalist at NBC. "Single-sex schools existed for affluent girls and parochial girls and Yeshiva girls," Tisch says, "but not for inner-city girls." So in 1996, with the blessing of then-Mayor Rudolph Giuliani and a team of lawyers who assured her a single-sex school would not violate Title IX, she went to East Harlem and opened a public school for girls. The results, Tisch says, have been stunning: In its six graduating classes, the Harlem school has produced a 100 percent graduation rate, a 100 percent rate of enrollment in four-year colleges, and an 82 percent retention rate once the girls enter college.

Even in 2001, the Harlem program had already impressed Hilary Rodham Clinton, who talked about the school on the floor of the Senate. "We could use more schools such as this," Clinton declared, joining Sen. Kay Bailey Hutchison in proposing an amendment to the No Child Left Behind education reform act that would make this possible. That amendment is responsible for last week's changes.

---

amendment /əˈmɛndmənt/ *n.* a small change or improvement that is made to law or document; the process of changing law and a document
peril /ˈpɛrəl/ *n.* serious and immediate danger
affluent /ˈæfluənt/ *adj.* having a lot of money and a good standard of living
parochial /pəˈroʊkiəl/ *adj.* [usually before noun] [formal] connected with a church parish
retention /rɪˈtɛnʃən/ *n.* the action of keeping sth. rather than losing it or stopping it

The increased **flexibility** of these revised Title IX regulations ordered in No Child Left Behind did not become official federal policy until last week, but the original NCLB laws already had initiated some changes anyway. As of this past September, 241 public schools were offering single-sex classes, and 51 of them were fully sex-segregated, according to the National Association for Single Sex Public Education, which Sax runs.

Some of these attempts have come under fire. This August, a school district in Louisiana dropped plans to offer single-sex classes in two junior high schools after the American Civil Liberties Union brought a case against it. Years before, the ACLU's New York **affiliate** group joined with the National Organization for Women to file a Title IX complaint against Tisch's Harlem school, but the Department of Education "never issued a ruling one way or another," says Emily Martin, deputy director of the ACLU Women's Rights Project.

Both NOW and the ACLU are members of the National Coalition for Women and Girls on Education, whose members have been circulating e-mails about how to respond to the new regulations. "There are actually more differences within the sexes than there are between them," says Lisa Maatz, director of public policy and government relations at the American Association of University Women, another **coalition** member.

Separation may not only be unnecessary, they say, but it could have **adverse** effects such as increasing gender inequality over the long term or **perpetuating stereotypes**. A culture of equality, NOW President Kim Gandy says, requires that males and females learn to work together early on. "How can you expect a boy who's never been beaten by a girl on an **Algebra** test to think that it's OK for a girl to be his boss?" she asks. "Our experience has been, when it comes to separating girls and boys and men and women, separation has not been equal. At every turn, women and girls are the ones who are **shortchanged**."

A review by the Department of Education concluded research is too limited to be definitive in favor of either argument. But advocates of the gender separation options say the **anecdotal** evidence already is **compelling** enough. DeMary of Virginia, who retired from the Virginia schools last December and now directs the Center for School Improvement at Virginia Commonwealth University, describes a young girl-only middle school classroom in Virginia who spoke to the state Department of Education. She said, 'I don't have to worry about the boys... I can focus on the content.'"

---

flexibility /ˌfleksəˈbɪlətɪ/ *n.* ability to change to suit new conditions or situation

affiliate /əˈfɪlɪˌeɪt/ *n.* a company, an organization, *etc.* that is connected with or controlled by another one

coalition /ˌkoəˈlɪʃən/ *n.* a group formed by people from several different groups, especially political ones, agreeing to work together for a particular purpose

adverse /ædˈvəːs/ *adj.* negative and unpleasant; not likely to produce a good result

perpetuate /pəˈpetʃuˌet/ *v.* to make sth. such as a bad situation, a belief continue for a long time

stereotype /ˈsterɪəˌtaɪp/ *n.* a fixed idea or image that many people have a particular person or thing, but which is not true in reality

algebra /ˈældʒəbrə/ *n.* a type of mathematics in which letters and symbols are used to represent quantities

shortchange /ˈʃɔːtˈtʃendʒ/ *v.* to cheat (someone) by giving insufficient money as change

anecdotal /ˌænɪkˈdotl:/ *adj.* based on anecdotes or possibly not true or accurate

compelling /kəmˈpelɪŋ/ *adj.* that makes one think it is true

Single-sex education is not a "silver bullet," DeMary says, but if it could help, why remove it from the tool kit of educational options? After all, she says, with state testing laws and federal No Child Left Behind policy, "we have enough accountability on student achievement that if it's not working—we're not going to keep doing it."

> kit /kɪt/ *n.* a set of tools or equipment that one uses for a particular purpose
> accountability /əˌkaʊntəˈbɪlɪti/ *n.* the fact or condition of being accountable; responsibility

Notes

For some of the terms in the following, no explanation is provided. You are required to explain them by making use of the library, the Internet or whatever sources accessible.

1. Title IX

Title IX of the Education Amendments of 1972 is a United States law enacted on June 23, 1972. It is the first comprehensive federal law to prohibit sex discrimination against students and employees of educational instructions. Title IX benefits both males and females, and is at the heart of efforts to create gender equitable schools. The law requires educational institutions to maintain policies, practices and programs that do not discriminate against anyone based on sex.

2. No Child Left Behind Amendment

3. NWLC: National Women's Law Center

The National Women's Law Center was founded in 1972 as a non-profit advocacy organization working to advance the progress of women, girls, and families with emphasis on employment, education, reproductive rights, and health and family issues.

4. Young Women's Leadership School

5. ACLU

The American Civil Liberties Union (ACLU) is a major American non-profit organization with headquarters in New York City, whose stated mission is "to defend and preserve the individual rights and liberties guaranteed to every person in this country by the Constitution and laws of the United States". It works through litigation, legislation, and community education. According to its annual report, the ACLU had over 500,000 members at the end of 2005.

6. Kim Gandy

Kim Gandy is an American feminist, and currently the President of the National Organization for Women (NOW). Gandy was born in Louisiana in 1954, and graduated from Louisiana Tech University with a Bachelor's of Science in mathematics.

Comprehension Questions

Please answer the following questions based on what you have learnt in the text.

1. What did Demary do after reading the book "Why Gender Matters?"
2. Why did Demary cancel his project later?
3. Does co-president of NWLC see eye to eye with Sax on the legitimacy of single-sex education?
4. Was Harlem program a successful one? Why?
5. What is the attitude of NOW and ACLU toward gender separation?
6. How do you understand Demary's words: "Single-sex education is not a silver bullet, but if it could help, why remove it from the tool kit of education options?"

Writing Practice

High-quality education is critical to the competitiveness of a nation. Recently, there are lots of accounts of "America's competitiveness crisis," "innovation shortfall," or how the United States is "losing its edge." A growing number of Americans from all walks of life have expressed the concern that the waning education standards are threatening U.S. competitiveness. Now you are supposed to express your view on the relationship between higher education and the future of a nation.

Further Study

This is the end of Unit 4; but you can also gain more knowledge by accessing the following resources.

1. Please visit the following websites for knowledge about general conditions of education around the world.
   http://www.fff.org/freedom/fd0606e.asp (Public School Have Flunk Out)
   http://www.fff.org/freedom/fd0601b.asp (Who Made the State the Ultimate Parent?)
   http://www.fff.org/freedom/fd0412d.asp (The Great Voucher Fraud)

2. Film recommended: *Waiting for "Superman"*—It is a 2010 documentary film from director Davis Guggenheim and producer Lesley Chilcott. It examines America's failing public education system and calls on Americans to do something about it. It shows to the audience the horrifying experiences of students across the country (mostly fifth and eighth graders), exposing the policies that led to those experiences, and  providing statistics that measure the extent to which U.S. public school system has failed. As part of the exposé, the movie includes several compelling interviews with educators, addressing issues such as the failure of the *No Child Left Behind* program, the purpose and effects of teachers' unions, the incredibly high dropout rates among public school students, and the impact of failing schools on U.S. economy and society.

Unit 5

Biography

Unit Goals

Upon completing the texts in this unit, students should be able to:
- have a better understanding of Ernest Hemingway both as an ordinary human being and as a famous writer;
- distinguish between autobiography and biography;
- use prefixes of time and order and locative prefixes correctly to form new words.

Before Reading

Hands-on Activities and Brainstorming

1. A good biography brings the person to life, and arouses readers' interest in learning more about him/her. Go to the library or surf on the Internet for biographies of a well-known figure and share with others what you have learned about him/her.
2. Biography is different from autobiography. How much do you know about their differences? Do they have anything in common? If yes, then in what way are they similar?
3. Visit the website http://www.ernest.hemingway.com for more information about Ernest Hemingway and his works.

A Glimpse at Words and Expressions

Please read the following sentences. Pay attention to the underlined part in each sentence and to how it is used in the sentence and then decide on its meaning. Write down the meaning in the brackets.

1. In this context, Hemingway's childhood pursuits (   )
   fostered the interests which would blossom into literary achievements.

2. Hemingway also had an aptitude for physical (   )
   challenge that engaged him through high school.

3. Hemingway would witness firsthand the cruelty and (   )
   stoicism required of the soldiers he would portray
   in his writing when covering the Greco-Turkish
   War in 1920 for *the Toronto Star*.

4. The famous description of this "Lost Generation" (   )
   was born of an employee's remark to Hemingway.

5. At this point he had no writing that was not (   )
   committed to publication.

6. In addition to personal experiences with war and (   )
   death, Hemingway's extensive travel in pursuit of
   hunting and other sports provided a great deal of
   material for his novels.

7. "Papa" was both a legendary celebrity and a sensitive (   )
   writer, and his influence, as well as some unseen
   writings, survived his passing.

8. ... the passions of the man are equaled only by those (   )
   in his writing.

Text A

Ernest Hemingway

Anonymous
(Abridged and Edited)

Ernest Hemingway was born on July 21, 1899, in suburban Oak Park, IL to Dr. Clarence and Grace Hemingway. Ernest was the second of six children to be raised in the quiet suburban town. His father was a physician and his mother
5 was devout and musical. In this context, Hemingway's childhood pursuits fostered the interests which would blossom into literary
10 achievements.

Although Grace hoped her son would be influenced by her musical interests, young Hemingway preferred to accompany his father

suburban /sə'bɜːbən/ *adj.* in or connected with a suburb
physician /fɪ'zɪʃən/ *n.* [formal, especially AmE] a doctor, especially one who is a specialist in general medicine and not surgery
devout /dɪ'vaʊt/ *adj.* (of a person) believing strongly in a particular religion and obeying its law and practices
musical /'mjuːzɪkəl/ *adj.* (of a person) with a natural skill or interest in music
foster /'fɒstə/ *v.* to encourage sb. to develop
blossom /'blɒsəm/ *v.* to become more healthy, confident or successful

on hunting and fishing trips. This love of outdoor adventure would be reflected later in many of Hemingway's stories, particularly those featuring protagonist Nick Adams.

Hemingway also had an aptitude for physical challenge that engaged him through high school, where he both played football and boxed. Because of permanent eye damage contracted from numerous boxing matches, Hemingway was repeatedly rejected from service in World War I. Boxing provided more material for Hemingway's stories, as well as a habit of likening his literary feats to boxing victories.

Hemingway also edited his high school newspaper and reported for the *Kansas City Star*, adding a year to his age after graduating from high school in 1917.

After this short stint, Hemingway finally was able to participate in World War I as an ambulance driver for the American Red Cross. He was wounded on July 8, 1918, on the Italian front near Fossalta di Piave. During his convalescence in Milan, he had an affair with nurse Agnes von Kurowsky. Hemingway was given two decorations by the Italian government, and he joined the Italian infantry. Fighting on the Italian front inspired the plot of *A Farewell to Arms* in 1929. Indeed, war itself is a major theme in Hemingway's works. Hemingway would witness firsthand the cruelty and stoicism required of the soldiers he would portray in his writing when covering the Greco-Turkish War in 1920 for the *Toronto Star*. In 1937 he was a war correspondent in Spain, and the events of the Spanish Civil War inspired For *Whom the Bell Tolls*.

Upon returning briefly to the United States after the First World War, Hemingway worked for the *Toronto Star* and lived for a short time in Chicago. There, he met Sherwood Anderson and married Hadley Richardson in 1921. On Anderson's advice, the couple moved to Paris, where he served as foreign correspondent for the *Star*. As Hemingway covered events on all of Europe, the young reporter interviewed important leaders such as Lloyd George, Clemenceau, and Mussolini.

The Hemingways lived in Paris from 1921 to 1926. This time of stylistic development for Hemingway reached its zenith in 1923 with the publication of *Three Stories and Ten Poems* by Robert McAlmon in Paris and the birth of his son John. This time in Paris also inspired the novel *A Moveable Feast*, published posthumously in 1964.

---

feature /'fiːtʃə/ *v.* to include a particular person or thing as a special feature

protagonist /prə'tægənɪst/ *n.* [formal] the main character in a play, film/movie or book

aptitude /'æptɪˌtjuːd/ *n.* natural ability or skill at doing sth.

contract /'kɒnˌtrækt/ *v.* [formal or medical] to get an illness

liken /'laɪkən/ *v.* to consider or describe as similar, equal, or analogous

stint /stɪnt/ *n.* a period of time that you spend working somewhere or doing a particular activity

convalescence /ˌkɒnvə'lesns/ *n.* a period of time when one gets well again after an illness or a medical operation; the process of getting well

decoration /ˌdekə'reɪʃən/ *n.* a medal that is given to sb. as an honor

infantry /'ɪnfəntri/ *n.* soldiers who fight on foot

stoicism /'stəʊɪˌsɪzəm/ *n.* [formal] the fact of not complaining or showing what one is feeling when he is suffering

cover /'kʌvə/ *v.* to report on an event for television, a newspaper, etc.; to show an event on television

Greco- combining form (North American English) = Graeco-

correspondent /ˌkɒrɪ'spɒndənt/ *n.* a person who reports news from a particular country or on a particular subject for a newspaper or a television or radio station

stylistic /staɪ'lɪstɪk/ *adj.* connected with the style an artist uses in a particular piece of art, writing or music

zenith /'zenɪθ/ *n.* [formal] the time when sth. is strongest and most successful

posthumous /'pɒstʃəməs/ *adj.* happening, done, published, etc. after a person has died

In January 1923 Hemingway began writing sketches that would appear in *In Our Time*, which was published in 1924. In August of 1923 he and Hadley returned to Toronto where he worked once again for the *Star*. At this point he had no writing that was not committed to publication, and in the coming months his job kept him from starting anything new. But this time off from writing gave him renewed energy upon his return to Paris in January of 1924.

During his time in Toronto he read Joyce's *Dubliners*, which forever changed his writing career. By August of 1924 he had the majority of *In Our Time* written. Although there was a period when his publisher Horace Liverwright wanted to change much of the collection, Hemingway stood firm and refused to change even one word of the book.

In Paris, Hemingway used Sherwood Anderson's letter of introduction to meet Gertrude Stein and enter the world of expatriate authors and artists who inhabited her intellectual circle. The famous description of this "Lost Generation" was born of an employee's remark to Hemingway, and it became immortalized as the epigraph for his first major novel, *The Sun Also Rises*.

This "Lost Generation" both characterized the postwar generation and the literary movement it produced. In the 1920s, writers such as Anderson, F. Scott Fitzgerald, James Joyce, Ezra Pound, and Gertrude Stein decried the false ideals of patriotism that led young people to war, only to the benefit of materialistic elders. These writers held that the only truth was reality, and thus life could be nothing but hardship. This tenet strongly influenced Hemingway.

The late 1920s were a time of many publications for Hemingway. In 1926, *The Torrents of Spring* and *The Sun Also Rises* were published by Charles Scribner's Sons.

In 1927 Hemingway published a short story collection, *Men without Women*. In the same year he divorced Hadley Richardson and married Pauline Pfieffer, a writer for *Vogue*. In 1928 they moved to Key West, where sons Patrick and Gregory were born in 1929 and 1932. 1928 was a year of both success and sorrow for Hemingway. In this year *A Farewell to Arms* was published, and his father committed

---

sketch /skɛtʃ/ *n.* a short report or story that gives only basic details about sth.

expatriate /ɛkˈspetriˌet/ *adj.* of a person living in a country that is not their own

inhabit /ɪnˈhæbɪt/ *v.* to live in a particular place

intellectual /ˌɪntlˈɛktʃuəl/ *n.* a person who is well educated and enjoys activities in which one has to think seriously about things

immortalize /ɪˈmɔrtlˌaɪz/ *v.* to prevent sb./sth. from being forgotten in the future, especially by mentioning them in literature, making films/movies about them, painting them, etc.

epigraph /ˈɛpɪˌgræf/ *n.* a line of writing, short phrase, etc. on a building or statue, or as an introduction to part of a book

decry /dɪˈkraɪ/ *v.* [formal] to strongly criticize sb./sth., especially publicly

patriotism /ˈpetriəˌtɪzəm/ *n.* love of one's country and willingness to defend it

tenet /ˈtɛnɪt/ *n.* [formal] one of the principles or beliefs that a theory or larger set of beliefs is based on

torrent /ˈtɔrənt/ *n.* a large amount of water moving very quickly

suicide. Clarence Hemingway had been suffering from hypertension and diabetes. This painful experience is reflected in the pondering of Robert Jordan in *For Whom the Bell Tolls*.

In addition to personal experiences with war and death, Hemingway's extensive travel in pursuit of hunting and other sports provided a great deal of material for his novels. Bullfighting inspired *Death in the Afternoon*, published in 1932. In 1934, Hemingway went on safari in Africa, which gave him new themes and scenes on which to base *The Snows of Kilamanjaro* and *The Green Hills of Africa*, published in 1935.

In 1937 he traveled to Spain as a war correspondent, and he published *To Have and Have Not*. After his divorce from Pauline in 1940, Hemingway married Martha Gelhorn, a writer. They toured China before settling in Cuba at Finca Vigia (Look-out Farm). *For Whom the Bell Tolls* was published in the same year.

During World War II, Hemingway volunteered his fishing boat and served with the U.S. Navy as a submarine spotter in the Caribbean. In 1944, he traveled through Europe with the Allies as a war correspondent and participated in the liberation of Paris. Hemingway divorced again in 1945 and then married Mary Welsh, a correspondent for *Time* magazine, in 1946. They lived in Venice before returning to Cuba.

In 1950 he published *Across the River and Into the Trees*, though it was not received with the usual critical acclaim. In 1952, however, Hemingway proved the comment "Papa is finished" wrong, in that *The Old Man and the Sea* won the Pulitzer Prize in 1953. In 1954, he won the Nobel Prize for Literature.

In 1960, the now aged Hemingway moved to Ketchum, Idaho, where he was hospitalized for uncontrolled high blood pressure, liver disease, diabetes, and depression.

On July 2, 1961, he died of self-inflicted gunshot wounds. He was buried in Ketchum. "Papa" was both a legendary celebrity and a sensitive writer, and his influence, as well as some unseen writings, survived his passing. In 1964, *A Moveable Feast* was published; in 1969, *The Fifth Column and Four Stories of the Spanish Civil War*; in 1970, *Islands in the Stream*; in 1972, *The Nick Adams Stories*; in 1985, *The Dangerous Summer*; and in 1986, *The Garden of Eden*.

Hemingway's own life and character are as fascinating as any in his stories. On one level, Papa was a legendary adventurer who enjoyed his flamboyant lifestyle and celebrity

---

commit /kəˈmɪt/ *v.* to do sth. wrong or illegal
hypertension /ˌhaɪpəˈtɛnʃən/ *n.* [medical] blood pressure that is higher than is normal
safari /səˈfɑːri/ *n.* a trip to see or hunt wild animals, especially in east or southern Africa
submarine /ˈsʌbməˌriːn/ *n.* a ship that can travel underwater
spotter /ˈspɒtə/ *n.* one who looks for a particular type of thing or person, as a hobby or job
acclaim /əˈkleɪm/ *n.* praise and approval for sb./sth., especially an article achievement
hospitalize /ˈhɒspɪt(ə)laɪz/ *v.* to send sb. to a hospital for treatment
inflict /ɪnˈflɪkt/ *v.* to cause (a blow, penalty, etc) to be suffered (by sb)
flamboyant /flæmˈbɔɪənt/ *adj.* (of people or their behavior) different, confident and exciting in a way that attracts attention

status, but deep inside lived a disciplined author who worked tirelessly in pursuit of literary perfection. His success in both living and writing is reflected in the fact that Hemingway is a hero to intellectuals and rebels alike; the passions of the man are equaled only by those in his writing.

> disciplined /'dɪsəplɪnd/ *adj.* obeying the rules
> rebel /rɪ'bɛl/ *n.* one who does not like to obey rules or who does not accept normal standards of behavior, dress, etc.

Better Know More

1. Nick Adams

Nick Adams is a fictional character, the protagonist of two dozen short stories by American author Ernest Hemingway, written in the 1920s to the 1930s. Adams is partly inspired by Hemingway's own experiences. Most of these stories were collected in a 1972 book titled *The Nick Adams Stories*.

2. Kansas City Star

The *Kansas City Star* is a newspaper based in Kansas City, Missouri, the United States. The paper has won eight Pulitzer Prizes since it was published in 1880. The *Star* is most notable for exerting great influence on the career of President Harry Truman.

3. Greco-Turkish War

The Greco-Turkish War of 1919 to 1922, also called the War in Asia Minor, was a series of military events occurring during the partitioning of the Ottoman Empire in the wake of World War I. The war was fought between Greece and Turkish revolutionaries of the Turkish National Movement that would later build up the Republic of Turkey.

4. Toronto Star

The *Toronto Star* is Canada's highest-circulation newspaper, though its print edition is distributed almost entirely within the province of Ontario. *The Star* (originally known as *The Evening Star* and then *The Toronto Daily Star*) was created in 1892 by striking *Afternoon News* printers and writers. It is possessed by Toronto Star Newspapers Ltd., a division of Star Media Group, a subsidiary of Torstar Corporation.

5. Sherwood Anderson (1876–1941)

Sherwood Anderson, an American novelist and short story writer, is recognized for his memorable work, the short story sequence *Winesburg, Ohio*. Writers who have been influenced include Ernest Hemingway, William Faulkner, John Steinbeck, J. D. Salinger, and Amos Oz, among others.

6. Dubliners

The author, James Augustine Aloysius Joyce (1882—1941), an Irish novelist and poet, was one of the most influential writers in the early 20th century. Joyce's best known work *Ulysses* (1922) is a landmark novel which perfected his stream of consciousness technique.

Dubliners, a collection consisting of 15 short stories, was first published in 1914. The fifteen stories depicted the Irish middle class life in and around Dublin in the early years of the 20th century. The stories were written at the time when Irish nationalism was at its zenith, and a search for a national identity was raging.

7. Gertrude Stein (1874–1946)

Gertrude Stein, an American writer and thinker who spent most of her life in France, was well-known for her writing, her art collection, and many famous people whom were invited to her salon in Paris. She is accredited with coining the term *Lost Generation* as description of her many expatriate acquaintances in France and Italy during the 1920s and 1930s.

8. Charles Scribner's Sons

Charles Scribner's Sons, or Scribner, is a New York City publisher which is best known for publishing a number of celebrities of American literature including Ernest Hemingway, F. Scott Fitzgerald, Kurt Vonnegut, Stephen King, and so forth.

9. Lost Generation

Lost Generation refers to the group of U.S. writers who came of age during World War I and established their reputations in the 1920s. In a more broad sense, it includes the entire post World War I American generation. The term was coined by Gertrude Stein in a remark to Ernest Hemingway. The writers who considered themselves "lost" found their inherited values could not operate in the postwar world and they felt spiritually alienated from a country they considered hopelessly provincial and emotionally barren. The term embraces Hemingway, F. Scott Fitzgerald, John Dos Passos, E.E. Cummings, Archibald MacLeish, and Hart Crane, among others.

10. F. Scott Fitzgerald (1896–1940)

F. Scott Fitzgerald was an American author of novels and short stories, whose works are the model writings of the Jazz Age, a term he coined himself. Fitzgerald is considered a member of the "Lost Generation" of the 1920s. He finished four novels, *This Side of Paradise, The Beautiful and Damned, Tender Is the Night* and his most famous, the celebrated classic, *The Great Gatsby*.

11. Ezra Pound (1885–1972)

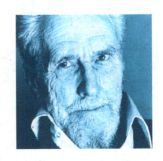

Ezra Weston Loomis Pound was an American expatriate poet and critic, and a major figure in the early modernist movement in poetry. He was well-known for his role in developing Imagism, which favored tight language, unadorned imagery, and a strong correspondence between the verbal and musical qualities of the verse and the mood it expressed. His best-known works include *Ripostes* (1912), *Hugh Selwyn Mauberley* (1920), and his unfinished 120-section epic, *The Cantos*, which was published in his middle and late career between 1917 and 1969.

12. Pulitzer Prize

Pulitzer Prizes are a series of 21 awards for outstanding achievements in drama, letters, music, and journalism. In 20 of these, each winner receives a certificate and a US $10,000 cash award. The winner in the public service category of the journalism competition is awarded a gold medal, which always goes to a newspaper, although an individual may be named in the citation. They were established by the will of Joseph Pulitzer, publisher of the *New York World*. They have been awarded annually since 1917 by Columbia University on recommendation of the Pulitzer Prize Board.

Check Your Understanding

Please answer the following questions based on what you have learnt in the text.

1. What was reflected in many of Hemingway's stories, particularly those featuring protagonist Nick Adams?
2. What changed Hemingway's writing style forever?
3. What did the term "Lost Generation" characterize?
4. What inspired Hemingway to compose novels in addition to his personal experiences with war and death?
5. How did Hemingway prove "Papa is finished" wrong?
6. How does the author of the text evaluate Hemingway?

A Sip of Word Formation

Prefixes of Degree or Size

Pre-, *post-*, *ex-*, and *re-* are prefixes of time and order.
1. *Pre-* is added to nouns, adjectives, verbs with the meaning of "before" (e.g. *pre-marital, prehistory, precaution, preconceive, premature*).
2. *Post-* is added to nouns, verbs and adjectives with the meaning of "after" (e.g. *postpone, postwar, postscript, postmodernism, posthumous*).
3. *Ex-* is added to nouns with the meaning of "former" (e.g. *ex-boyfriend, ex-husband, ex-wife, ex-president, ex-criminal*).
4. *Re-* is added to nouns, verbs, adjectives, adverbs with the meaning of again (e.g. *refill, reexamine, reaffirmed, refreshingly*).

Locative Prefixes

Sub-, *inter-*, and *trans-* are locative prefixes.
1. *Sub-* means "under" (e.g. *subway, submarine*), or "less than" (e.g. *sub-zero* temperature, *sub-standard*);
2. *Trans-* means "across" (e.g. *transcontinental, transmigrate*);
3. *Inter-* means "between" (e.g. *interbreed, intergalactic*).

Build Your Vocabulary

For each of the following sentences, a word is provided in the brackets. Use the appropriate form of the word to fill in the blank in the sentence, so that the sentence is logical and grammatical.

1. The long _____ period of times is divided into different ages named from the material which man used in the manufacture of his weapons and tools. (history)
2. It was not until the _____ period in Germany that many honors were given to Einstein for his brilliant achievements in the domain of physics. (war)
3. Is it necessary to _____ and redesign elite education in Singapore? (examine)
4. Human beings aren't meant to operate like machines continuously. By contrast, we're designed to be rhythmic, and to intermittently _____ ourselves. (fuel)
5. As President, he proposes to _____ income between the rich and the poor. (distribute)
6. Only when we have rid ourselves of our _____ ideas are we able to make right judgment at the critical moment. (conceive)
7. A present survey shows _____ babies have problems with motor skills, learning ability and eyesight later in life. (mature)
8. Martin Luther attached lighted candles to a small evergreen tree, trying to _____ the reflections of the starlit heaven. (create)

9. This country is rich in natural resources and its _____ resources occur at widely scattered locations. (soil)
10. Unless saving and investment are done in kind, a financial _____ must link savers and investors. (media)
11. The stake of this battle was nothing less than control of most of the western _____ railroads. (continent)
12. We will explore several questions about how specific _____ environments are designed and implemented, as well as how they impact classroom dynamics and student learning. (action)

You'd Like to Be

 ## A Skilled Text Weaver

Fill in the blanks with the words you have learnt in this text, one word for each blank. You are advised to read the text carefully until you have become very familiar with it before starting to work on this task.

Mark Twain was born in Florida, Missouri, of a Virginian family on November 30, 1835. At school, according to his own words, he had only _____ for spelling. After his father's death in 1847, Twain was apprenticed to a printer. He started his career as a journalist by writing for the *Hannibal Journal*. Later he worked as a licensed Mississippi river-boat pilot.

Twain moved to Virginia City, where he spent two years _____ for *Territorial Enterprise*. In 1864 Twain left for California, where he worked in San Francisco as a _____. A story he heard about a frog during that period _____ his *The Celebrated Jumping Frog of Calaveras County, and Other Sketches*, which marked the beginning of his literary career.

His fame reached its _____ in 1870 when *The Innocents Abroad* was received with a popular _____. Subsequently, he published several masterpieces: *The Prince and The Pauper, Life on the Mississippi* and *Huckleberry Finn*. From 1896 to 1900, he _____ mainly in Europe. During the _____, his favorite daughter died of spinal meningitis. The death of his wife in 1904 in Florence and that of his second daughter darkened the author's life, which was also seen in the writings and his _____ published autobiography. Twain's view of human nature had never been very optimistic, but during the final years, he became even bitter.

Mark Twain has been _____ to Walt Whitman who is one of the most American writers, and is highly respected as "Father of Literature." Although he suffered many losses in his life including his children and accumulated debts, at the time of his death, he had grown to be a _____ adventurer, dutiful reporter and keen observer.

A Sharp Interpreter

Please paraphrase the following sentences. Change the sentence structure wherever necessary.

1. In this context, Hemingway's childhood pursuits fostered the interests which would blossom into literary achievements.
2. Hemingway also edited his high school newspaper and reported for the *Kansas City Star*, adding a year to his age after graduating from high school in 1917.
3. Hemingway would witness firsthand the cruelty and stoicism required of the soldiers he would portray in his writing when covering the Greco-Turkish War in 1920 for *The Toronto Star*.
4. In Paris, Hemingway used Sherwood Anderson's letter of introduction to meet Gertrude Stein and enter the world of expatriate authors and artists who inhabited her intellectual circle.
5. The "Lost Generation" both characterized the postwar generation and the literary movement it produced.
6. In 1952, however, Hemingway proved the comment "Papa is finished" wrong, in that *The Old Man and the Sea* won the Pulitzer Prize in 1953.
7. Papa was both a legendary celebrity and a sensitive writer, and his influence, as well as some unseen writings, survived his passing.

A Solid Sentence Constructor

The following is a list of words and expressions you have learnt in the text. Please make a sentence with each of them.

1. to foster
2. to accompany
3. to feature
4. to commit to
5. to ponder
6. to volunteer
7. flamboyant

A Careful Writer

The following are three groups of words. You are required to study the words in each group carefully and then use them to write a paragraph of your own. Make sure that the paragraphs you have written are grammatical and coherent.

1. engage   repeatedly   correspondent   ambulance

2. reject   decry   acclaim   ponder

📖 A Superb Bilingualist

Please translate the following sentences into English using words or expressions provided in the brackets.

1. 在贫病交加的困境下，梵高(Van Gogh)依然保持了色彩鲜明、笔法粗犷的绘画特点。(characterize)
2. 他在路透社从事编辑工作期间，结识了很多来自世界各地的专业作家。(stint)
3. 欧洲许多国家反对对电子贸易征税，认为这会自毁经济。(commit)
4. 在他发表评论以后的几天里，合法移民协会在线发起请愿，谴责他的种族主义言论。(decry)
5. 承德避暑山庄(The Mountain Resort in Chengde)在植物配置上体现了追求古朴、体现自然的艺术特色。(in pursuit of)
6. 圣诞节是人们互赠礼物表示关爱的日子。每到这个时候，商店的橱窗陈列都会显得格外引人注目。(fascinating)
7. 对一些人而言，正是生活中的困难和坎坷激发了他们的斗志，从而取得了卓越的成就。(inspire)
8. 罢工给经济带来了严重损失。(inflict)

Text B

Joseph Heller
Anonymous
(Abridged and edited)

American writer, who gained world fame with his satirical, anti-war novel *Catch-22* (1961), set in the World War II Italy. The book was partly based on Heller's own experiences and influenced among others Robert Altman's comedy *Mash*, and the subsequent long-running TV series, set in the Korean War. The phrase "catch-22" has entered the English language to signify a no-win situation, particularly one created by a law, regulation or circumstance.

All over the world, boys on every side of the bomb line were laying down their lives for what they had been told was their country, and no one seemed to mind, least of all the boys who were laying down their young lives. There was no end in sight. (from Catch-22)

Joseph Heller was born in Brooklyn, New York, as the son of poor Jewish parents. His Russian-born father, who was a bakery truck driver, died in 1927. After graduating from Abraham Lincoln High School in 1941, Heller joined the Twelfth Air Force. He was stationed in Corsica, where he flew 60 combat missions as a B-25 bombardier. In 1949 Heller received his M.A. from Columbia University. He was a Fulbright scholar at Oxford in 1949—1950. Heller worked as a teacher at Pennsylvania State University (1950—1952), copywriter for the magazines *Time* (1952—1956), *Look* (1956—1958), and promotion manager for McCall's. He left McCall's in 1961 to teach fiction and dramatic writing at Yale University and the University of Pennsylvania.

His first stories Heller sold already during his student times. They were published in such magazines as *Atlantic Monthly* and *Esquire*. In the early 1950s he started working on *Catch-22*. At that time Heller was employed as a copywriter at a small advertising agency. Most of the book he wrote in the foyer of a West End Avenue apartment. "As I've said and repeated, I wrote the first chapter in longhand one morning in 1953, hunched over my desk at the advertising agency (from ideas and words that had leaped into my mind only the night before); the chapter was published in the quarterly *New World Writing #7* in 1955 under the title "*Catch-18*."

satirical /ˈsætɪrɪkəl/ *adj.*	using satire to criticize sb./sth.
subsequent /ˈsʌbsɪkwənt/ *adj.*	happening or coming after someone else
regulation /ˌrɛɡjəˈleɪʃən/ *n.*	an official rule made by a government or some other authority
bakery /ˈbeɪkəri/ *n.*	a place where bread and cakes are made and/or sold
bombardier /ˌbɑmbəˈdɪr/ *n.*	the person on a military plane in the US air force who is responsible for aiming and dropping bombs
foyer /ˈfɔɪə/ *n.*	an entrance hall in a private house or flat/apartment
longhand /ˈlɔŋˌhænd/ *n.*	ordinary writing; not typed or written in shorthand

I received twenty-five dollars. The same issue carried a chapter from Jack Kerouac's On the Road, under a pseudonym.
40 (from Now and Then, 1998)

The novel went largely unnoticed until 1962, when its English publication received critical praise. And in *The New York World-Telegram* Richard Starnes opened his
45 column with the prophetic words: "Yossarian will, I think, live a very long time." An earlier reviewer called the book "repetitious and monotonous," and another "dazzling performance that will outrage nearly as many
50 readers as it delights."

The protagonist is Captain John Yossarian, lead bombardier of the 256th squadron, who is stationed at an airstrip on the fictitious island off the coast of Italy during
55 WW II. Other characters include the conman Milo Minderbinder, company mess officer, who creates a successful black-market business, Major Major, Lieutenant Scheisskopf, who wants to turn his men into perfect parade
60 ground robots, Chief White Halfoat, whose family is constantly chased and evicted by oil companies, and mail clerk Wintergreen, who is really running the war. Yossarian, struggles to retain his sanity and hopes to get a medical
65 discharge by pretending to be insane. The story centers on the USAF regulation which suggests that willingness to fly dangerous combat missions must be considered insane, but if the airmen seek to be relieved on
70 grounds of mental reasons, the request proves their sanity. Heller's absurd world follows the rules of Samuel Beckett and Lewis Carroll's Wonderland:

"Oh, you can't help that," said the Cat: "we're all mad here. I'm mad. You're mad."
75 "How do you know I'm mad?" said Alice.
"You must be," said the Cat, "or you wouldn't have come here."

And as Alice, Yossarian eventually rejects the irrational logic of his rabbit hole after his friends are killed or missing. But instead of waking up, Yossarian decides to desert to Sweden. The non-chronological, fragmented narrative underlines the surreal experience of

---

pseudonym /ˈsudnˌɪm/ *n.* a name used by sb., especially a writer, instead of their real name
prophetic /prəˈfɛtɪk/ *adj.* [formal] correctly stating or showing what will happen in the future
repetitious /ˌrɛpɪˈtɪʃəs/ *adj.* involving sth. that is often repeated
monotonous /məˈnɑtnəs/ *adj.* never changing and therefore boring
dazzling /ˈdæzlɪŋ/ *adj.* of impressing sb. a lot with one's beauty, skill, knowledge, etc.
outrage /ˈaʊtˌrɛdʒ/ *v.* to make sb. shocked and angry
squadron /ˈskwɑdrən/ *n.* a group of military aircraft or ships forming a section of a military force
airstrip /ˈɛrˌstrɪp/ *n.* a narrow piece of cleared land that an aircraft can land on
fictitious /fɪkˈtɪʃəs/ *adj.* invented by sb. rather than true
conman /kɑnmæn/ *n.* [informal] a man who tricks others into giving him money, etc.
mess /mɛs/ *n.* food or a meal served to a group of people, usually soldiers or sailors
lieutenant /luˈtɛnənt/ *n.* an officer of middle rank in the army, navy, or air force
parade ground a large flat area where soldiers march and practise military movements
evict /ɪˈvɪkt/ *v.* to force sb. to leave a house or land, especially when one has the legal right to do so
sanity /ˈsænɪti/ *n.* the state of having a normal healthy mind
discharge /dɪsˈtʃɑrdʒ/ *n.* the act of officially allowing sb. or of telling sb., to leave somewhere, especially sb. in a hospital or the army
insane /ɪnˈseɪn/ *adj.* seriously mentally ill and unable to live in normal society
relieve /rɪˈliv/ *v.* to dismiss sb. from a job, position, etc.
absurd /əbˈsəd/ *adj.* completely ridiculous; not logical and sensible
irrational /ɪrˈræʃənəl/ *adj.* not based on, or not using clear, logical thought
desert /ˈdɛzət/ *v.* to leave the armed force without permission

the characters and the contrast between real life and illogicalities of war. It has been noted, that Heller's characters have similarities with Louis Falstein's novel *The Sky is a Lonely Place*, which was published earlier. Falstein depicts combat missions above Mediterranean during WW II. However, Heller's tone is comic. The publication of *Catch-22* signaled a more experimental approach to the war novel, anticipating such works as Thomas Pynchon's *V.* (1963) and Kurt Vonnegut's *Slaughter-house-Five* (1969). Heller also expressed the emerging rebelliousness of the Vietnam generation and criticism of mass society.

Catch-22 has enjoyed a steady sale since its publication. Mike Nichols's movie version of the novel from 1970 is considered disappointing, although its good cast tried its best. Nichols emphasized the absurdity of war, and as Heller, he rejected American militarism. Orson Welles, who also was interested in filming the book, was in the role of General Dreedle. After writing *Catch22*, Heller worked on several Hollywood screenplays, such as *Sex and the Single Girl*, *Casino Royale*, and *Dirty Dingus Magee*, and contributed to the TV show *McHale's Navy* under the pseudonym Max Orange. In the 1960s Heller was involved with the anti-Vietnam war protest movement.

Heller waited 13 years before publishing his next novel, *Something Happened* (1974). It portrayed a corporation man Bob Slocum, who suffers from insomnia and almost smells the disaster mounting toward him. Slocum's life is undramatic, but he feels that his happiness is threatened by unknown forces. "When an ambulance comes, I'd rather not know for whom." He does not share Yossarian's rebelliousness, but he act cynically as a "wolf among a pack of wolves". Heller's play-within-a-play, *We bombed in New Haven* (1968), was written in part to express his protest against the Vietnam war. It was produced on Broadway and ran for 86 performances. *Catch-22* has also been dramatized. It was first performed at the John Drew Theater in East Hampton, New York, July 13, 1971.

Heller's later works include *Good as Gold* (1979), where the protagonist Bruce Gold tries to regain the Jewishness he has lost. Readers hailed the work as a return to puns and verbal games familiar from Heller's first novel. *God Knows* (1984) was a modern version of the story of King David and an allegory of what it is like for a Jew to survive

chronological /ˌkrɒnəˈlɒdʒɪkəl/ *adj.* (of a number of events) arranged in the order in which they happened
fragmented /ˈfræɡməntɪd/ *adj.* of breaking or making sth. break into small pieces or parts
surreal /səˈriəl/ *adj.* very strange; more like a dream than reality, with ideas and images mixed together in a strange way
depict /dɪˈpɪkt/ *v.* to describe sth. in words, or give an impression of sth. in words or with a picture
rebelliousness /rɪˈbeljəsn/ *n.* an intentionally contemptuous behavior or attitude
cast /kæst/ *n.* all the people who act in a play or film/movie
absurdity /əbˈsɜːdɪti/ *n.* state of being completely ridiculous; not being logical and sensible
militarism /ˈmɪlɪtəˌrɪzəm/ *n.* the belief that a country should have great military strength in order to be powerful
insomnia /ɪnˈsɒmniə/ *n.* the condition of being unable to sleep
mount /maʊnt/ *v.* to gradually increase, rise, or get bigger
cynically /ˈsɪnɪkli/ *adv.* believing that people only do things to help themselves rather than for good or honest reasons
hail /heɪl/ *v.* to describe sb./sth. being very good or special, especially in newspaper, etc.
pun /pʌn/ *n.* the clever or humorous use of a word that has more than one meaning, or of words that have different meanings but sound the same
allegory /ˈælɪˌɡɒri/ *n.* a story, play, picture, etc. in which each character or event is a symbol representing an idea or a quality, such as truth, evil, death, etc.; the use of such symbols

in a hostile world. David has decided that he has been given one of the best parts of the Bible. "I have suicide, regicide, patricide, homicide, fratricide, infanticide, adultery, incest, hanging, and more decapitations than just Saul's."

No Laughing Matter (1986), written with Speed Vogel, was a surprisingly cheerful account of Heller's experience as a victim of Guillain-Barré syndrome. During his recuperation Heller was visited among others by Mario Puzo, Dustin Hoffman and Mel Brooks. *Closing Time* (1994) is a sequel to *Catch-22*, depicting the current lives of its heroes. Yossarian is now 40 years older and as preoccupied with death as in the earlier novel. "Thank God for the atom bomb," says Yossarian. *Now and Then* (1998) is Heller's autobiographical work, evocation of his boyhood home, Brooklyn's Coney Island in the 1920s and the 1930s.

"It has struck me since — it couldn't have done so then — that in Catch-22 and in all my subsequent novels, and also in my one play, the resolution at the end of what narrative there is evolves from the death of someone other than the main character." (from Now and Then)

Heller had two children by his first marriage. His divorce was recounted in *No Laughing Matter*. In 1989 Heller married Valerie Humphries, a nurse he met while ill. Heller died of a heart attack at his home on Long Island on December 13, 1999. His last novel, *Portrait of an Artist as an Old Man* (2000), was about a successful novelist who seeks an inspiration for his book.

"A lifetime of experience had trained him never to toss away a page he had written, no matter how clumsy, until he had gone over it again for improvement, or had at least stored it in a folder for safekeeping or recorded the words on his computer." (from Portrait of an Artist as an Old Man)

---

hostile /'hɑstəl/ *adj.* very unfriendly or aggressive and ready to argue or fight

regicide /'rɛdʒɪˌsaɪd/ *n.* [formal] the crime of killing a king or queen; a person who is guilty of this crime

patricide /'pætrɪˌsaɪd/ *n.* [formal] the crime of killing your father ; a person who is guilty of this crime

fratricide /'frætrɪˌsaɪd/ *n.* [formal] the crime of killing your brother or sister; a person who is guilty of this cime

infanticide /ɪn'fæntɪˌsaɪd/ *n.* [formal] the crime of killing a baby; a person who is guilty of this crime

adultery /ə'dʌltəri/ *n.* sex between a married person and sb. who is not their husband or wife

incest /'ɪnˌsɛst/ *n.* involving sex between two people in a family who are very closely related

decapitation /dɪˌkæpɪˈteʃən/ *n.* cutting off sb's head

recuperation /rɪˌkupəʃən/ *n.* getting back one's health, strength or energy after being ill/sick, tired, injured, etc.

sequel /'sikwəl/ *n.* a book, film/movie, play, etc. that continues the story of an earlier one

evocation /ˌɛvəˈkeʃən/ *n.* imaginative re-creation

recount /rɪˈkaʊnt/ *v.* [formal] to tell sb. about sth. , especially sth. that one has experienced

toss /tɔs, tɑs/ *v.* to throw sth. lightly or carelessly

clumsy /'klʌmzi/ *adj.* (of actions and statements) done without skill or in a way that offends people

folder /'foldə/ *n.* a cardboard or plastic cover for holding loose papers, etc.

Notes

For some of the terms in the following, no explanation is provided. You are required to explain them by making use of the library, the Internet or whatever sources accessible.

1. Robert Altman (1925–2006)

Robert Altman was an American film director known for making films that are highly naturalistic, but with a stylized perspective. In 2006, he was given Academy Honorary Award.

2. Fulbright Scholar

3. Look

Look stands for *Love of Our Kind*. Its target audience is African-American urban college students. It was a bi-weekly, general-interest magazine published in Des Moines, Iowa from 1937 to 1971, putting more emphasis on photographs rather than articles.

4. McCall's

McCall's was a monthly American women's magazine that enjoyed great popularity in the 20th century, peaking at a readership of 8.4 million in the early 1960s. It was originally established as a small-format magazine called *The Queen* in 1873. In 1897 it was renamed *McCall's Magazine—The Queen of Fashion* (later shortened to *McCall's*) and subsequently developed to become a large-format glossy. It was one of the "Seven Sisters" group of women's service magazines.

5. The New York World-Telegram

6. Samuel Beckett (1906–1989)

Samuel Beckett was an Irish avant-garde writer, dramatist and poet, writing in English and French. His plays are concerned with human suffering and survival, and his characters are struggling with meaninglessness and the world of the Nothing. He was awarded Nobel Prize for Literature in 1969.

7. Lewis Carroll (1832–1898)

8. Thomas Pynchon

9. Kurt Vonnegut

Comprehension Questions

Please answer the following questions based on what you have learnt in the text.

1. When did Heller start working on Catch-22?
2. What does the phrase "Catch-22" signify in English?
3. What does the non-chronological, fragmented narrative underline in Heller's novels?
4. How many years did Heller wait before publishing his novel, Something Happened (1974)?
5. Where did Catch-22 perform in 1971?
6. What does Closing Time depict as a sequel to Catch-22?

Writing Practice

A biography is simply the story of a life. Very short biographies tell the basic facts of someone's life and importance. Longer biographies include not only these basic facts, but also a lot more details. In addition, longer biographies may tell a good story. A biography, long or short, covers the following parts:

1. Introduction, which can grab the readers' attention and tells them who the subject of the biography is;
2. Information about the subject's childhood;
3. Talents and accomplishments of the subject;
4. Conclusion which highlights the subject's influence.

It is usually organized chronologically. The author of Text A introduces Ernest Hemingway's life involving his experiences and achievements according to time sequence.

Choose a person you are interested in, famous or ordinary, and write about him/her in the third person and present tense by following the above pattern.

Further Study

This is the end of Unit 5; but you can also gain more knowledge by accessing the following resources.

Recommended film: *The Old man and the Sea*—*The Old Man and the Sea* tells a story of an aging fisherman, Santiago, under attack by starvation and weeks of misfortune. Santiago, a strong and proud man, in his youth, is going to battle a giant marlin in the following days. The battle, seen actually as the battle for his life, enables him to regain his self-esteem, confidence and youth, as well as his peer's admiration.

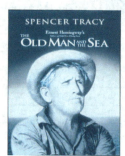

Unit 6

Reflections on Life

Unit Goals

Upon completing the texts in this unit, students should be able to:
- know that the better way to deal with problems in life is to "look inside the square";
- understand the importance of learning to approach problems from a new perspective;
- use the conversion prefixes correctly to form new words.

Before Reading

Hands-on Activities and Brainstorming

1. Life is full of ups and downs. How we see them often decides the outcome. Do you agree to this argument? Give examples to support your view.
2. Life is often compared to a journey. How do you understand this comparison? Why?
3. Visit the website http://en.wikipedia.org/wiki/Helen_Keller for information about Helen Keller and http://www.lkwdpl.org/wihohio/sull-ann.htm for information about her teacher Annie Sullivan to understand how our life philosophy can affect us. It is highly recommended that you make what you have learned about them into a presentation.

A Glimpse at Words and Expressions

Please read the following sentences. Pay attention to the underlined part in each sentence and to how it is used in the sentence and then decide on its meaning. Write down the meaning in the brackets.

1. He graciously accepted and sat down in one of the cushioned chairs, albeit slightly uneasy.　　　　　　(　　　　)
2. He sighed, took a sip of his coffee and began to tell me how much he was becoming disillusioned with work and the whole scheme of things.　　　　　　(　　　　)

3. It seemed that the bottom line of the matter was that he was tired of pulling the weight for his family and wanted out. (   )

4. The worry in his eyes was evident and I felt the urge to fix things, as was my nature when it comes to helping people... (   )

5. What has happened here is that when you first got married, you had the tendency to think "outside of the square". (   )

6. Basically, Elmer, you're a walking time bomb, ready to explode anytime and it doesn't have to be that way. (   )

7. I took up cycling like I used to do in my twenties. (   )

8. I see not having to worry over bills and having a chance to enjoy life instead of always fretting over what's going to get paid this month and what isn't. (   )

9. After that, I joined a gym and chewed the fat with my buddies there. (   )

10. The positive attitude will offset any negative energies that might arise ... (   )

Text A

Think inside the Square to Keep Those Love Fires Burning

Anonymous
(Abridged and Edited)

I was sitting in my sanctuary in my back yard contemplating the world's mysteries and minding my own business when a fellow neighbor walked up to me and started a conversation. As he looked a little distressed, I invited him into my little spiritual oasis and offered him a cup of

sanctuary /ˈsæŋktʃuˌɛri/ *n.* refuge or safety from pursuit, persecution, or other dangers
contemplate /ˈkɑntəmˌplet/ *v.* to think about sth. deeply and at length
fellow /ˈfɛlo/ *adj.* [only before noun] used to describe sb. who is the same as you in some way, or in the same situation
distressed /dɪˈstrɛst/ *adj.* suffering from extreme anxiety, sorrow, or pain
oasis /oˈesɪs/ *n.* a pleasant place or period of time in the middle of sth. unpleasant or difficult

coffee. He graciously accepted and sat down in one of the cushioned chairs, albeit slightly uneasy. I could tell by looking at him that he was troubled and I asked him what the matter was. He sighed, took a sip of his coffee and began to tell me how much he was becoming disillusioned with work and the whole scheme of things. It seemed that the bottom line of the matter was that he was tired of pulling the weight for his family and wanted out.

"Elmer," I said, "how long have you been married?"

"Too long," was his reply. "I'm working two jobs while she's sitting home, doing nothing. The spark has gone out of my marriage and I see no other alternative than to end it."

He took a sip of his coffee and put it back down on the patio table. The worry in his eyes was evident and I felt the urge to fix things, as was my nature when it comes to helping people not only find their soul mates, but keep them as well.

"Elmer," I began, "when I tell you this, you have to keep in mind that I'm telling you from a professional standpoint and not as a friend. You understand, don't you?"

"I'm listening," he said. "You remember when you married Fran and all the world was a happy and blissful place?" I asked him.

"Sure, I remember."

"What has happened here is that when you first got married, you had the tendency to think 'outside of the square'," I said.

"Outside of the square?"

"Yes, instead of focusing on yourself, you took on responsibilities such as caring for your family and all those other obligations that entails when one agrees to marry. You put your own needs aside to make sure that your wife and children were well cared for. What has happened is reality crashed down upon you and you have no inner resources left in which to restore things to the way they were. Basically, Elmer, you're a walking time bomb, ready to explode anytime and it doesn't have to be that way."

"It doesn't?"

"Of course, it doesn't. It's time to think 'inside the square', Elmer. It's time you focused on what makes you happy in order to make the rest of your family happy."

---

graciously /ˈgreɪʃəsli/ *adv.* in a gracious manner; courteously; benignantly

cushion /ˈkʊʃən/ *v.* to make sth. soft with a cushion

albeit /ɔːlˈbiːɪt/ *conj.* [formal] although

uneasy /ʌnˈiːzi/ *adj.* feeling worried or unhappy about a particular situation, especially because one thinks that sth. bad or unpleasant may happen or because one is not sure that what he is doing is right

sigh /saɪ/ *v.* to emit a long, deep audible breath expressing sadness, relief, tiredness, or similar

disillusioned /ˌdɪsɪˈluːʒənd/ *adj.* disappointed because the person one admired or the idea one believed to be good and true now seems without value

pull one's weight to do one's fair share of work

spark /spɑːrk/ *n.* a special quality of energy, intelligence or enthusiasm that makes one very imaginative, amusing, etc.

alternative /ɔːlˈtɜːnətɪv/ *n.* sth. that one can choose to do or has out of two or more possibilities

patio /ˈpætiˌoʊ/ *n.* a flat hard area outside, and usually behind, a house where people can sit

evident /ˈɛvɪdənt/ *adj.* clearly seen or understood; obvious

urge /ɜːdʒ/ *n.* a strong desire or impulse to do sth.

fix /fɪks/ *v.* to put (a bad or unwelcome situation) right

standpoint /ˈstændˌpɔɪnt/ *n.* an opinion or a way of thinking about ideas or situations

tendency /ˈtɛndənsi/ *n.* if sb./sth. has a particular tendency, they are likely to behave or act in a particular way

entail /ɛnˈteɪl/ *v.* to involve sth. that cannot be avoided

resources /ˈriːˌsɔːrs/ *n.* personal qualities such as courage and imagination that help you deal with difficult situations

walking time bomb a person whose behavior is very erratic and unpredictable and is about to lose his/her temper at any time

explode /ɪkˈsploʊd/ *v.* to suddenly become very angry or dangerous

"You've got a point there," he said. "You've got to begin with what makes Elmer happy," I continued. "Look at you. You're working two jobs and you come home and all you can do is eat a little dinner and go to bed. Then, you get back up and do it all over again. It's no wonder that you're distressed. What we have here, Elmer, is not disillusionment with your marriage; it's disillusionment with yourself and you don't even realize it."

"But, I have to work two jobs," he interrupted. "There's the mortgage, the kid's college tuition, car payments."

"Elmer, stop right there," I interrupted. "What you are doing is looking 'outside of the square' again. Look 'inside of the square' and what do you see?"

Elmer stopped and thought for a moment. "I see someone who wants good things in life," he said. "I see not having to worry over bills and having a chance to enjoy life instead of always fretting over what's going to get paid this month and what isn't."

"Okay, Elmer," I said, "what can you do to make this happen for you?"

"Tell my wife to get a job?"

"Yes, that would certainly help, but we're not talking about your wife right now; we're talking about you. What can you do for yourself to keep your marriage alive and become a happier person within?"

"Accept the things I cannot change and focus on the things I can?"

"And how do you do that?" I asked.

"By looking 'inside the square' and not blaming others for my unhappiness?"

"Exactly."

Elmer is but one of the millions of people in the world that think running away from their problems is the solution to finding happiness within themselves. And they're dead wrong. Running away only prolongs the problem and, in fact, can intensify the very problem that you need to fix. Once Elmer understands what he has to fix about himself, only positive energy will flow, which will eradicate the negativities in his life.

I saw Elmer a week later while I was pruning my shrubs and he stopped for a bit to tell me his good news.

"I just have to tell you," he said, out of breath. "I took your advice and started thinking 'inside the square'. I took up cycling like I used to do in my twenties. After that, I told my wife that from now on, I'm going to do this twice a week. She looked at me in astonishment, but then said, 'Elmer, that's wonderful!' I was so surprised that she would approve of this.

---

mortgage /ˈmɔːrɡɪdʒ/ n. a legal agreement by which a bank or similar organization lends one money to buy a house, etc., and one pays the money back over a particular number of years; the sum of money that one borrows

tuition /tuˈɪʃən/ n. the money that one pays to be taught, especially in a college or university

dead /dɛd/ adv. completely; exactly

prolong /prəˈlɔŋ/ v. to make sth. last longer

intensify /ɪnˈtɛnsəˌfaɪ/ v. to increase in degree or strength; to make sth. increase in degree or strength

eradicate /ɪˈrædɪˌket/ v. to destroy or get rid of sth. completely, especially sth. bad

negativity /ˌnɛɡəˈtɪvɪti/ n. a tendency to consider only the bad side of sth./sb.; a lack of enthusiasm or hope

prune /pruːn/ v. to cut off some of the branches from a tree, bush, etc. so that it will grow better and stronger

shrub /ʃrʌb/ n. a large plant that is smaller than a tree and that has several stems of wood coming from the ground

After that, I joined a gym and chewed the fat with my buddies there. I've never been happier!"

"That's wonderful, Elmer," I said. "And, how is your marriage?"

"Oh, that's the best part," he said, excitedly. "My wife looks at me like I'm a new man. It seems my positive attitude was contagious and even her own attitude has changed. She's thinking of joining me for a long-distance cycling trip to the mountains! And, even better than that, she's willing to join me for a budgeting class so that we can manage our bills better!"

"I'm so happy for you, Elmer," I said. "Just remember this—whenever things start getting bad, think 'inside the square' and do something good for yourself. The positive attitude will offset any negative energies that might arise and through bonding with your wife again, you will find that over time, it can only get better."

I watched Elmer walk back to his house and it could have been my imagination, but I do believe there was a step in his gait that wasn't there before.

Sometimes life gets in the way of maintaining a positive outlook on life, but if you stop for a moment and "fix" things within your own self, everything will come together not only for you, but for the loved ones in your family, too!

> **chew the fat** to chat in a leisurely and prolonged way
> **buddy** /ˈbʌdi/ *n.* a close friend
> **contagious** /kənˈtedʒəs/ *a.* spreading or tending to spread from one to another; infectious
> **budget** /ˈbʌdʒɪt/ *v.* to allow or provide a particular amount of money in a budget
> **offset** /ɔfˌsɛt/ *v.* to use one cost, payment or situation in order to cancel or reduce the effect of another
> **bond** /bɑnd/ *v.* to establish a relationship or link with someone based on shared feelings, interests, or experiences
> **gait** /get/ *n.* a way of walking
> **outlook** /ˈaʊtˌlʊk/ *n.* a person's point of view or general attitude to life

Better Know More

Dorothy Thompson

She is editor-in-chief, CEO and founder of *The Writer's Life* Publications and *The Writer's Life* ezine which was in the list of *Writer's Digest* magazine's top 101 websites for writers in 2003. Her first printed book *Romancing the Soul* was published by Zumaya Publications in 2004. Then she began writing on the subject of soul mate and one of her relationship columns was published by *Quilter's Home* magazine in 2006. Dorothy has also been a special guest on many radio programs including *Lifetime Radio*, *Single Talk* (*World Talk Radio*), and *Cuzin Eddie Show*, etc.

Check Your Understanding

Please answer the following questions based on what you have learnt in the text.

1. What was the author doing when a fellow neighbor walked up to her and started a conversation?
2. Why did the author invite her neighbor into her little spiritual oasis and offer him a cup of coffee?
3. What happened in Elmer's life that distressed him so much?
4. How do you understand "think 'outside the square'"?
5. In the author's opinion, what were the causes of and solutions to Elmer's marital problem?
6. What can Elmer do for himself to keep his marriage alive and become a happier person within?
7. How was Elmer's marriage after he took the author's advice?
8. Why was there a step in Elmer's gait that wasn't there before?

A Sip of Word Formation

Conversion Prefixes

Prefixes modify the meaning of the stem, but usually do not change the part of speech of the original word. Exceptions are the prefixes *be-* and *en-* (or *em-*), which will change the part of speech of the stem when they are attached to the original word. For example:

1. *be-*   numb (*adj.*) → *benumb* (*v.*)   friend (*n.*) → *befriend* (*v.*)
2. *en-* (*em-*)   slave (*n.*) → *enslave* (*v.*)   body (*n.*) → *embody* (*v.*)
3. *a-*   sleep (*n.*) → *asleep* (*adj.*)   blaze (*n.*) → *ablaze* (*adj.*)

Build Your Vocabulary

For each of the following sentences, a word is provided in the brackets. Use the appropriate form of the word to fill in the blank in the sentence, so that the sentence is logical and grammatical.

1. The Prime Minister vowed to support reforms to _____ the poor, but said the ultimate responsibility for change lay with themselves. (power)
2. Many white people supported the abolishment of slavery because they showed compassion for the _____ black men and women who were subjected to violence and discrimination. (slave)
3. _____ employees' efforts and ignoring employees' moods can hurt a lot more than their feeling. (little)

4. How to _____ and assess the value of humor therapy has been the recent focus of medical researchers and practitioners. (body)
5. Jeremy and Steven, two professional Jet-Ski riders, expected to raise awareness of _____ and funds for cancer research by trying to set a new record of long distance ride _____ their personal watercrafts. (board)
6. Due to economic recession, many small businesses are struggling to keep _____ by selling their assets or getting a bank loan. (float)
7. Mathew was _____ with love for the Little Mermaid and ran toward the sea, holding her in arms. (witch)
8. Royal Albert Hall stands right _____ Kensington Road from Albert Memorial. (cross)

You'd Like to Be

A Skilled Text Weaver

Fill in the blanks with the words you have learnt in this text, one word for each blank. You are advised to read the text carefully until you have become very familiar with it before starting to work on this task.

When Dillon proposed to Caren, he knew that it would not mark the beginning of a marriage that _____ responsibilities and _____. It marked the end. Instead of marrying Caren, Dillion flew to New York on Thursday to bury her. Caren died from the effects of nerofibromatosis type 2 (NF2)(2型神经纤维瘤病), a genetic disorder that causes tumors. Both Dillon and Caren suffered from NF2. Caren was diagnosed at 17, and Dillon discovered he had the illness at 20 when he started to have abnormal _____ and lose his hearing.

"I never loved anybody like I loved Caren," Dillion said, "We were so meant for each other. We are _____." They met during a NF2 conference and became pen pals and Internet pals later. After keeping in contact for about six years, they confessed their love to each other. "She had an optimistic _____ on life and a playfulness in her spirit that were _____," Dillon said. Then Caren left her family and friends and moved from New York to Las Vegas to be with Dillon. NF2 is such a terrible disorder that would prevent most people from leaving the house. But they didn't like to be confined to the _____ of their house, so they got out and stayed active. Caren even worked 8 years for a college degree that would normally takes two years. Unfortunately, her illness progressed more quickly than expected. She eventually lost her hearing, sight and had tumors along her spine. They had no other _____ than to send her to a hospital in New York. Four months later she passed away, _____ she dealt with the illness courageously.

Caren and Dillon's joy of life and great _____ _____ under the worst circumstances inspired everyone they encountered. Even though tortured by such terrible disabilities, they tried to make every day count and never became _____ with life and the whole _____ of things. Their life story is so inspirational to _____.

A Sharp Interpreter

Please paraphrase the following sentences. Change the sentence structure wherever necessary.

1. I was sitting in my sanctuary in my back yard contemplating the world's mysteries and minding my own business when a fellow neighbor walked up to me and started a conversation.
2. He sighed, took a sip of his coffee and began to tell me how much he was becoming disillusioned with work and the whole scheme of things.
3. It seemed that the bottom line of the matter was that he was tired of pulling the weight for his family and wanted out.
4. The worry in his eyes was evident and I felt the urge to fix things.
5. What has happened is reality crashed down upon you and you have no inner resources left in which to restore things to the way they were.
6. The positive attitude will offset any negative energies that might arise and through bonding with your wife again, you will find that over time, it can only get better.
7. Sometimes life gets in the way of maintaining a positive outlook on life, but if you stop for a moment and "fix" things within your own self, everything will come together not only for you, but for the loved ones in your family, too.

A Solid Sentence Constructor

The following is a list of words and expressions you have learnt in the text. Please make a sentence with each of them.

1. distressed
2. to bond with
3. to chew the fat
4. to care for
5. to intensify
6. to take up
7. to approve of

A Careful Writer

The following are three groups of words. You are required to study the words in each group carefully and then use them to write a paragraph of your own. Make sure that the paragraphs you have written are grammatical and coherent.

1. standpoint   keep ... in mind   take on   put aside   negativity

2. spark   patio table   uneasy   budget   restore... to...

A Superb Bilingualist

Please translate the following sentences into English using words or expressions provided in the brackets.

1. 倘若传媒一味明哲保身，而不如实报道，那么新闻自由将会荡然无存。(mind one's own business)
2. 在新的团队里，我努力尽到自己的职责，来回报同事们对我的理解和支持。(pull one's weight)
3. 随着《珍爱人生》(Precious)和《弱点》(The Blind Side)两部影片的上映，很多非裔美国人开始担心美国电影中的黑人形象被僵化了。(fret about/over)
4. 尽管苔丝(Tess)极力与生活抗争，但是她注定无法摆脱作为一个生活在维多利亚时代女人的命运。(entail)
5. 学生们的热情表明，他们显然很乐于参与课外活动，为走向社会做好准备。(evident)
6. 自古雅典时期起，人们就相信社会本身具有向前发展的内在趋势。(have a tendency to)

Text B

Learn How to Face Difficulty

By Deanna Mascle
(Abridged and Edited)

"It is not because things are difficult that we do not dare; it is because we do not dare that they are difficult."—Seneca the Younger

This is a great quote to both contemplate and to apply to your life.

5   How often do you hear people complain?

> quote /kwot/ *n.* a phrase or short piece of writing taken from a longer work of literature, poetry, etc. or what someone else has said

91

Pick a topic—love, friendship, careers, etc. The list of issues that people complain about is endless. You and I are no different. Perhaps we don't complain about each of these things but more than likely there is something that we complain about with great regularity.

Now, sometimes complaints are simply a way to vent some frustration at the moment but we don't really want anything to change in this area. However, more often than not, someone regularly complains about one specific problem.

If I had a dollar for every time I heard one friend complain about the difficulty of finding a good man I could throw her a huge wedding bash or perhaps simply buy her a husband in some small third-world country. When I thought about my friend Donna's problem and applied Seneca's quote to it a light bulb suddenly appeared above my head just like in the cartoons!

It was true! Donna is having difficulty finding a good man simply because she isn't daring enough. Sure she goes out on dates and tries to maintain an active social life, however she holds herself aloof emotionally. She isn't willing to dare much at all when it comes to her heart—so how can she hope that someone else will do so for her? Sure, there might be someone, somewhere, but she is also missing out on relationships, at least friendships, with some really great guys simply because she is too afraid to dare to care.

That is sad. We all know that love is marvelous but it is also frightening, however we have to take risks in order to experience it fully. Sometimes we might get hurt, however, more often than not, we will find the rewards outweigh the risks. There is no guarantee that Donna opens herself up and dares to love and that she will find the love of her life—however, there is certainly a guarantee that a life filled with love is more rewarding than one that is not.

I have another friend who is also afraid to dare. Jeff hates his job. No, that's not exactly right. He loves the work itself but he really hates the company that he works for. He finds the management very difficult to work for (and if even a small percentage of the stories he tells are true then he's right, it is a horrible place to work).

However, every time I suggest he look for a job somewhere else he comes up with some excuse about how difficult it would be. True the job market isn't great, but he's a skilled worker in a high-demand field so I'm sure he could find something. He's doomed his job

regularity /ˌregjəˈlærəti/ *n.* the state or quality of being regular
vent /vɛnt/ *v.* to express feelings, especially anger, strongly
more often than not usually; in a way that is typical of sb./sth.
bash /bæʃ/ *n.* a large party or celebration
light bulb a rounded glass container with a thin thread of metal inside which produces light when an electric current goes through it 电灯泡
daring /ˈdɛrɪŋ/ *adj.* brave; willing to do dangerous or unusual things; involving danger or taking risks
marvelous /ˈmɑrvələs/ *adj.* causing great wonder; extraordinary
outweigh /aʊtˈweɪ/ *v.* to be heavier, greater, or more significant than
guarantee /ˌgærənˈti/ *n.* something that makes sth. else certain to happen
rewarding /rɪˈwɔrdɪŋ/ *adj.* providing satisfaction; gratifying
doom /dum/ *v.* to make sb./sth. certain to fail, suffer, die, etc.

⁵⁰ search before he even started it because he's not daring enough.

> **complaisant** /kəmˈpleɪsənt/ *adj.* ready to accept other people's actions and opinions and to do what other people want

It wouldn't be fair to share my friends' examples without pointing to my own shortcomings. Probably the greatest difficulty in my own life is within my marriage and that ⁵⁵ is simply because I don't dare enough emotionally there. I have become too complaisant and take my husband and marriage for granted. I need to dare more emotionally.

So think about the difficulties in your own life and apply Seneca's rule then decide if you can be more daring! All the ⁶⁰ best!

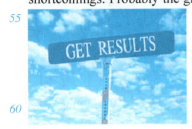

Notes

For some of the terms in the following, no explanation is provided. You are required to explain them by making use of the library, the Internet or whatever sources accessible.

1. Deanna Mascle

Deanna Mascle is a writer as well as a writing instructor at Morehead State University. She has been writing and publishing online since more than a decade ago. She publishes trivia and inspirational ezines and newsletters about preschool education, Internet marketing, and writing.

You can find more information at *Inspiration* by Dawggone and her inspirational magazines *Words of Inspiration Online* and *Daily Quote Online*.

2. Seneca the Younger

_____
_____
_____
_____
_____
_____

Comprehension Questions

Please answer the following questions based on what you have learnt in the text.

1. How do you understand "It is not because things are difficult that we do not dare; it is because we do not dare that they are difficult"?

2. What does the author mean by "You and I are no different"?
3. According to the author, why does "someone regularly complain about one specific problem"?
4. What does the author find out when she applies Seneca's quote to Donna's problem?
5. According to the author, what is the characteristic of love and what is the right attitude that we should hold towards love?
6. Why is Jeff's job search doomed?
7. How does the author explain her own shortcomings with Seneca's quote?

Writing Practice

Life is a journey that is not always full of happy moments. Sometimes we are not given what we think we deserve. Life can at times appear beset with problems in marriage, career or relationship, etc. It is impossible to have an easy life. For some, a life that is too easy would not be worth living. Whatever attitude we may develop toward life, facing difficulties negatively is simply not the right way to solve problems. Happiness and true success depend upon how we handle the troubles and difficulties. The author of this article contends that we should face difficulties in life with a brave heart.

Now you are supposed to write on how to overcome difficulties in life. Precise diction, clear viewpoint and good organization are highly valued.

Further Study

This is the end of Unit 6; but you can also gain more knowledge by accessing the following resources.

Recommended film: *Shawshank Redemption*—Andy Dufresne, a smart and caring banker, is accused and convicted of murdering his wife and her lover. But Andy claims that he is innocent. He is sent to Shawshank State Prison and spends nearly two decades there. During the time in prison, he becomes friends with Red and is used by Warden Norton to launder his money. Andy sees the possibility of a new trial since he finds evidence to prove his innocence, but only to be sent to solitary confinement. Though life has changed a lot, Andy never loses hope. This film is adapted from *Rita Hayworth and Shawshank Redemption* written by Stephen King.

Unit 7

Renowned Universities

Unit Goals

Upon completing the texts in this unit, students should be able to:
- ☞ understand the history and the development of Oxford University;
- ☞ understand about the university ideas and the concept of the Wisconsin Idea;
- ☞ use reversative or privative prefixes correctly to form new words.

Before Reading

📖 Hands-on Activities and Brainstorming

1. Oxford University and Cambridge University are renowned universities. It would be interesting to access the live information released by the official websites of the two universities. The websites can be located at http://www.ox.ac.uk and http://www.cam.ac.uk. You can also rely on the library for collecting information. You are encouraged to develop the information that you have collected on Oxford University or Cambridge University into a presentation.
2. Oxford has produced such outstanding figures as Indira Gandhi, Margaret Thatcher and Bill Clinton. Go to the library or Google for more facts about them. If possible, you could focus on their life at Oxford.

📖 A Glimpse at Words and Expressions

Please read the following sentences. Pay attention to the underlined part in each sentence and to how it is used in the sentence and then decide on its meaning. Write down the meaning in the brackets.

1. The university was given a boost in 1167 when, for   (   )
political reasons, Henry II of England ordered all
English students at the University of Paris to return
to England.

2. From the start there was friction between "town and gown". ( )

3. Rioting in the 13th century between students and local people hastened the establishment of primary halls of residence. ( )

4. What set Oxford (and Cambridge) apart from most other universities is the collegiate system and the tutorial system. ( )

5. The collegiate system fosters a sense of community between tutors and students. ( )

6. Most students find their tutors understanding and approachable, and the ones who will encourage then to work hard and achieve their best by stimulating their interest rather than coercion. ( )

7. Today Oxford University is comprised of thirty-nine colleges and six permanent private halls. ( )

8. Oxford's teaching and research is consistently in the top rank nationally and internationally. ( )

Text A

Oxford University

By M. Boyanova
(Abridged and Edited)

England is famous for its educational institutes. There were many different kinds of schools in Medieval England and English universities were one of the most significant creations. The students who attended either Oxford or Cambridge Universities set an intellectual standard that contrasted strongly with the norm of medieval England. Today both universities are internationally renowned centers for teaching and research, attracting students and scholars from all over the world.

The University of Oxford, located in the city of Oxford is one of the oldest and most highly respected Universities in Europe. It was the first university established in Britain. Oxford is situated about 57 miles north-west of

institute /ˈɪnstɪˌtuːt/ *n.* a society or organization for the promotion of science, education
contrast with to show a clear difference when compared with
norm /nɔːm/ *n.* a standard of behavior that is typical of or accepted within a particular group or society
renowned /rɪˈnaʊnd/ *adj.* famous and respected

London in its own county of Oxfordshire. The story of Oxford is one of war, plague, religious persecution, heroes and the emergence of one of the greatest universities in the world. Known as the city of "Dreaming Spires," Oxford is dominated by the university's medieval architecture and exquisite gardens.

According to legend, Oxford University was founded by King Alfred the Great in 872 when he happened to meet some monks there and had a scholarly debate that lasted several days. A more realistic version is that it grew out of efforts begun by Alfred to encourage education and establish schools throughout his territory.

Long after Alfred, during the late 11th or early 12th century, it is known that Oxford became a centre of learning for clerics, from which a school or university could have sprung. The university was given a boost in 1167 when, for political reasons, Henry II of England ordered all English students at the University of Paris to return to England. Most of the returning students gathered at Oxford and the University began a period of rapid development.

Oxford differs from many other universities in that there is no central university campus. Instead, the University consists of a large number of colleges and associated buildings, scattered throughout the city. Most students took lodgings with local people, who soon realized that they could charge them higher than average rent.

However, it was a strain on the resources of the community to have to provide for the large number of people from elsewhere.

From the start there was friction between "town and gown." In 1209, a woman was accidentally killed by one of the gownsmen; three students were at once executed by the citizens, in revenge for the woman's death. In protest at the hanging, the University of Oxford went into voluntary suspension, and scholars moved to a number of other locations, including the pre-existing school at Cambridge, which is situated about 50 miles north of London. It is now widely agreed that these scholars from Oxford started Cambridge's life as a University in 1209.

Rioting in the 13th century between students and local people hastened the establishment of primary halls of residence. These were succeeded by the first of Oxford's

county /ˈkaʊnti/ n.	a territorial division exercising administrative, judicial, and political functions in Great Britain and Ireland
persecution /ˌpɜːsɪˈkjuːʃən/ n.	a treatment that is cruel and unfair especially because of race, religion or political beliefs
emergence /ɪˈmɜːdʒəns/ n.	the act of coming out; becoming apparent
spire /spaɪr/ n.	a tall pointed structure on the top of a building, especially a church
dominate /ˈdɑməˌnet/ v.	to be the most important or noticeable feature of sth.
exquisite /ˈɛkskwɪzɪt/ adj.	extremely beautiful and carefully designed
realistic /ˌriəˈlɪstɪk/ adj.	of or relating to the representation of objects, actions, or social conditions as they actually are
cleric /ˈklɛrɪk/ n.	a member of the people ordained for religious service
associated /əˈsoʊʃiˌeɪtɪd/ adj.	connected
scattered /ˈskætərd/ adj.	spread far apart over a wide area
lodging /ˈlɑdʒɪŋ/ n.	temporary accommodation
strain /streɪn/ n.	pressure or stress
friction /ˈfrɪkʃən/ n.	disagreement among people who have different opinions
gownsman /ˈɡaʊnzmən/ n.	the faculty and student body of a university
execute /ˈɛksɪˌkjut/ v.	to kill sb. as a legal punishment
riot /ˈraɪət/ v.	to behave in a violent way in a public place, often as a protest
primary /ˈpraɪˌmɛri/ adj.	developing or happening first hall of residence dormitory
succeed /səkˈsid/ v.	to come next after sb./sth. and take their/its place or position

colleges whose architectural splendor, together with the University's libraries and museums, give the city its unique character.

The first college, University College, was founded in 1249 by William of Durham. Other notable colleges include All Souls, founded in 1438, Christ Church, founded in 1546 and Lady Margaret Hall, founded in 1878, which was the first women's college. Since 1974, all but one of Oxford's colleges has changed their statutes to admit both men and women. St. Hilda's remains the only women's college and the rest enroll both men and women.

What set Oxford (and Cambridge) apart from most other universities is the collegiate system and the tutorial system. According to the collegiate system, each college is an organized corporation under its own head, and enjoying the fullest powers of managing its own property and governing its own members. All colleges and halls have the same privileges as to receiving undergraduate members, and no one can be admitted into Oxford University by the central authority until he has been accepted by one of the colleges.

The collegiate system fosters a sense of community between tutors and students, and among students themselves. The colleges provide a certain number of rooms within their own walls for students, with the remainder living in the city. Meals are served either in the college halls or in the students' rooms; and attached to every college is a chapel where daily service is held during the term according to the forms of the Church of England.

The system of tutorials in college is a central part of undergraduate teaching in Oxford for all subjects. Undergraduate teaching at Oxford combines centrally organized lectures and seminars with weekly or twice weekly tutorials or classes. The college is an academic society in which students study under the guidance of college tutors, who will determine the week's study schedule, usually involving some reading and writing an essay or solving some problems. They will also go through the work with each individual student (or with one or two other undergraduates) and advise them on how to organize their studies, which lectures to attend, on the choice of optional papers, and so on. As students' work becomes more specialized, the tutor may arrange tutorials with appropriate experts elsewhere in the university. Most students find their tutors understanding and approachable, and the ones who will encourage them to work hard and achieve their best by stimulating their interest rather than by coercion.

Today Oxford University is comprised of thirty-nine colleges and six permanent private halls, founded between 1249 and 1996, whose

notable /ˈnotəbəl/ adj. (for sth.) deserving to be noticed or to receive attention; important
statute /ˈstætʃut/ n. an established law or rule
collegiate system a college-based higher education system
tutorial system an instructional system that requires the active exchange of ideas between students and their tutor during student learning process
corporation /ˌkɔːpəˈreɪʃən/ n. a body that is granted a charter legally recognizing it as a separate legal entity having its own rights, privileges, and liabilities distinct from those of its members
privilege /ˈprɪvəlɪdʒ/ n. a special right or advantage that a particular person or a group of people has
undergraduate /ˌʌndəˈɡrædʒuɪt/ n. a college or university student who has not yet received a bachelor's or similar degree
seminar /ˈsɛməˌnɑːr/ n. a small group of students in a college or graduate school engaged in original research or intensive study under the guidance of a professor who meets regularly with them to discuss their reports and findings
approachable /əˈprotʃəbəl/ adj. friendly and easy to talk to
stimulate /ˈstɪmjəˌlet/ v. to encourage
coercion /koʊˈɜːʒən/ n. the action of making sb. do sth. that they do not want to do, the act of using force or of threatening to use force
comprise /kəmˈpraɪz/ v. to consist of

architectural grandeur, together with that of the University's libraries and museums, gives the city its unique character. More than 130 nationalities are represented among a student population of over 18,000.

Many famous people have studied at Oxford University and they include John Locke, Adam Smith, Percy Bysshe Shelley, Lewis Carroll, Oscar Wilde, Indira Gandhi, Baroness Margaret Thatcher, Bill Clinton, Rupert Murdoch, Rowan Atkinson (Mr. Bean), and Hugh Grant. Oxford has produced four British and eight foreign kings, 47 Nobel prize-winners, 25 British Prime Ministers, 28 foreign presidents and prime ministers, seven saints, 86 archbishops, 18 cardinals, and one pope. Seven of the last eleven British Prime Ministers have been Oxford graduates.

Oxford's teaching and research is consistently in the top rank nationally and internationally, and is at the forefront of medical, scientific and technological achievement. Amongst the University's old members are many widely influential scientists. Contemporary scientists include Stephen Hawking, Richard Dawkins and Tim Berners Lee, inventor of the World Wide Web.

grandeur /ˈɡrændʒə/ n.	magnificence
archbishop /ɑːtʃˈbɪʃəp/ n.	大主教
graduate /ˈɡrædʒuˌet/ n.	one who has received an academic degree or diploma
forefront /ˈfɔːˌfrʌnt/ n.	the position of most importance and prominence
influential /ˌɪnfluˈɛnʃəl/ adj.	having a great influence or power
contemporary /kənˈtɛmpəˌrɛri/ adj.	living or occurring at the same time

Better Know More

1. Oxford University

Oxford is the oldest university in the English-speaking world and lays claim to nine centuries of continuous existence. As an internationally renowned centre for teaching and research, Oxford now enrolls 18,000 students with almost a quarter of the students from overseas, representing 130 nationalities across the world.

Oxford is a collegiate university, with 39 self-governing colleges related to the university in a type of federal system. There are also seven Permanent Private Halls, founded by different Christian denominations. Thirty colleges and all halls admit students for both undergraduate and graduate degrees. Seven other colleges are for graduates only; one has Fellows only, and one specializes in part-time and continuing education.

2. King Alfred (849–899)

King Alfred was the king of the southern Anglo-Saxon kingdom of Wessex from 871 to 899. Alfred is noted for his defense of the kingdom against the Danish Vikings, becoming the only English King to be awarded the epithet "The Great." As a learned man, Alfred encouraged education and improved the kingdom's legal system.

3. Cambridge University

Cambridge University has suffered comparison over the years from being the relative newcomer to elder sister Oxford. The term "relative" is worth noting, as Cambridge University dates back to the early 13th century. Some stories tell that the university was begun by masters and students fleeing one of the periodic outbreaks of "town vs. gown" tension which plagued Oxford from time to time. Whatever its origins, it did not take Cambridge long to evolve its own unique history and architectural heritage.  Its reputation for outstanding academic achievement is known world-wide and reflects the intellectual achievement of its students, as well as the world-class original research carried out by the staff of the university and the colleges.

There are 31 colleges in Cambridge. Each college is an independent institution with its own property and income. The colleges appoint their own staff and are responsible for selecting students, in accordance with university regulations. The teaching of students is shared between the colleges and university departments. Degrees are awarded by the university. A college is the place where students live, eat and socialize. It is also the place where they receive small group teaching sessions, known as supervisions. The supervision system is one of the main reasons for the University's success in the external reviews of learning and teaching.

4. Town and Gown

The relationship of Oxford University to the town of Oxford has a rocky history, spotted with outbreaks of rioting and violence. One of the most infamous outbreaks came on St. Scholastrica's Day (February 10) in 1354. It started innocently enough, when some students drinking at the Swyndlestock Tavern, accused the landlord of serving them "indifferent wine." The argument escalated until townsfolk came to the defense of the innkeeper. The bells of St. Mary's church called townsfolk to arms, and for three days they beat and killed students and ransacked the colleges. The fallout from the riot was severe. The city had to pay for repairs to the colleges, and the Mayor and burgesses of Oxford had to swear allegiance to the chancellor of the university every year and pay token damages in a special ceremony. The ceremony continued well into the Victorian period.

5. **Early universities in the world**

The University of Bologna in Italy and the University of Paris are now considered the oldest universities in the world, founded about one thousand years ago. It is not very clear when the first university of the United Kingdom was formed, but we know that nearly one thousand years ago, some teaching existed at Oxford. It was not until 1167, when Henry II banned English students from attending the University of Paris that the University of Oxford began to develop rapidly. Scholars from the University of Paris founded the University of Oxford and students from Oxford founded the University of Cambridge in the 13th century. John Harvard from Cambridge then founded America's first university, the University of Harvard. The chain link of founding and establishing universities continued and spread to other parts of the world.

Check Your Understanding

Please answer the following questions based on what you have learnt in the text.

1. Where is the University of Oxford located?
2. According to legend, who was the founder of the University of Oxford?
3. In what situation in the 12th century was the University of Oxford given a boost?
4. What is the relationship between the University of Oxford and the University of Cambridge?
5. What makes the University of Oxford stand out from other universities?
6. Toward the end of this article, the author gives a long list of elites who once studied at the University of Oxford. Can you figure out who's who?
7. Which aspect of the University of Oxford impresses you most? Can you state why?
8. With which of the following views do you agree more strongly? And why?
    A) Quality universities make quality students.
    B) Quality students make quality universities.

A Sip of Word Formation

Reversative or Privative Prefixes

Reversative prefixes are prefixes that take the meanings of reversing the action. Commonly found reversative or privative prefixes are *un*-, *de*-, and *dis*-.
1. Unlike the negative prefix *un*-, this prefix *un*-is used with verbs and indicates "opposite action" (e.g. *uncovered*).
2. *De*- combines with verbs to form new verbs; it indicates actions which have the opposite effect of the process described by the original verb (e.g. *depersonalize*). It also combines with nouns to form verbs which indicate that the thing referred to by the noun is removed (e.g. *defrost*).

3. *Dis*- closely related semantically to *un*- and *de*-, the prefix *dis*- forms reversative verbal bases (e.g. *disconnected*).

Build Your Vocabulary

For each of the following sentences, a word is provided in the brackets. Use the appropriate form of the word to fill in the blank in the sentence, so that the sentence is logical and grammatical.

1. His friends are trying to _____ him of his trouble. (burden)
2. Do not _____ the seatbelt before the plane stops completely. (fast)
3. The factory that _____ its waste into the river paid a ￡50,000 fine. (charge)
4. We shall not allow minor reverses to _____ us from moving boldly forward. (courage)
5. The president made it clear that he would not hesitate to _____ the currency if it became necessary. (value)
6. People can _____ very quickly in the desert. (hydrate)
7. It is reported that scientists have succeeded in _____ entire genetic code for two of the most common cancers. (code)
8. Education and training is the key that will _____ our nation's potential. (lock)

You'd Like to Be

A Skilled Text Weaver

Fill in the blanks with the words you have learnt in this text, one word for each blank. You are advised to read the text carefully until you have become very familiar with it before starting to work on this task.

The _____ "Financial Crisis and Sino-American Relations" was held in the Center for American Studies yesterday. The participants _____ about 20 scholars from domestically _____ universities. After making in-depth discussions concerning the issue how China and U.S. should _____ a win-win relationship at a time when the international financial crisis continued to spread and develop, all the scholars reached an unanimous agreement that the _____ common interest of China and U.S. was to broaden and deepen economic cooperation, and properly handle possible _____ and differences, on the basis of respecting international law and _____ governing international relations, to _____ economic recovery and emerge from the crisis. What's more, China and U.S. should continue to _____ good working relations of various government departments and _____ dialogue and exchanges of legislatures, _____ and business communities and media organizations between the two counties. As for the Taiwan-related issues, all the scholars insisted that Taiwan was an inalienable part of China's _____ and no matter how the situation across the Taiwan Straits may evolve, China would never waiver in its commitment to the One-China principle and the U.S. side was expected to honor its commitments, and take concrete actions to support the peaceful development of cross-Straits relations.

A Sharp Interpreter

Please paraphrase the following sentences. Change the sentence structure wherever necessary.

1. The story of Oxford is one of a war, plague, religious persecution, heroes and the emergence of one of the greatest universities in the world.
2. However it was a strain on the resources of the community to have to provide for the large number of people from elsewhere.
3. From the start there was friction between "town and gown."
4. What set Oxford (and Cambridge) apart from most other universities is the collegiate system and the tutorial system.
5. Most students find their tutors understanding and approachable, and the ones who will encourage them to work hard and achieve their best by stimulating their interest rather than by coercion.
6. Oxford's teaching and research is consistently in the top rank nationally and internationally, and is at the forefront of medical, scientific and technological achievement.
7. The colleges provide a certain number of rooms within their own walls for students, with the remainder living in the city.

A Solid Sentence Constructor

The following is a list of words and expressions you have learnt in the text. Please make a sentence with each of them.

1. to contrast with
2. to be dominated by
3. to take lodgings with
4. in revenge for
5. in protest at
6. to set apart from
7. to be comprised of
8. to give ... the unique character
9. to be at the forefront of

A Careful Writer

The following are three groups of words. You are required to study the words in each group carefully and then use them to write a paragraph of your own. Make sure that the paragraphs you have written are grammatical and coherent.

1. territory   scattered   emergence   contrast with   privilege   execute

   _____
   _____
   _____
   _____

2. comprise   foster   execute   approachable   hasten   friction

   _____
   _____
   _____
   _____

A Superb Bilingualist

Please translate the following sentences into English using words or expressions provided in the brackets.

1. 天津位于北京东南120公里处。(be situated)
2. 这个国家的历史充斥着战争、杀戮、阴谋和报复。(be one of)
3. 作为律师,大卫收费不高,又平易近人,是村民们公认的"穷人的律师"。(known as, approachable)
4. 新政策有力地推动了这个地区的经济发展。(boost)
5. 地震过后,又爆发了大面积的瘟疫,导致了数万人丧生。(succeed, plague)
6. 在这所大学,普通导师和知名学者享有同样的权利。(tutor, renowned, privilege)

Text B

What Is the Wisconsin Idea?

By Bassam Z. Shakhashiri
(Abridged and Edited)

The Wisconsin Idea proclaims, "The boundaries of the University are the boundaries of the state." It means that the University should not be an ivory tower institution but should serve all the people of the state in relevant ways. This may seem obvious today, but in the mid-nineteen century it was revolutionary. At that time, most institutions of higher education were private schools which emphasized a "classical" education in Greek and Latin, and few people were able to attend.

No one knows who coined the phrase "Wisconsin Idea" or when, but as early as 1858 a state legislative committee defined the role of a state-supported university:

> The general government has made a generous donation to the people of Wisconsin. They have an unquestioned right to demand that it shall primarily be adapted to popular needs, that its courses of instruction shall be arranged to meet as fully as possible the wants of the greatest number of our citizens.

In 1906, University President Charles Van Hise said, "I shall never be content until the beneficent influence of the University reaches every family in the state."

The Wisconsin Idea became nationally famous. In 1912, Theodore Roosevelt, impressed by the way in which Wisconsin had achieved substantial improvements without resorting to sweeping experiments, declared that "all through the Union we need to learn the Wisconsin lesson of scientific popular self-help, and of patient care in fundamental legislation."

In recent decades the borders of the University have expanded to the borders of the nation, the world and beyond. Today the University draws students from around the world, sends researchers to every part of the world, and sends experiments into space.

Among the University's pioneering efforts:

- In 1860, the University introduced continuing education for professionals by offering a short-term course for teachers.
- The University admitted its first full-time women students in 1863.
- The University established an experimental farm in 1866.

University Extension was founded in 1907 and soon had agriculture agents in every

---

Wisconsin /wɪsˈkɑnsɪn/ 威斯康星（美国五十州之一）
proclaim /prəˈkleɪm/ v. to publicly and officially make known
boundary /ˈbaʊndəri/ n. sth. that indicates or fixes a limit or extent
coin /kɔɪn/ v. to invent a new word or phrase that other people then begin to use
legislative /ˈlɛdʒɪˌsleɪtɪv/ adj. [formal] connected with the act of making and passing laws
beneficent /bəˈnɛfɪsənt/ adj. showing kindness
resort /rɪˈzɔːt/ v. (~ to) to do sth. difficult because of no other choice
pioneering /ˌpaɪəˈnɪərɪŋ/ adj. taking the initiative in the development of

county. It pioneered correspondence courses and is now promoting distance education. Today the University offers more than 400 extended hours' classes after 4 PM and on weekends and thousands of websites providing information to the public.

The Wisconsin Idea has also fostered a long partnership between the University and government. University of Wisconsin Law School graduates Robert M. La Follette Sr. and his wife Belle Case La Follette founded the Progressive Party which promoted many reforms including civil service, primary elections, and direct election of US senators. "Fighting Bob" La Follette served as Wisconsin governor and U.S. senator. Belle Case La Follette was the first woman to graduate from the University of Wisconsin Law School, in 1885. In the early 1900s, Professor John R. Commons drafted the state's first civil service law and helped draft the nation's first worker's compensation law. In the 1930s, University Professor Edwin Witte, along with other faculty and graduate students, drafted the nation's first unemployment compensation law and Social Security legislation. Law Professor Frank Turkheimer served as a special counsel for the Congressional Watergate hearings in 1974. More recently, Political Science Professor Don Kettle chaired governor's blue ribbon commissions on campaign finance reform and the relationship between state and local governments. These are just a few of the many faculties who have advised governments. Many University graduates have held government positions. In 1976, Shirley S. Abrahamson (S.J.D. 1962) became the first woman to serve on the state Supreme Court. In 1996 she became the first woman Chief Justice. Tommy G. Thompson (B.S. 1963, J.D. 1966) was the longest-serving Wisconsin governor (1987—2001) and now serves as Secretary of Health and Human Services. Eight of Wisconsin's last ten governors were graduates of the U.W.-Madison. Some 2250 University graduates have entered the Peace Corps, more than any other university.

"I want to contribute to the place where I live. I'm in a great position to do that because I'm both doing the research and going out to talk to farmers about it." - Kent Weigel

The University is a leader in research which has often led to applications that have improved the quality of life for everyone. For example, Wisconsin's dairy industry would not be possible without the pioneering agricultural research conducted by University faculty starting in the 1880s and continuing today. Many University faculty saw no clear dividing line between basic research and applied research. Much of their research has been aimed at solving specific problems, but they assumed that all research would eventually provide concrete benefits. In 1933, some farmers asked Professor Karl Paul Link why eating spoiled sweet clover made their cows bleed to death. Link found and synthesized

correspondence course a course of study that one does at home, using books and exercises sent by post/mail
compensation /ˌkɑmpənˈseʃən/ n. something especially money to give for the damage or hurt to others
faculty /ˈfækəlti/ n. all the teachers of a university or college
counsel /ˈkaʊnsəl/ n. a lawyer to represent sb. in court
chair /tʃɛr/ v. to act as a chairman
blue ribbon an award or honor given for excellence
dairy /ˈdɛri/ n. a business for processing or selling milk and milk products
concrete /kɑnˈkrit/ adj. real
sweet clover 草木樨
synthesize /ˈsɪnθɪˌsaɪz/ v. to form or produce by chemical processing from simpler elements

dicumarol, a blood thinner which impedes coagulation. Eventually, link made more than 100 variants of dicumerol. Some are used in
85 human medicine and have saved the lives of thousands of people in danger from blood clots. Another variation, Warfarin, is one of the most efficient rat poisons ever invented and is used around the world. Warfarin was
90 named for the Wisconsin Alumni Research Foundation. Link gave the patent to the Foundation, which has made tens of millions of dollars from it and used the money to fund more research.
95   Wisconsin has also been a leader in the environmental movement. John Muir is considered the father of the national park system and founded the Sierra Club. Professor Aldo Leopold founded the study of
100 wildlife ecology and his 1949 best-selling book *A Sand County Almanac* (referring to Adams County, Wisconsin) is a classic which still sells briskly today. Former Wisconsin governor and U.S. Senator Gaylord Nelson
105 (LL.B. 1942) founded Earth Day.

dicumarol /daiˈkuːmərəl/	n. 一种抗血凝剂
thinner /ˈθɪnə/	n. a substance that is added to sth. to make it less thick
coagulation /kəʊˌæɡjuˈleɪʃən/	n. a soft or solid mass caused by the transformation of a liquid 凝结物
variant /ˈvɛərɪənt/	n. a thing that is a slightly different form or type of sth. else 变体
clot /klɒt/	n. a thick mass of blood 血凝物
Warfarin /wɔːfərɪn/	n. 灭鼠灵
ecology /ɪˈkɒlədʒɪ/	n. the science of the relationships between organisms and their environments
oncology /ɒnˈkɒlədʒɪ/	n. the part of medical science that deals with tumors and cancer
retrovirus /ˌrɛtrəʊˈvaɪrəs/	n. 逆转录酶病毒(一种致肿瘤病毒)
stem cell	干细胞
strain /streɪn/	n. breed or type (of animal, insect or plant)
accreditation /əˌkrɛdɪˈteɪʃən/	n. the act of accrediting or the state of being accredited, especially the granting of approval to an institution of learning by an official review board after the school has met specific requirements
co-ordination /coʊ-ˌɔːdɪnˈeɪʃən/	n. the act of making parts of sth., groups of people, etc. work together in an efficient and organized way
outreach /aʊtˈriːtʃ/	n. extent of reach

    Three Nobel Prize winners carried out their research at the U.W.-Madison. In 1958 Professor Joshua Lederberg won the Nobel for discoveries relating to genetic recombination. In 1970, Biochemistry Professor Har Gobind Khorana won the Nobel for the first synthesis
110 of a gene. In 1975, oncology Professor Howard Temin won the prize for discovering retroviruses. Today the University is a world leader in stem cell research under Professor James Thomson, who was the first to develop a replicating strain of stem cells.
    The University renewed its commitment to the Wisconsin Idea in 2000 with the creation of the William T. Evjue Distinguished Chair for the Wisconsin Idea, endowed by the Evjue
115   Foundation. Professor Shakhashiri was appointed the first holder of the chair in 2001. The University also established Wisconsin Idea Fellowships. As part of the re-accreditation process and expansion of the Wisconsin Idea under Chancellor David Ward and Provost (now Chancellor) John Wiley, the University
120   re-organized and increased co-ordination of the outreach efforts already under way by many schools and departments of the University.

Notes

For some of the terms in the following, no explanation is provided. You are required to explain them by making use of the library, the Internet or whatever sources accessible.

1. Ivory Tower

_____
_____
_____
_____
_____

2. Theodore Roosevelt (1858–1919)

Theodore Roosevelt was the 26th President of the United States. He is noted for his energetic personality, range of interests and achievements. Before becoming President (1901—1909), he held offices at the municipal, state, and federal level of government. Roosevelt's achievements as a naturalist, explorer, hunter, author, and soldier are as much a part of his fame as any office he held as a politician. On the world stage, his policies were characterized by his slogan "speak softly and carry a big stick." He was the first American to win the Nobel Peace Prize.

Comprehension Questions

Please answer the following questions based on what you have learnt in the text.

1. What is the meaning of Wisconsin Idea?
2. What are the university's pioneering efforts mentioned in the text?
3. Can you give an example to illustrate "the university is a leader which has often led to applications that have improved the quality of life for everyone"?
4. Can you talk about the three Nobel Prize winners carrying out their research at the UW-Madison?

Writing Practice

Given the fact that university education is aggrandizing its attraction to more and more people from different backgrounds, it is interesting to know the rationale behind this encouraging phenomenon.

You are asked to write an essay on the topic: Why Do People Attend University? Use specific reasons and examples to support your view.

Further Study

This is the end of Unit 7; but you can also gain more knowledge by accessing the following resources.

1. Recommended film: *Miracle at Oxford*—It tells a story of how Oxford's rowers won a boat race—a traditional competition between Oxford and Cambridge—after many failures. This film will enable you to understand the history of Oxford and Cambridge from another perspective.
2. Access the website at http://www.blanchflower.org/alumni/ and find out about the alumni of Oxford and Cambridge.

Unit 8

Poverty

Unit Goals

Upon completing the texts in this unit, students should be able to:
- understand the urgency of combating child trafficking and child labor in Africa;
- understand the roots of poverty and what can be done to reduce poverty;
- use suffixes of status and domain correctly to form new words.

Before Reading

Hands-on Activities and Brainstorming

1. Our world has been fighting against human trafficking and child labor for centuries. Still we cannot say we are close to the end of the fighting. What are the root causes of human trafficking and child labor? What are the effective measures that can be taken to stop them? Do you know anything about human trafficking and child labor? You can surf the Internet or simply google to read stories about human trafficking and child labor and share your stories with others.
2. Go to the library or visit certain websites to gather information about global poverty. Besides, try to find at least three reasons for the problem of poverty in Africa and figure out some solution to ease the problem. Develop what you have gathered into a presentation.

A Glimpse at Words and Expressions

Please read the following sentences. Pay attention to the underlined part in each sentence and to how it is used in the sentence and then decide on its meaning. Write down the meaning in the brackets.

1. Since the problem is closely <u>linked to</u> the continent's poverty, and can only be eliminated with increases in family incomes and children's educational opportunities.   (   )

2. Trafficking is beginning to get on the policy agenda.　　(　　)
3. An ILO study issued in June found that child　　(　　)
   trafficking in West and Central Africa is on the rise.
4. In a paper presented to a conference on "human　　(　　)
   trafficking" held in Nigeria in February, 2001 ...
5. Over the past year, however, African countries have　　(　　)
   been moving more systematically to counter this
   trend.
6. Africa has the highest incidence of child labor in the　　(　　)
   world.
7. Poor infrastructure, low teacher spirits and the　　(　　)
   introduction of school fees under the country's
   structural adjustment program have contributed to
   higher dropout and absence rates.
8. ... ILO draws a distinction between normal family　　(　　)
   obligations and work which gives rise to exploitation
   and abuse.

Text A

Child Labour Rooted in Africa's Poverty

By Ernest Harsch
(Abridged and Edited)

Across Africa, there are an estimated 80 million child workers, a number that could rise to 100 million by 2015. Since the problem is closely linked to the continent's poverty, and can only be eliminated with increases in family incomes and children's educational opportunities, UNICEF, the ILO and other groups are focusing initially on the "worst forms" of child labour. These include forced labour and slavery, prostitution, employment in the drug trade and other criminal activities, and occupations that are especially dangerous to children's health and security.

Mr. Alec Fyfe, a senior adviser on child labour for UNICEF told *Africa Recovery*, "Trafficking is beginning to get on the policy agenda." Because trafficking tears children away from the protection of their families and communities, it is especially dangerous to

> initially /ɪˈnɪʃəlɪ/ *adv.* at the beginning
> prostitution /ˌprɒstɪˈtjuːʃən/ *n.* the work of a person who has sex for money
> traffick /ˈtræfɪk/ *v.* to deal illegally
> agenda /əˈdʒɛndə/ *n.* a list of items to be discussed at a meeting

their well-being. An ILO study issued in June found that child trafficking in West and Central Africa is on the rise. Reports from many countries in Africa suggest that most of the children are sent to other countries for domestic service, or put to work on plantations, in petty trade and as beggars. The trafficking of children for commercial sexual exploitation was also reported.

Trafficked children, the study found, were working between 10 and 20 hours a day, carrying heavy loads and operating dangerous tools. They often lack adequate food and drink. Nigeria reported that one out of five children trafficked in that country died of illness or accidents. Others contracted sexually transmitted diseases, including HIV/AIDS. Although parents were sometimes persuaded by recruiters to send their children away to earn some extra income, often neither the children nor the parents were paid.

In a paper presented to a conference on "human trafficking" held in Nigeria in February, Dr. Salah, a UNICEF regional director for West and Central Africa, agreed with the ILO assessment that child labour trafficking has become a "substantial problem" in the region. Among the reasons influencing the phenomenon, the paper listed:

- Poverty, a major and ever-present causal factor, which greatly limits vocational and economic opportunities in rural areas in particular and pushes families to use all available means to increase their meagre incomes;

- Inadequate educational opportunities. In order to help their children search for the opportunity for education, parents willingly move them from the protective envelope of the family;

- Ignorance among families and children about the risks of trafficking;

- Migration of adults from villages to urban slums, which exposes their children to greater risks;

- High demand among employers for cheap and submissive child labour;

- Ease of travel across regional borders;

- The desire of young people themselves to travel and explore;

- Inadequate political commitment, legislation and judicial mechanisms to deal with child traffickers.

Over the past year, however, African countries have been moving more systematically to counter this trend.

Child trafficking is only one of the more harmful aspects of a much broader problem. Africa has the highest incidence of child labour in the world. According to the ILO, 41 percent

---

well-being /ˈwɛlˈbiːɪŋ/ n. general health and happiness
domestic service n. work performed in a household by someone who is not a member of the family 家政服务
plantation /plænˈteɪʃən/ n. a large area of land where crops are grown
petty /ˈpɛti/ adj. little; minor
exploitation /ˌɛksplɔɪˈteɪʃən/ n. a situation in which sb. treats others in an unfair way, especiallly in order to make money from their work
Nigeria /naɪˈdʒɪriə/ 尼日利亚（非洲中西部国家）
transmit /trænsˈmɪt/ v. to pass sth. from one person to another
assessment /əˈsɛsmənt/ n. a carefully thought opinion or a judgment about sb./sth.
ever-present /ˈɛvəˈprɛznt/ adj. existing everywhere
vocational /voˈkeɪʃənəl/ adj. connected with the skills, knowledge, etc. that people need to have in order to do a particular job
meagre /ˈmiːɡə/ adj. small in quantity and poor in quality
slum /slʌm/ n. an area of a city that is very poor and where the houses are dirty and in bad condition
submissive /səbˈmɪsɪv/ adj. obedient
legislation /ˌlɛdʒɪˈsleɪʃən/ n. a law or a set of laws passed by a parliament, congress or government body
judicial /dʒuˈdɪʃəl/ adj. connected with a legal judgment
mechanism /ˈmɛkəˌnɪzəm/ n. a system of the parts in sth. or an organization that together perform a particular function

of all African children between the ages of 5 and 14 are involved in some form of economic activity, compared with 21 per cent in Asia and 17 percent in Latin America. Among girls, the participation rate also is the highest: 37 percent in Africa, 20 percent in Asia and 11 percent in Latin America.

It is no coincidence that Africa also is the poorest region, with the weakest school systems. And among African children, those from poorer families are far more likely to seek work. A 1999 Child Labour Survey in Zimbabwe, conducted by the ILO, found that about 88 percent of economically active children aged 5—17 came from households with incomes below 36 US dollars per month.

coincidence /kəʊˈɪnsɪdəns/ n.	the fact of two things happening at the same time by chance, in a surprising way
Zimbabwe /zɪmˈbɑbwi/	津巴布韦(非洲南部国家)
Tanzania /ˌtænzəˈniə/	坦桑尼亚(东非国家)
deterioration /dɪˌtɪrɪəˈreɪʃən/ n.	the state of growing worse
infrastructure /ˈɪnfrəˌstrʌktʃə/ n.	the basic systems and services that are necessary for a country or an organization
drop-out /ˈdrɒpˌaʊt/ n.	a person who leaves school or college before they have finished their studies
site /saɪt/ n.	a place where a building, town, etc. is situated
distort /dɪˈstɔːt/ v.	to change the shape, appearance or sound of sth.
mobilize /ˈməʊbəˌlaɪz/ v.	to assemble, marshal, or coordinate for a purpose

According to an ILO study on Tanzania, the incidence of child labour in the country has risen partly because of the deterioration of the school system, itself a result of economic decline. Poor infrastructure, low teacher spirits and the introduction of school fees have contributed to higher drop-out and absence rates. This has brought down Tanzania's once-high primary enrolment rate: from 90 percent in 1980 to 77.8 percent in 1996. Thirty percent of all children between 10 and 14 are not attending school, and many end up working. In villages around mining sites, the school drop-out rate is around 30—40 percent.

Recognizing that the roots of child labour lie in family poverty, and that it cannot simply be legislated out of existence, the ILO draws a distinction between normal family obligations and work which gives rise to exploitation and abuse. The UNICEF study on Eastern and Southern Africa similarly admits that African culture allows children to work within the family and community, but economic hardships, HIV/AIDS and other disasters have distorted traditional forms of child work into exploitative practices.

Since the conditions do not yet exist to end all types of child labour, the immediate challenge is to educate the public about the dangers to children of the most exploitative and abusive forms of child labour and to mobilize governments and societies to combat them.

Better Know More

1. UNICEF

United Nations International Children's Emergency Fund (UNICEF) is an affiliated agency of the United Nations. It was established in 1946 as the United Nations International

Children's Emergency Fund to provide relief to children in countries devastated by World War II. Now, UNICEF is concerned with assisting children and adolescents throughout the world, particularly in devastated areas and developing countries. Unlike most UN agencies, UNICEF is financed through voluntary contributions from governments and individuals, rather than by regular assessments. It was awarded the Nobel Peace Prize in 1965.

2. The ILO

Founded in 1919, The International Labour Organization (The ILO) is the UN specialized agency which seeks the promotion of social justice and internationally recognized human and labour rights. It formulates international labour standards in the form of conventions and recommendations, setting minimum standards of basic labour rights: freedom of association, the right to organize, collective bargaining, abolition of forced labour, equality of opportunity and treatment, etc.

3. Africa Recovery

Africa Recovery (now known as *Africa Renewal*) was a renowned magazine and first appeared in 1987. It was one of the major items produced by the Africa Renewal information program. The program, produced by the Africa Section of the United Nations Department of Public Information, provides up-to-date information and analysis of the major economic and development challenges facing Africa today. It also produces a range of public information materials, including backgrounds, press releases and feature articles. It works with the media in Africa and beyond to promote the work of the United Nations, Africa and the international community to bring peace and development to Africa.

Check Your Understanding

Please answer the following questions based on what you have learnt in the text.

1. How many child workers are there across Africa?
2. What are the "worst forms" of child labour? Why are international organizations focusing on the "worst forms" of child labour?
3. What are the possible causes of child labour?
4. What happened to those trafficked children?
5. What caused child labour trafficking to become a substantial problem in West and Central Africa?
6. How is child labour related to educational problems in Tanzania?
7. What is the immediate challenge to combating child labour?
8. What's your view on the relationship between poverty and education?

A Sip of Word Formation

Reversative or Privative Prefixes

1. Similar in meaning to -*dom*, -*hood* derivatives express concepts such as "state" (e.g. *adulthood*, *childhood*, *farmerhood*), and "collectivity" (e.g. *beggarhood*, *Christianhood*). As with other suffixes, metaphorical extensions can create new meanings, for example the sense "area" in the highly frequent *neighborhood*, which originates in the collectivity sense of the suffix.
2. The suffix -*ship* forms nouns denoting "state" or "condition", similar in meaning to derivatives in -*age*, -*hood* and -*dom*. Base words are mostly person nouns as in *friendship*, *membership*, *statesmanship*, *vicarship*. Extensions of the basic senses occur, for example "office", as in *postmastership*, *professorship*, or "activity", as in *courtship* "courting" or *censorship* "censoring".
3. The native suffix -*dom* is semantically closely related to -*hood*, and -*ship*, which expresses similar concepts. -*dom* attaches to nouns to form nominals which can be paraphrased as "state of being X" as in *apedom*, *clerkdom*, *slumdom*, *yuppiedom*, or which refers to collective entities, such as *professordom*, *studentdom*, or denote domains, realms or territories as in *kingdom*, *cameldom*, *maoridom*.

Build Your Vocabulary

For each of the following sentences, a word is provided in the brackets. Use the appropriate form of the word to fill in the blank in the sentence, so that the sentence is logical and grammatical.

1. It is commonly believed that a lie in childhood may lead to a crime in _____. (adult)
2. The Party must be on full alert against corrosion by all decadent ideas and maintain the purity of its _____. (member)
3. For his treason, not only was everything taken away from him, but also his German _____. (citizen)
4. The Federal Government's plan to introduce a mandatory Internet _____ has met with strong opposition from the IT and Telecommunications industries. (censor)
5. A liar begins with making _____ appear like truth, and ends with making truth itself appear like _____. (false)
6. Surely there should have been some mention of the shocking misjudgment on the part of _____. (official)
7. Throughout the University of California system, the university _____ recognizes the special achievements of outstanding scholars. (professor)
8. After an incredibly short _____, she accepted his marriage proposal. (court)

You'd Like to Be

A Skilled Text Weaver

Fill in the blanks with the words you have learnt in this text, one word for each blank. You are advised to read the text carefully until you have become very familiar with it before starting to work on this task.

There is a growing awareness that climate change can no longer be considered simply an environmental issue. More importantly, it puts at risk the protection and improvement of human health and _____. Climate-sensitive diseases attracted less attention in the world in the past, but now they have become an _____ challenge worldwide. According to the U.K. government report in 2008, U.K. was to be hit by regular malaria outbreak more seriously within five years. It is _____ that malaria kills almost 1 million people in the world annually and the number is still _____ _____ _____. The _____ of the situation mainly _____ in fatal heat waves resulted from global warming. A prudent strategy for _____ the problem is to set a high priority on reducing the _____ of climate-sensitive _____ disease through first _____ research and then taking relevant measures such as vector control efforts, vaccination programs as well as improving sanitary _____ such as water treatment program.

A Sharp Interpreter

Please paraphrase the following sentences. Change the sentence structure wherever necessary.

1. ...UNICEF, the ILO and other groups are focusing initially on the "worst forms" of child labour.
2. ...Dr. Salas, a UNICEF regional director for West and Central Africa, agreed with the ILO assessment that child labour trafficking has become a "substantial problem" in the region.
3. In order to help their children search for the opportunity for education, parents willingly move them from the protective envelope of the family.
4. According to an ILO study on Tanzania, the incidence of child labour in the country has risen partly because of the deterioration of the school system, itself a result of economic decline.
5. Recognizing that the roots of child labour lie in family poverty, and that it cannot simply be legislated out of existence, the ILO draws a distinction between normal family obligations and work which gives rise to exploitation and abuse.
6. Since the conditions do not yet exist to end all types of child labour, the immediate challenge is to educate the public about the dangers to children of the most exploitative and abusive forms of child labour and to mobilize governments and societies to combat them.

A Solid Sentence Constructor

The following is a list of words and expressions you have learnt in the text. Please make a sentence with each of them.

1. to be linked to
2. to focus on
3. on the agenda
4. to tear ... away from
5. to be exposed to
6. to counter

A Careful Writer

The following are three groups of words. You are required to study the words in each group carefully and then use them to write a paragraph of your own. Make sure that the paragraphs you have written are grammatical and coherent.

1. exploit   recruiter   submissive   coincidence   conduct

2. assessment   traffick   transmit   meagre   household

A Superb Bilingualist

Please translate the following sentences into English using words or expressions provided in the brackets.

1. 这个女孩子从厌学、辍学到走上犯罪的道路绝非偶然。(coincidence, end up)
2. 由于我校增加了热门专业,与去年相比,学生入学人数增加了15%。(compared with, enrolment)
3. 我们清醒地认识到解决贫困问题会是艰难而漫长的。(combat, be likely to)

4. 贫困的根源在于教育的缺失。要消除贫困，我们就要办好教育。(root, the lack of)
5. 博彩成瘾会引发人们不劳而获的错误思想，扭曲人生观，有时甚至会导致道德水准的下降。(give rise to, misconception, distorted, contribute to)

Text B

Understanding Poverty

Anonymous
(Abridged and Edited)

Poverty is hunger. Poverty is lack of shelter. Poverty is being sick and not being able to see a doctor. Poverty is not having access to school and not knowing how to read. Poverty is not having a job, is fear for the future, living one day at a time. Poverty is losing a child to illness brought about by unclean water. Poverty is powerlessness, lack of representation and freedom.

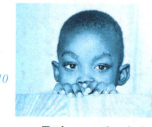

Poverty has many faces, changing from place to place and across time, and has been described in many ways. Most often, poverty is a situation people want to escape. So poverty is a call to action—for the poor and the wealthy alike—a call to change the world so that many more may have enough to eat, adequate shelter, access to education and health, protection from violence, and a voice in what happens in their communities.

To know what helps to reduce poverty, what works and what does not, what changes over time, poverty has to be defined, measured, and studied—and even experienced. As poverty has many dimensions, it has to be looked at through a variety of indicators—levels of income and consumption, social indicators, and indicators of vulnerability to risks and of socio/political access.

Much work has been done using consumption or income-based measures of poverty, but also on non-income dimensions of poverty, most notably in the Human Development Report prepared annually by the United Nations Development Program.

A common method used to measure poverty is based on incomes or consumption levels. A person is considered poor if his or her consumption or income level falls below some minimum level necessary to meet basic needs. This minimum level is usually called the "poverty line." What is necessary to satisfy basic needs varies across time and societies. Therefore, poverty lines vary in time and place, and each country uses lines which are appropriate to its level of development,

---

access /ˈæksɛs/ *n.* a way of entering or reaching a place
representation /ˌrɛprɪzɛnˈteʃən/ *n.* the fact of having representatives who will speak or vote for someone or on his behalf
dimension /dɪˈmɛnʃən/ *n.* an aspect
indicator /ˈɪndɪˌketə/ *n.* a sign that shows what sth. is like or how a situation is changing
consumption /kənˈsʌmpʃən/ *n.* the act of buying and using products
vulnerability /ˌvʌlnərəˈbɪləti/ *n.* weakness, easily to be attacked or hurt
minimum /ˈmɪnəməm/ *n.* the smallest or lowest amount that is possible, required or recorded

societal norms and values.

Information on consumption and income is obtained through sample surveys, in which households are asked to answer detailed questions on their spending habits and sources of income. Such surveys are conducted more or less regularly in most countries. These sample survey data collection methods are increasingly being complemented by participatory methods, where people are asked what their basic needs are and what poverty means to them. Interestingly, new research shows a high degree of concordance between poverty lines based on objective and subjective assessments of needs.

When estimating poverty worldwide, the same reference poverty line has to be used and expressed in a common unit across countries. Therefore, for the purpose of global aggregation and comparison, the World Bank uses reference lines set at $1 and $2 per day. It has been estimated that in 2001, 1.1 billion people had consumption levels below $1 a day and 2.7 billion lived on less than $2 a day. These figures are lower than earlier estimates, indicating that some progress has taken place, but they still remain too high in terms of human suffering, and much more remains to be done.

While much progress has been made in measuring and analyzing income poverty, efforts are needed to measure and study the many other dimensions of poverty. Work on non-income dimensions of poverty—defining indicators where needed, gathering data, assessing trends—is presented in the World Development Report (WDR) 2000 *Attacking Poverty*. This work includes assembling comparable and high-quality social indicators for education, health, access to services and infrastructure. It also includes developing new indicators to track other dimensions—for example risk, vulnerability, social exclusion, access to social capital—as well as ways to compare a multi-dimensional conception of poverty, when it may not make sense to aggregate the various dimensions into one index.

In addition to expanding the range of indicators of poverty, work is needed to integrate data coming from sample surveys with information obtained through more participatory techniques, which usually offer rich insights into why programs work or do not. Participatory approaches illustrate the nature of risk and vulnerability, how cultural factors and ethnicity interact and affect poverty, how social exclusion sets limits to people's participation in development, and how barriers to such participation can be removed. Work on integrating analyses of poverty based on sample surveys and on participatory techniques is presented in the WDR.

The uneven progress of development is worrying. The flows of trade and capital that

---

societal /səˈsaɪətl/ *adj.* connected with society and the way it is organized

norm /nɔːm/ *n.* standards of behaviour that are typical of or accepted within a particular group or society

complemented /ˈkɒmpləmentɪd/ *adj.* supplementary

participatory /pɑːˈtɪsəpəˌtɔri/ *adj.* sharing or taking part in

concordance /kənˈkɔːdns/ *n.* the state of being similar to sth. or consistent with it

aggregation /ˌægrɪˈgeɪʃən/ *n.* several things grouped together or considered as a whole

assemble /əˈsembəl/ *v.* to come together as a group; to bring people or things together as a group

conception /kənˈsepʃən/ *n.* an understanding or a belief of what sth. is or what sth. should be

index /ˈɪnˌdeks/ *n.* a sign or measure that sth. else can be judged by 指数

integrate /ˈɪntɪˌgreɪt/ *v.* to combine two or more things so that they work together

illustrate /ˈɪləˌstreɪt/ *v.* to make the meaning of sth. clearer by using examples, pictures, etc.

ethnicity /eθˈnɪsɪti/ *n.* the fact of belonging to a particular race

barrier /ˈbæriə/ *n.* a blocking object or problem; obstacle

uneven /ʌnˈiːvən/ *adj.* organized in a way that is not regular and/or fair

integrate the global economy may bring benefits to millions, but poverty and suffering *persist*. Responding to such concerns, governments and international development agencies have
80 begun to re-examine the way they operate. In September 2000, 189 countries signed the *Millennium Declaration*, which has established a set of eight goals for which 18 *numerical* targets have been set and over 40 *quantifiable*
85 indicators have been *identified*. The goals are: eliminate extreme poverty and hunger; achieve universal primary education; promote gender equality and empower women; reduce child *mortality*; improve *maternal* health; combat
90 HIV/AIDS, *malaria*, and other diseases; ensure environmental *sustainability*; and develop a global partnership for development.

While each goal is important in its own right, they should be viewed together as they
95 are mutually reinforcing. Achieving them will require building *capacity* for effective, democratic, and accountable *governance*, protection of human rights, and respect for the rule of law.

> **persist** /pəˈsɪst/ *v.* to continue to exist
> **millennium** /məˈlɛniəm/ *n.* a period of 1000 years
> **numerical** /nuˈmɛrɪkəl/ *adj.* expressed in numbers
> **quantifiable** /ˈkwɑntəfaɪəbl/ *adj.* that can be described or expressed as an amount or a number
> **identify** /aɪˈdɛntəˌfaɪ/ *v.* to recognize sb./sth. and be able to say who or what they are
> **mortality** /mɔːˈtæləti/ *n.* the number of deaths in a particular situation or period of time
> **maternal** /məˈtɜːnəl/ *adj.* connected with being a mother
> **malaria** /məˈlɛriə/ *n.* 疟疾
> **sustainability** /səˌsteɪnəˈbɪləti/ *n.* the ability in continuing or being continued for a long time
> **capacity** /kəˈpæsɪti/ *n.* the ability to understand or to do sth.
> **governance** /ˈɡʌvənəns/ *n.* the activity of governing a country or controlling a company or an organization; the way in which a country is governed or a company or institution is controlled

Notes

For some of the terms in the following, no explanation is provided. You are required to explain them by making use of the library, the Internet or whatever sources accessible.

1. The Human Development Report

The Human Development Report is an independent report commissioned by the United Nations Development Programme (UNDP). It is the product of a selected team of leading scholars, development practitioners and members of the Human Development Report Office of UNDP. It was first launched in 1990 with the single goal of putting people back at the center of the development process in terms of economic debate, policy and advocacy. Each report talks about a topical theme and provides significant analysis and policy recommendations. The report is translated into more than a dozen languages and publicized in more than 100 countries annually.

2. The World Bank

Comprehension Questions

Please answer the following questions based on what you have learnt in the text.

1. What are the indicators of poverty?
2. Why is there the necessity to measure and study non-income poverty?
3. What ways have been adopted by governments and international development agencies to collect information on consumption and income?
4. What are the goals for *Millennium Declaration* signed by 189 countries in 2000?

Writing Practice

  This unit presents to the readers a general picture of the problem of child labor and child trafficking in Africa and the root causes. From the texts, we have learnt that inadequate educational opportunities and a higher demand of cheap labor deprived the children of the rights to receive education and led to ignorance of the risk of child trafficking. You are supposed to express your views on poverty and give your suggestions on how to draw public attention to this issue and combat the tragic trend.

Further Study

  This is the end of Unit 8; but you can also gain more knowledge by accessing the following resources.

1. Please visit the official website of the non-profit organization—Cooperative for Assistance and Relief Everywhere (CARE) located at http://www.care.org/ to find out what it has contributed to the cause of poverty reduction.
2. Please watch the recommended film *Yesterday*—It tells a poor, young HIV-positive mother struggling to raise her daughter alone in an isolated village. It gives audiences an in-depth insight into life in South Africa.

Unit 9

Tragedy

Unit Goals

Upon completing the texts in this unit, students should be able to:
- understand the great ancient Greek cultural achievements in the Classical Period, especially the elements and features of tragedy;
- develop the ability to appreciate Sophocles' skillful untangling of the plot complication;
- use verb and adjective suffixes correctly to form new words.

Before Reading

Hands-on Activities and Brainstorming

1. Visit the website http://www.theatrehistory.com/ancient/OEDIPUS001.html to gain some basic knowledge about ancient Greek tragedy and Sophocles' *Oedipus Rex*.
2. Have a group discussion on the theme of *Oedipus Rex*.
3. *Oedipus Rex* is a tragedy created in strict accordance with "the Three Unities". Do you think the creation of plays should always follow this principle? Why?
4. Some believe "Men's determination can conquer Nature," while others have faith in "fatalism." What is your opinion? It is highly recommended that you develop it into a presentation.

A Glimpse at Words and Expressions

Please read the following sentences. Pay attention to the underlined part in each sentence and to how it is used in the sentence and then decide on its meaning. Write down the meaning in the brackets.

1. As he approached the city, he came to an intersection where three roads <u>converged</u>, and encountered there an old man riding along the path who refused to <u>give way</u>. (   )

2. A horrendous monster called the Sphinx was choking the city off from the rest of the world.   (   )
3. In shock and rage, the Sphinx threw itself off a cliff.   (   )
4. A Corinthian shepherd takes Oedipus to Polybus and Merope, the King and Queen of Corinth who adopt the baby and pass him off as their own child.   (   )
5. The god demands that the murderer be discovered and rooted out.   (   )

Text A

Sophocles and *Oedipus Rex*

By Frances B. Titchener
(Abridged and Edited)

Sophocles belongs to the generation of Athenian playwrights who followed in Aeschylus' wake and built upon his successes. Born around 495 BCE and dying in 406 BCE, Sophocles' life encompassed almost the entire of the fifth century BCE, the Golden Age of Classical Athens. And indeed, if anyone was, Sophocles was Athens' "golden boy."

No play shows better Sophocles' mastery of dense expression than *Oedipus Rex*. Like a gathering of Olympian deities, the audiences in the Theatre of Dionysus look down from their mountain vantage upon the hapless mortals below struggling vainly against fate

---

Sophocles /ˌsɔfəˈkliːz/ n. Greek dramatist
Athenian /əˈθiːnɪən/ adj. of Athens
playwright /ˈpleɪˌraɪt/ n. one who writes plays; a dramatist
Aeschylus /ˈɛskələs/ n. Greek dramatist
encompass /ɛnˈkʌmpəs/ v. to form a circle or ring around; surround
Oedipus /ˈɛdəpəs/ n. the son of Jocasta and of Laius, king of Thebes
deity /ˈdiəti/ n. a god or goddess
Dionysus /ˌdaɪəˈnaɪsəs/ n. a Greek god, son of Zeus and Semele
vantage /ˈvæntɪdʒ/ n. a place or position affording a good view of something
hapless /ˈhæplɪs/ adj. (especially of a person) unfortunate

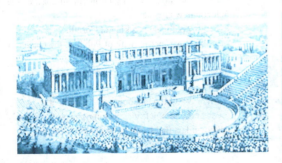

and, because the viewers know where the characters will end up ultimately, they can see how the gods work, how impossible it is for humans to escape their destiny.

    The myth of Oedipus revolves around a man destined by the gods to suffer the most horrible fate. Oedipus' story takes place, for the most part, in the city of Thebes in northern
20 Greece, where he was born. When he was still in his mother's womb, Oedipus' parents Laius and Jocasta asked the oracle of Apollo at Delphi about their unborn child. The oracle's reply was terrifying, that the boy would grow up to kill his father and marry his mother.

    Because of this horrifying portent, Jocasta and Laius did what many people with unwanted children did in antiquity. They had the baby's feet spiked—Oedipus' name means in Greek
25 "swollen foot," the result of this injury—and ordered a faithful herdsman who worked in the mountains near Thebes to carry the child off into the wild and abandon it, an act called exposure. With this, they thought they had sidestepped fate but, in fact, their actions proved to be part of its unfolding.

    The herdsman felt pity for the helpless
30 babe so, instead of leaving it to rot in the wild or serve as fodder for wild animals, he handed it over to another herdsman from the neighboring city of Corinth. This man, in turn, gave it to his king and queen, Polybus and Merope, who
35 were childless and raised Oedipus as their own. Thus, the boy grew up in Corinth believing himself the natural-born offspring of the royal family, until one day when he heard from a visiting stranger that he wasn't the
40 legitimate son of Polybus and Merope. After his parents refused to tell him one way or the other, Oedipus stormed off to Delphi to demand the truth of Apollo. As before, the oracle delivered its gruesome verdict on his
45 fate.

    Stunned by the revelation that he was destined one day to marry his mother and kill his father, he vowed never to return to Corinth

Thebes /θiːbz/ n. a city in Greece, in Boeotia, north-west of Athens
Laius /ˈlaɪjəs/ n. a king of Thebes, the father of Oedipus and husband of Jocasta
Jocasta /dʒoˈkæstə/ n. a Theban woman, the wife of Laius and mother and later wife of Oedipus
oracle /ˈɔrəkəl/ n. 1. a priest or priestess acting as a medium through whom advice or prophecy was sought from the gods in classical antiquity
2. a response or message given by an oracle, especially an ambiguous one
Apollo /əˈpɑlo/ n. a god, son of Zeus and Leto and brother of Artemis
Delphi /ˈdɛlˌfaɪ/ n. one of the most important religious sanctuaries of the ancient Greek world, dedicated to Apollo and situated on the lower southern slopes of Mount Parnassus above the Gulf of Corinth
portent /ˈpɔrˌtɛnt/ n. a sign or warning that a momentous or calamitous event is likely to happen
antiquity /ænˈtɪkwɪti/ n. the ancient past, especially the period of classical and other human civilizations before the Middle Ages
spike /spaɪk/ v. to impale on or pierce with a sharp point
sidestep /ˈsaɪdˌstɛp/ v. to avoid (someone or something) by stepping sideways
fodder /ˈfɑdə/ n. food, especially dried hay or straw, for cattle and other livestock
Corinth /ˈkɔrɪnθ/ n. a city on the north coast of the Peloponnese, Greece
Polybus /ˈpɔlibʌs/ n. a king of Corinth
Merope /ˈmɔrope/ n. wife of Polybus, the Queen of Corinth
gruesome /ˈgrusəm/ adj. causing repulsion or horror; grisly
verdict /ˈvɜdɪkt/ n. an opinion or judgment
revelation /ˌrɛvəˈleʃən/ n. a surprising and previously unknown fact that has been disclosed to others

but instead headed down a different road leading out of Delphi and ended up eventually near Thebes. As he approached the city, he came to an intersection where three roads converged, and encountered there an old man riding along the path who refused to give way. Their quarrel quickly escalated to violence, and in the primordial act of road rage he knocked the obstructive gaffer out of his wagon and killed him.

When he reached Thebes, Oedipus discovered a city under siege. A horrendous monster called the Sphinx ("Strangler") was choking the city off from the rest of the world. It refused to let anyone pass who couldn't answer its riddle: "What walks on four legs in the morning, two legs at noon, and three in the evening?" Being naturally quick-witted, Oedipus figured out that the answer was Man, who crawls when young, walks upright as an adult and uses a cane in old age. In shock and rage, the Sphinx threw itself off a cliff.

Oedipus entered Thebes a triumphant savior, winning both throne and queen. His wife was, of course, the newly widowed Jocasta, and as was later revealed, his own mother. When the full truth about Oedipus' birth at long last came to light and she realized that through her actions her son-and-husband had committed unspeakable acts, Jocasta killed herself. Soon thereafter, blinded and forlorn, Oedipus went into exile from Thebes. So goes Sophocles' version of the myth.

One of the most intriguing aspects of this play is its plot, often heralded as the first great detective story. Sophocles has ingeniously scrambled the plot elements so that the dramatic climax will shock even those who know the story well. Here are the basic elements of the plot arranged in order chronologically:

1. FIRST ORACLE: At or before Oedipus' birth an oracle tells Laius and Jocasta that their child "will kill his father and marry his mother."

2. EXPOSURE: The cursed baby is "exposed," left to die on Mount Cithaeron near Thebes.

converge /kənˈvɜːdʒ/ v. (of lines) to tend to meet at a point

primordial /praɪˈmɔːdiəl/ adj. existing at or from the beginning of time ; primeval

gaffer /ˈɡæfə/ n. a person in charge of others; a boss

siege /siːdʒ/ n. a military operation in which enemy forces surround a town or building, cutting off essential supplies, with the aim of compelling those inside to surrender

horrendous /həˈrendəs/ adj. extremely unpleasant, horrifying, or terrible

Sphinx /sfɪŋks/ n. a winged monster of Thebes, having a woman's head and a lion's body

choke sth. off to prevent or inhibit the occurrence or development of

forlorn /fəˈlɔːn/ adj. pitifully sad and abandoned or lonely

herald /ˈherəld/ v. to acclaim

ingeniously /ɪnˈdʒiːnjəsli/ adv. (of a person) clever, original, and inventive

scramble /ˈskræmbəl/ v. to make (sth.) jumbled or muddled

Cithaeron /sɪˈθiːrən/ n. a mountain located in South East Greece

3. 3a. RESCUE and 3b. ADOPTION of the baby: A Corinthian shepherd takes Oedipus to Polybus and Merope, the King and Queen of Corinth who adopt the baby and pass him off as their own child.

TIME PASSES: Oedipus grows up in Corinth.

4. THE STRANGER: A visitor to Corinth tells Oedipus that he is not the biological son of Polybus and Merope, the people he believes are his parents.

5. SECOND ORACLE: Oedipus goes to Delphi to learn the full truth from Apollo's oracle. There he receives a shocking reply to the question of his parentage, that he will kill his father and marry his mother.

6. FLIGHT FROM CORINTH: Thinking Polybus and Merope are his true parents, Oedipus avoids returning to Corinth and instead heads for Thebes.

7. MURDER: Oedipus meets and kills an old man at a crossroads. This man turns out to be his biological father Laius.

8. SPHINX: Oedipus proceeds on to Thebes which the monstrous Sphinx is at that moment besieging. Oedipus solves its famous riddle, saves Thebes and is given the kingdom and queen in marriage as his reward. The queen is Jocasta, his really widowed mother.

TIME PASSES: Oedipus rules Thebes. He and Jocasta have four children.

9. PLAGUE: Apollo sends a plague on Thebes. Jocasta's brother Creon brings back a THIRD ORACLE that demands expiation for Laius' murder. The god demands that the murderer be discovered and rooted out.

10. REVELATION OF THE TRUTH: When investigation shows that Oedipus is the culprit, Jocasta commits suicide. Oedipus blinds himself and goes into exile.

In spite of all these plot elements, the dramatic setting of the play encompasses only elements 9 and 10, from the plague to the final revelation of the truth. That is, by the time in which the play takes place, all the other elements 1—8 have already happened and are revealed to the audience through exposition, the process of informing the viewers about the background of the plot.

But that exposition, especially the order in which Sophocles presents the first eight elements, is a hallmark of this play, artfully circuitous in its design much like a well-written murder mystery. The play opens with element 9, Plague. Soon thereafter, element 8, Sphinx is mentioned but then Sophocles holds back the exposition and allows much time to pass on stage as Oedipus quarrels with first Teiresias and then Creon. Finally, in the middle of the play Jocasta casually mentions elements 1 and 2, the first oracle and the exposure of her baby, which inspires Oedipus to narrate elements 4—7, how he left Corinth and murdered the old man on the road.

With that, the only missing element in the prehistory of the plot is 3, the dramatic linchpin identifying the accursed child as Oedipus. This element is divided into 3a, the baby's rescue and 3b, its adoption. Contrary to chronological order, the Corinthian messenger first

---

pass sb. off as to falsely represent a person or thing as (sth. else)

besiege /bɪˈsiːdʒ/ v. to surround (a place) with armed forces in order to capture it or force its surrender

Creon /crəon/ n. a king of Thebes, Jocasta's brother

expiation /ˌɛkspiˈeʃən/ n. the act of making amends or reparation for guilt or wrongdoing; atonement

culprit /ˈkʌlprɪt/ n. a person who is responsible for a crime or other misdeed

circuitous /s əˈkjuːɪtəs/ adj. (of a route or journey) longer than the most direct way

Teiresias /taɪˈrisiəs/ n. a blind prophet in Thebes

linchpin /ˈlɪntʃˌpɪn/ n. a person or thing vital to an enterprise or organization

reveals 3b, Oedipus' adoption. Then after yet another delay encompassing more than a hundred lines, the old herdsman to whom Laius had entrusted the task of exposing the new-born Oedipus confesses at last that he saved the baby. With that, the final element 3a, Oedipus' rescue, is made known, and the full truth, element 10, is revealed.

> lurch /ləːtʃ/ v. to make an abrupt, unsteady, uncontrolled movement or series of movements; stagger
> singe /sɪndʒ/ v. to burn (sth.) superficially or lightly

So, the elements come in this order: 9, 8, 1, 2, 4, 5, 6, 7, 3b, 3a, 10. This lurching about in the plot gives the viewers much the same sense of confusion the characters are experiencing as the play proceeds, which helps the audience feel as if they're participating in the process of uncovering the truth, the way a good detective story does. Yet unlike the characters on stage but instead more like readers and gods, the viewers sit safe above the din and disaster unfolding below them, hovering just close enough to the tragedy to feel its heat but not be singed.

Better Know More

1. Sophocles

Sophocles was one of the three ancient Greek tragedians whose work has survived. His first plays were written later than those of Aeschylus and earlier than those of Euripides. According to a 10th century encyclopedia, Sophocles wrote 123 plays during the course of his life, but only seven have survived in a complete form: *Ajax, Antigone, Trachinian Women, Oedipus Rex, Electra, Philoctetes and Oedipus at Colonus.* Sophocles' fame and many works earned him a crater on the surface of Mercury named after him.

2. Aeschylus

Aeschylus was the first of the three ancient Greek tragedians whose work has survived and is often recognized as the father of tragedy. His name derives from a Greek word, meaning "shame." According to Aristotle, he expanded the number of characters in plays to allow for conflict among them; previously, characters interacted only with the chorus. Only seven out of 70—90 tragedies said to have been written by Aeschylus have survived intact: *The Persians, Seven against Thebes, The Suppliants,* the trilogy known as *The Oresteia,* consisting of the three tragedies *Agamemnon, The Libation Bearers* and *The Eumenides,* and *Prometheus Bound* (whose authorship is disputed).

3. Timeline

475 BC–221 BC The Contention of Numerous Schools of Thoughts in the Warring States Period

- 221 BC The Warring States Period Ended
- 286 BC Zhuangtzu died
- 289 BC Mencius died
- 318 BC Hui Shi died
- 322 BC Aristotle died
- 323 BC The Classical Period Ended
- 323 BC Alexander the Great died
- 332 BC Alexander conquered Egypt
- 333 BC Alexander defeated Persians at Battle of Issus
- 335 BC Aristotle's *Poetics*
- 338 BC Shang Yang died
- 347 BC Plato died
- 359 BC Shang Yang reformed
- 369 BC Zhuangtzu was born
- 370 BC Hui Shi was born
- 371 BC Mencius was born
- 376 BC Motze died
- 380 BC Plato established the Athens' Academy
- 384 BC Aristotle was born
- 386 BC Plato founded the Academy
- 390 BC Shang Yang was born
- 399 BC Socrates was executed
- 406 BC Sophocles died
- 408 BC Epicurus died
- 428 BC Plato was born
- 441 BC Euripides wrote his first tragedy
- 456 BC Aeschylus died
- 468 BC Sophocles wrote his first tragedy
- 468 BC Motze was born
- 476 BC The Warring States Period Began
- 476 BC The Spring and Autumn Period Ended
- 479 BC Confucius died
- 483 BC Gautama Buddha died
- 484 BC Epicurus was born
- 496 BC Sophocles was born
- 500 BC The Greek Classical Period Began
- 500 BC Laotze died
- 525 BC Aeschylus was born
- 551 BC Confucius was born
- 580 BC Laotze was born
- 770 BC The Spring and Autumn Period Began
- 1100 BC Mycenaean Culture Suppressed
- 1200 BC Mycenaean Power Declined

4.   The Golden Age of Classical Athens

The Golden Age of Classical Athens, also known as Fifth Century Athens, refers to the Greek city-state Athens in period of roughly 480 BCE–404BCE. This was a period of Athenian political hegemony, economic growth and cultural flourishing formerly known as Classical Greece, and The Age of Pericles. Athens produced some of the most influential and enduring cultural artifacts of the Western tradition at that time. The playwrights Aeschylus, Sophocles and Euripides all lived and worked in fifth century Athens. The Golden Age also featured the most renowned Western philosophers of all time. Chief among them were Socrates, whose ideas exist only in a series of dialogues by his student Plato, who mixed them with his own; Plato; and later, Plato's student, Aristotle. Athens therefore earned the title of "school of Greece" and was deemed the capital of world eloquence.

5.   *Oedipus Rex*

Oedipus Rex is an Athenian tragedy by Sophocles that was first performed in 429 BCE. It was the second of Sophocles' three Theban plays to be produced, but it comes first in the internal chronology, followed by *Oedipus at Colonus* and then *Antigone*. Over the centuries, it has come to be regarded by many as the best Greek tragedy. The story of Oedipus seems rather paradoxical as much of Oedipus' misfortune was the result of his own will, revealing that free will and predestination are by no means mutually exclusive.

6.   The Theatre of Dionysus

The Theatre of Dionysus is one of the earliest preserved open-air theatre in Athens. The theatre was dedicated to Dionysus, the god of wine and the patron of drama, frequently used to host the City Dionysia festival. Amongst those who competed were the dramatists of the classical era, Aeschylus, Sophocles, Euripides, Aristophanes, and Menander. Mathematics played an important role in the construction of The Theatre of Dionysus, as the designers had to be able to create good acoustics in it so that the actors' voices could be heard throughout the theatre, including the very top row of seats. The theatre was enormous, able to seat up to 25,000 viewers.

7.   Oracle

The word "Oracle" in the text carries two meanings. The Oracle of Apollo of Delphi was the priestess at the Temple of Apollo at Delphi, located on the slopes of Mount Parnassus. She was widely credited for her prophecies inspired by Apollo, a prominence unusual for a woman in male-dominated ancient Greece. In other situations, oracle also refers to the prophecies or the messages delivered by the priestess.

8. The Sphinx

The sphinx, in Greek tradition, has the haunches of a lion, the wings of a great bird, and the face and breast of a woman. She is treacherous and merciless: those who cannot answer her riddle suffer a fate typical in such mythological stories: they are gobbled up whole and raw, eaten by this ravenous monster.

Check Your Understanding

Please answer the following questions based on what you have learnt in the text.

1. When was the Golden Age of Classical Athens?
2. In terms of literature, what characterized the Golden Age?
3. In what sense was Sophocles Athens' "golden boy"?
4. How do you understand "how impossible it is for humans to escape their destiny"?

A Sip of Word Formation

Verb Suffixes

There are four suffixes which derive verbs from other categories (mostly adjectives and nouns), *-ify*, *-ize*, *-en*, and *-ate*.

1. *-ate* means "to make, to cause, or to act," etc.; such as, "to make propitious" (e.g. *propitiate*); or "to give life to" (e.g. *animate*).
2. The Germanic suffix *-en* attaches mostly to adjectives (e.g. *blacken, ripen*), but a few nouns can also be found (e.g. *lengthen*). The meaning of *–en* formations is "to make" or "become."
3. *-ify* usually attaches to some adjectives, which means "to make" (e.g. *purify*) or "become" (e.g. *specify*).
4. *-ize* means "to become," "make" (e.g. *Americanize*), or "make like" (e.g. *fossilize*).

Adjective Suffixes

-ful, *-less*, *-ly*, *-y*, *-ish*, *-some*, *-able*, *-al*, *-ous*, *-ic*, and *-ive* are adjective suffixes.

1. *-ful* is usually added to nouns with the meaning of (1) full of (e.g. *wishful*); (2) having the qualities of (e.g. *graceful*); or (3) tending to (e.g. *successful*).
2. *-less* is a negative suffix with the meaning of (1) without; or (2) not doing; not affected by. Usually they can be added to the same root while having the opposite meaning (e.g. *helpful–helpless*).
3. *-ly* is added to nouns with the meaning of having the qualities (e.g. *friendly, scholarly*). Note: hourly, daily, weekly, monthly, etc. can be adjectives or adverbs.

4. *-y* is added to nouns and changes the nouns into adjectives (e.g. *greedy, salty*).
5. *-ish* is added to nouns with the meaning of (1) from the country mentioned (e.g. *Turkish*); (2) [sometimes disapproving] having the nature of; like (e.g. *childish*); or (3) fairly, approximately (e.g. *thirtyish*).
6. *-some* is added to a word with the meaning of producing; likely to (e.g. *fearsome, quarrelsome*).
7. *-able* (BrE also *-ible*) often means that something can be done (e.g. *washable*).
   Note: not all adjectives ending in -able/-ible have this meaning (e.g. *pleasurable, valuable*).
8. *-al* can be added to a noun with the meaning of connected with (e.g. *magical, verbal*).
9. *-ous* combines with nouns meaning having the nature or quality (e.g. *dangerous, famous*).
10. *-ic* is added to a noun with the meaning of (1) connected with (e.g. *scenic*); or (2) that performs the action mentioned (e.g. *artistic*).
11. *-ive* is usually combined with a word with the meaning of (1) tending to (e.g. *explosive*); or (2) having the nature of (e.g. *prescriptive*).

Build Your Vocabulary

For each of the following sentences, a word is provided in the brackets. Use the appropriate form of the word to fill in the blank in the sentence, so that the sentence is logical and grammatical.

1. Our client called yesterday, saying that the original design of the advertisement had to be _____. (modifiable)
2. According to an April, 2009 Field Poll, 56 percent of Californians favor _____ _____ marijuana for social use and taxing the sales proceeds. (legal)
3. Are you an interesting person? Writing cartoon captions is a great way to _____ your humor skills. (sharp)
4. Everybody loves _____ gifts which are very special to both the giver and receiver. (person)
5. For many, the hardest part of socializing with strangers is _____ conversation. (initiative)
6. It is important to follow the maintenance guidelines to help _____ the life of your battery. (length)
7. Japanese violinist and educationist Shinichi Suzuki believes that every child has unlimited potential and that no one, if taught in a scientific way, is _____ of improvement. (hope)
8. In order to attract more tourists to our city, we need to design attractive and _____ _____ brochures. (information)
9. Ted Turner, one of the individuals on the Forbes 400 list, suggested in 1996 that the rich give bigger part of their wealth away to support _____ charities. (worth)
10. President Reagan's 1984 speech depicts the _____ attack on the beaches of Normandy during World War II. (hero)

11. After years of bilateral disputes, the two nations finally agreed to build a good _____ relationship and partnership. (neighbor)
12. If you want to persuade your audience, you'd better first make yourself sound _____ to them. (believe)
13. Recently, some major economies in East Asia have witnessed a _____ demand and a slow-down in their growth, which has affected trade and financial stability. (slug)
14. For non-English majors, it is difficult to tell who the _____ author of this book is, Mark Twain or Ernest Hemingway. (origin)
15. The poet enjoys walking on the _____ road every day after dinner. (lone)
16. Millions of the most _____ men, who would otherwise have made great contribution to human progress, were killed in wars. (courage)
17. One of the world's most successful luxury brands, Louis Vuitton uses limited availability as a _____ pricing strategy to make its image exclusive. (power)

You'd Like to Be

A Skilled Text Weaver

Fill in the blanks with the words you have learnt in this text, one word for each blank. You are advised to read the text carefully until you have become very familiar with it before starting to work on this task.

Greek literature boasts three great _____ of tragedy whose works are extant: Aeschylus, Sophocles, and Euripides. All of them have contributed a great deal to the development of tragedy in _____, which differentiates itself at modern times, and their works have established some important elements of tragedy, such as a _____ protagonist (悲剧主角), the _____ of an oracle, the abundance of _____, and the _____ for sins.

Aristotle said in his work Poetics that "tragedy is characterized by seriousness and dignity and involving a great person who experiences a reversal of fortune." This definition _____ the change of fortune from bad to good, and that from good to bad as well. However, according to Aristotle, the latter is always preferable, as in Oedipus Rex, because tragedy forces the spectator to pity and fear for himself when he observes the _____ outcome of the protagonist. In other words, the function of tragedy is to arouse the emotions of pity and fear, and to affect the catharsis (宣泄) of these emotions within the spectators, thus the process of catharsis can not only be an experience of the protagonist, the author, but also of the audience.

Catharsis is an integral part of the tragedy, but can it stand alone? Tragedy cannot exist solely on fear and pity; otherwise there would be little distinction between *Hamlet* and a mediocre revenge drama. A greatly stylized tragedy combines pity and fear with the "enlightenment", the protagonist's realization of his or her flaw, or the _____ of the truth. This enlightenment, another _____ of ancient Greek tragedy, exists in harmony with pity and fear; in fact, without it the actions and meaning of the play would have been superficial and fleeting (肤浅的). The enlightenment supports, or justifies, the emotional response and helps the viewer to remember the events and gain knowledge from those events.

A Sharp Interpreter

Please paraphrase the following sentences. Change the sentence structure wherever necessary.

1. Like a gathering of Olympian deities, the audiences in the Theatre of Dionysus look down from their mountain vantage upon the hapless mortals below struggling vainly against fate and, because the viewers know where the characters will end up ultimately, they can see how the gods work, how impossible it is for humans to escape their destiny.
2. With this, they thought they had sidestepped fate but, in fact, their actions proved to be part of its unfolding.
3. As before, the oracle delivered its gruesome verdict on his fate.
4. Then after yet another delay encompassing more than a hundred lines, the old herdsman to whom Laius had entrusted the task of exposing the new-born Oedipus confesses at last that he saved the baby.
5. This lurching about in the plot gives the viewers much the same sense of confusion the characters are experiencing as the play proceeds, which helps the audience feel as if they're participating in the process of uncovering the truth, the way a good detective story does.

A Solid Sentence Constructor

The following is a list of words and expressions you have learnt in the text. Please make a sentence with each of them.

1. to encompass
2. revelation
3. to converge
4. to choke... off
5. expiation
6. to storm off

A Careful Writer

The following are two groups of words. You are required to study the words in each group carefully and then use them to write a paragraph of your own. Make sure that the paragraphs you have written are grammatical and coherent.

1. playwright   deity   hapless   unfolding   exposure

2. portent   gruesome   go into exile   besiege   forlorn

A Superb Bilingualist

Please translate the following sentences into English using words or expressions provided in the brackets.

1. 虽然俄狄浦斯竭力逃避神谕所示的命运，但他的行为反成为神谕应验的一部分。(sidestep, oracle, unfolding)
2. 对于俄狄浦斯刺瞎双眼，自我放逐这一事件，人们已经谈论了太多太多。但以往的解释过多地强调其赎罪的心态，而忽视了这一行为具有深思熟虑、心理满足、自我肯定的因素——即对自我的超越。(exile, expiation)
3. 《俄狄浦斯王》以追查杀害前王凶手为开始，调查过程充满悬念。随着真相的逐步揭示，戏剧渐入高潮。(suspense, revelation of truth, climax)
4. 18世纪以前，亚里士多德式三一律(Aristotelian Three Unities)是所有戏剧必须遵从的准则。在这方面，《俄狄浦斯王》堪称典范。所谓三一律是指一部戏剧在情节(action)、时间与地点上的一致，也就是在舞台上完成一个发生在二十四小时内、同一地点的完整剧情。(herald)

Text B

Oedipus Rex

By Sophocles
First performed around 429 BC
Translated by George Theodoridis

OEDIPUS
(King of Thebes)
JOCASTA
(Queen of Thebes)
CREON
(Brother to Jocasta)

CREON:
All the folks respect me now. They greet me with a smile, they come to me whenever they need something from you because they know they can depend on me. Why then should I give all this up for the sake of your throne? Would it not be thoroughly unwise of me? In any case, Oedipus, believe me: murder is not in my nature—alone or with others!

Go ahead, go to Delphi, Oedipus! Check me out. Ask the oracle if I'm not telling the truth; and if you find out that Teiresias and I conspired against you, then kill me. In that I'll give you a hand but judge me with certain proof. Judging a good friend as evil without reason is bad work because sending away a good friend is like losing your own life and your own life is the most loved life of all.

Time, Oedipus, will show you the truth in this matter. Innocence takes time to be revealed; guilt can be announced far too quickly.

CHORUS:
He spoke well, my king. Those who hurry to judge, judge badly.

OEDIPUS:
When the schemer rushes with his scheme so must I with my decisions, otherwise his schemes win over my decisions.

CREON:
So what is it you want, Oedipus? To send me away from here?

---

check sb. out establish the truth or inform oneself about someone
conspire /kənˈspaɪr/ *v.* make secret plans jointly to commit an unlawful or harmful act
schemer /skiːmər/ *n.* a person who is involved in making secret or underhand plans

OEDIPUS:

Send you away? Absolutely not! I want you dead! Dead here, before me rather than alive elsewhere.

40 CREON:

Tell me first. What exactly are you afraid that I'll do to you?

OEDIPUS:

Are you disobeying me?

45 CREON:

I can see, your reasoning is bad, Oedipus!

OEDIPUS:

My reasoning is perfect.

CREON:

50 But your reasoning ought to be perfect in my mind also.

OEDIPUS:

Firstly, you can't be trusted.

CREON:

But what if you're wrong?

55 OEDIPUS:

You're still obliged to obey!

CREON:

Obey? An unjust command? Why should I?

OEDIPUS: *(Exasperated)*

60 O, Thebes, Thebes!

CREON:

Thebes is mine just much as she is yours!

(Enter Jocasta from door SL)

JOCASTA:

65 What is all this? What is all this silly squabbling? Are you not ashamed? The whole country is suffering the pains of a horrendous pestilence and you two—here you are, in front of the palace for all the people to see, arguing about your petty little affairs. Get back inside both of you, before you turn these little affairs into a something major. These petty squabbles of yours can bring about large and bitter consequences.

70 CREON:

Darling sister! Your husband here is threatening most seriously to either send me away from the land of my birth or to have me executed.

OEDIPUS:

Of course I do. I caught him plotting against me, Jocasta. An evil mind working evil
75 webs.

CREON:

Ah! If this is true then let me not enjoy a moment more of my life. Let me wander around the world, a cursed soul wherever I go!

JOCASTA:

80 By all the gods, Oedipus! Have some faith in him! At least have some faith in the gods

---

exasperated /ɪɡˈzæspəˌreɪtɪd/ *adj.* irritate intensely; infuriate

squabble /ˈskwɑbəl/ *n.* a noisy quarrel about sth. trivial

pestilence /ˈpɛstələns/ *n.* a fatal epidemic disease, especially bubonic plague

plot /plɑt/ *v.* secretly make plans to carry out (an illegal or harmful action)

by whom he swears; and then in me and in all these folk who stand before you!
CHORUS:
 I beg you king, listen and think! Think well!
85 OEDIPUS:
 And compromise upon what?
CHORUS:
 Trust Creon. He has never been untrustworthy before and now, you see, your faith in him is made all the more
90 secure by his oaths.
OEDIPUS:
 Do you know what you're saying?
CHORUS:
 I do, my king!
95 OEDIPUS:
 Tell me!
CHORUS:
 I'm saying you should never condemn a friend without proof.
OEDIPUS:
100 Know this well, old man: that if this is what you really want then you must also want my destruction or my exile from this land.
CHORUS:
 By Helios, the Sun, the first of all the gods! May I be cast asunder without gods or friends by my side if I desire such a thing! My poor, luckless heart, though, is hurt with
105 these new suffering of Thebes and all the more if upon them are added your own sufferings, my king.
OEDIPUS:
 Well, then, all right! Let him be exiled and not killed—even though, I know, it means my own death or my own exile in disgrace. It is your mouth that gained my sympathy, not
110 his. I shall hate him wherever he might be.
CREON:
 So much hatred in your compromise! Yet, when your anger subsides a little how you'll suffer! Souls like yours are their own worst enemy! Quite justly, too!
OEDIPUS:
115 Leave! Get out!
CREON:
 I shall. A foreigner to you, a friend to them.

(Exit Creon)

120 CHORUS:
 Queen, why don't you take your husband inside?
JOCASTA:
 First I need to know what's going on.

---

compromise /ˈkɑmprəˌmaɪz/ v. settle a dispute by mutual concession
Helios /ˈhiːliɔs/ the sun personified as a god, father of Phaethon
asunder /əˈsʌndə/ adv. apart
disgrace /dɪsˈgreɪs/ n. loss of reputation or respect as the result of a dishonorable action

125 CHORUS:
       Hollow suspicions from words, my Lady. Still, even the unjust word has a strong bite.
   JOCASTA:
       Hollow words from both?
130 CHORUS:
       Yes, madam.
   JOCASTA:
       But why?
   CHORUS:
135   Enough, my Lady, enough! Thebes is suffering enough. Let them end it where they've just stopped.
   OEDIPUS: *(To the Leader)*
       You see? An intelligent man like you, yet you see what you've done with my part of justice! You spat upon it with cold and uncaring heart!
140 CHORUS:
       But, my king, I've told you many times before: I would be mad to disobey you. You, Oedipus who, when this land was tortured by misfortune, you came and healed her well. Heal her again, my king, heal her!
   JOCASTA:
145   By the gods, Oedipus! Tell me, as well, what raised your anger so much?
   OEDIPUS:
       Your brother says I am Laius' murderer!
   JOCASTA:
       Who told him that? Or was it his own thinking?
150 OEDIPUS:
       He's sent that evil seer to me to tell me while he kept his own mouth free from such utterances.
   JOCASTA:
       Well, then! Oedipus, my king! Forget everything and listen to me. No mortal knows the
155 will of the gods. Let me show you proof of this. Once, an oracle came to Laius—I'm not saying from Apollo directly, but from his servants- that it was his Fate to die by the hand of his son—his and my son! However, word has it that Laius was killed by strangers, thieves, at a three-way cross road.
       As for the boy, three days after he was born, the king has his ankles pinned and gave
160 him to someone to take him to some forest where no human ever went. And so, neither the child was allowed by Apollo to kill his father, nor did Laius suffer murder in the hands of his own son.
       That was god's real intention, not what some seer said would happen. If the god wants something done he'll tell us himself.
165 OEDIPUS: *(highly disturbed by some new thought)*
       Ah, what a fear! What a trembling, cold panic has overtaken me, wife! Something from what you've just said ...

> seer /sɪr/ *n.* a person of supposed supernatural insight who sees visions of the future

JOCASTA:
   What fear, my king? Tell me.
170 OEDIPUS:
   I think... I think I've heard you say that Laius was killed at a tree-way crossing.
JOCASTA:
   That's what they said then and that's what they're still saying now.
OEDIPUS:
175   And where is this cross road exactly?
JOCASTA:
   The city is called Phocis. A divided road which splits all the way to the Delphi on one side and to Daulia on the other.
OEDIPUS:
180   How long ago did the murder happen?
JOCASTA:
   It was announced just a little before you arrived here and became king.
OEDIPUS:
   Oh, Zeus! Zeus! What do you have in store for me next?
185 JOCASTA:
   What is it, Oedipus? What memory disturbs your mind?
OEDIPUS:
   Ask me no more, wife, just tell me: What height what age was Laius then?
JOCASTA:
190   Tall... his hair just greying... looked quite like you do now.
OEDIPUS:
   O, what a wretched man I am! I think I've cursed hateful curses to myself without my knowing.
JOCASTA:
195   My king! What are you saying? What fear floods your face!
OEDIPUS:
   A dire fear! I fear that blind priest, that seer is truly Apollo's eye! You'll show me proof of this if you can tell me one more thing.
JOCASTA:
200   Ask, Oedipus! How frightened I am. Ask and I shall tell you.
OEDIPUS:
   When Laius went away, was he accompanied by a few or by many armed men?
JOCASTA:
   Five, including a herald. Laius was in a carriage.
205 OEDIPUS:
   Ah! So many clear signs, wife. Wife, who told you all this?
JOCASTA:
   A servant. He was the only survivor. He came
210 and told me.

Phocis /ˈfosɪs/ a city located in central Greece, upon the Gulf of Corinth
Daulia /ˈdɔːbə/ a municipality within the prefecture of Boeotia, in Greece, which is located on Mount Parnassos
dire /daɪr/ *adj.* extremely serious or urgent

OEDIPUS:
    Does he still live with us?
JOCASTA:
    No. As soon as he came and saw you upon Laius'
throne he disappeared. He begged me at the time to send him to the grazing lands, to be as far away from the city as possible. So I sent him. He was a good man and worthy of even greater reward so I granted him his wish.
OEDIPUS:
    Could we bring him here in a hurry?
JOCASTA:
    Of course, but why?
OEDIPUS:
    I'm afraid for myself, wife. I'm afraid I said too much against myself and I want to see him.
JOCASTA:
    Of course he'll come but I think I have the right to know what's going on.

> grazing /ˈɡreɪzɪŋ/ *n.* grassland suitable for pasturage

Notes

For some of the terms in the following, no explanation is provided. You are required to explain them by making use of the library, the Internet or whatever sources accessible.

1. Thebes

2. Laius

Comprehension Questions

Please answer the following questions based on what you have learnt in the text.

1. According to Frances B. Titchener, which element did Text B display?
2. What was Oedipus accused of by Creon? Why was Creon so sure about it?
3. Was Oedipus the murderer of his biological father?
4. How was this murder unfolded in the play?

Writing Practice

Wise arrangement of the plot elements forms the most outstanding feature of *Oedipus Rex*, which starts off with the investigation to find the murderer of the former king, the latter part of the story sequence, namely element 9 in Frances B. Titchener's idea. Write your own versions of *Oedipus Rex* by arranging the elements of the plot in other ways.

Further Study

This is the end of Unit 9; but you can also gain more knowledge by accessing the following resources.

Recommended Film—*Oedipus Rex* is a 1967 Italian film directed by Pier Paolo Pasolini. Pasolini adapted the screenplay from the Greek tragedy *Oedipus the King* written by Sophocles in 428 BC.

A son is born to a young couple in pre-war Italy. The father, motivated by jealousy, takes the baby into the desert to be abandoned, at which point the film's setting changes to the ancient world. The child is rescued, named Edipo by King Polybus and Queen Merope of Corinth...

Unit 10

Reflections on Wars

Unit Goals

Upon completing the texts in this unit, students should be able to:
- be aware of the social reality: the existence of terrorism, and learn how to face up to it;
- learn lessons from history;
- use adjective, adverb and diminutive suffixes correctly to form new words.

Before Reading

Hands-on Activities and Brainstorming

1. Visit the websites on Noam Chomsky to learn who he is.
2. Visit the sub-links of Talks and Debates of http: //www.chomsky.info/ and gather the information about his viewpoints concerning the September 11th attack. It would be interesting to compare his views with those of his peers or rivals. You may also rely on the library for collecting information. Develop your gathered information into a presentation.

A Glimpse at Words and Expressions

Please read the following sentences. Pay attention to the underlined part in each sentence and to how it is used in the sentence and then decide on its meaning. Write down the meaning in the brackets.

1. ...to alleviate the threat, which has been severe in the past... (   )
2. It is pointless to seek a truly precise definition of "terror." (   )
3. It is commonly claimed that critics of ongoing policies do not present solutions. (   )
4. Bringing up the record is an enlightening exercise. (   )

5. There is an accurate translation for that charge: "They present solution, but I don't like them."   (   )
6. Since the first War on Terror was waged by those now carrying out the re-declared war, or their immediate mentors, it follows...   (   )
7. Those are very sweeping statements.   (   )
8. To take one of these official definitions, terrorism is "the calculated use of violence or threat of violence to attain goals ..."   (   )

Text A

The Terrorist in the Mirror

By Noam Chomsky
(Abridged and Edited)

"Terror" is a term that rightly arouses strong emotions and deep concerns. The primary concern should, naturally, be to take measures to alleviate the threat, which has been severe in the past, and will be even more so in the future. To carry on in a serious way, we have to establish some guidelines. Here are a few simple ones: first, facts matter, even if we do not
5 like them; second, elementary moral principles matter, even if they have consequences that we would prefer not to face; and the last, relative clarity matters. It is pointless to seek a truly precise definition of "terror," or of any other concept outside of the hard sciences and mathematics, often even there. But we should seek enough clarity at least to distinguish terror from two notions that lie uneasily at its borders: aggression and legitimate resistance.
10   If we accept these guidelines, there are quite helpful ways to deal with the problems of terrorism, which are quite severe. It's commonly claimed that critics of ongoing policies do not present solutions. Check the record, and I think you will find that there is an accurate translation for that charge: "They present solutions, but I don't like them."
  Suppose, then, that we accept these simple guidelines. Let's turn to the "War on
15 Terror." Since facts matter, it matters that the War was not declared by George W. Bush on 9/11, but by the Reagan administration 20 years earlier. The campaign was directed to a particularly dangerous form of the plague: state-directed international terrorism. The main focus was Central America and the Middle East, but it reached to southern Africa
20 and Southeast Asia and beyond.
  A second fact is that the war was declared by pretty much the same people who are conducting the re-declared war on
25 terrorism. The military component of the

clarity /ˈklærɪti/ n. the quality of being expressed clearly
precise /prɪˈsaɪs/ adj. clear and accurate
  adv. precisely
border /ˈbɔːdə/ n. a part that forms the outer edge of sth.
legitimate /ləˈdʒɪtəmɪt/ adj. for which there is a fair and acceptable reason
component /kəmˈpəʊnənt/ n. one of several parts of which sth. is made

re-declared War was led by Donald Rumsfeld. During the first stage of the War on Terror, Rumsfeld was Reagan's special representative to the Middle East. There, his main task was to establish close relations with Saddam Hussein so that the US could provide him with large-scale aid, including means to develop WMD (Weapons of Mass Destruction), continuing long after the violence against the Kurds and the end of the war with Iran. The official purpose, not concealed, was Washington's responsibility to aid American exporters and "the markedly unanimous view" of Washington and its allies Britain and Saudi Arabia that "whatever the sins of the Iraqi leader, he offered the West and the region a better hope for his country's stability than did those who have suffered his repression."

Saddam is at last on trial for his crimes. The first trial, now underway, is for crimes he committed in 1982. 1982 happens to be an important year in US-Iraq relations. It was in 1982 that Reagan removed Iraq from the list of states supporting terror so that aid could flow to his friend in Baghdad. Rumsfeld then visited Baghdad to confirm the arrangements. Judging by reports and comments, it would be impolite to mention any of these facts, let alone to suggest that some others might be standing alongside Saddam before the bar of justice. Removing Saddam from the list of states supporting terrorism left a gap.

Since the first War on Terror was waged by those now carrying out the re-declared war, or their immediate mentors, it follows that anyone seriously interested in the re-declared War on Terror should ask at once how it was carried out in the 1980s. The topic, however, is under a practical ban. That becomes understandable as soon as we investigate the facts: the first War on Terror quickly became a murderous and cruel terrorist war, in every corner of the world where it reached; leaving shocked societies that may never recover. What happened is hardly obscure, but unacceptable, therefore protected from inspection. Bringing up the record is an enlightening exercise, with enormous implications for the future.

These are a few of the relevant facts, and they definitely do matter. Let's turn to the second of the guidelines: elementary moral principles. The most elementary is a deep truism: decent people apply to themselves the same standards that they apply to others, if not more severe ones. Adherence to this principle of universality would have many useful consequences. For one thing, it would save a

representative /ˌreprɪˈzentətɪv/ *n.* a person who has been chosen to speak or vote for sb. else or on behalf of a group
Saddam Hussein *n.* 萨达姆·侯赛因
conceal /kənˈsiːl/ *v.* [formal] to hide sb. or sth.
unanimous /juːˈnænəməs/ *adj.* agreed or shared by everyone in a group
ally /əˈlaɪ/ *n.* a state formally cooperating with another for a military or other purpose
Saudi Arabia 沙特阿拉伯
underway /ˌʌndəˈweɪ/ *adj.* ongoing
Baghdad /ˈbæɡdæd/ 巴格达(伊拉克首都)
wage /weɪdʒ/ *v.* to begin and continue a war, a battle, etc.
mentor /ˈmentɔːr/ *n.* an experienced person who advises and helps sb. with less experience over a period of time
ban /bæn/ *n.* an official rule which says that sth. is not allowed
obscure /əbˈskjʊr/ *adj.* difficult to understand
truism /ˈtruːɪzəm/ *n.* a statement that is clearly true and does not therefore add anything interesting or important to a discussion
adherence /ædˈhɪrəns/ *n.* the fact of behaving according to a particular rule, etc., or of following a particular set of beliefs, or a fixed way of doing

lot of trees. The principle would radically reduce published reporting and explanation on social and political affairs. It would almost eliminate the newly fashionable discipline of Just War theory. And it would wipe the record almost clean with regard to the War on Terror. The reason is the same in all cases: the principle of universality is rejected, for the most part tacitly, though sometimes clearly. Those are very sweeping statements. I purposely put them in a stark form to invite you to challenge them, and I hope you do. You will find, I think, that although the statements are somewhat overdrawn—purposely—they nevertheless are uncomfortably close to accurate, and in fact very fully documented. But try for yourselves and see.

Now, let's turn to the third background issue: defining "terror" and distinguishing it from aggression and legitimate resistance. I have been writing about terror for 25 years, ever since the Reagan administration declared its War on Terror. I've been using definitions that seem to be doubly appropriate: first, they make sense; and second, they are the official definitions of those waging the war. To take one of these official definitions, terrorism is "the calculated use of violence or threat of violence to attain goals that are political, religious, or ideological in nature...through intimidation, coercion, or instilling fear," typically targeting civilians. The British government's definition is about the same: "Terrorism is the use, or threat, of action which is violent, damaging or disrupting, and is intended to influence the government or intimidate the public and is for the purpose of advancing a political, religious, or ideological cause."

These definitions seem fairly clear and close to ordinary usage. There also seems to be general agreement that they are appropriate when discussing the terrorism of enemies.

There are ways to deal constructively with the threat of terror, though not those preferred by "bin Laden's indispensable ally," or who simply claim that no proposals are made when there are quite straightforward proposals that they do not like. The constructive ways have to begin with an honest look in the mirror, never an easy task, always a necessary one.

eliminate /ɪˈlɪməˌnet/ v. to remove or get rid of sth. sb.
tacit /ˈtæsɪt/ adj. understood or implied without being stated (adv. tacitly)
sweeping /ˈswipɪŋ/ adj. wide in range or effect
appropriate /əˈpropriˌet/ adj. suitable, acceptable or correct for the particular circumstances
ideological /ˌaɪdiəˈlɑdʒɪkəl/ adj. of or relating to a set of beliefs (n. ideology)
intimidate /ɪnˈtɪmɪˌdet/ v. to frighten or threaten sb. so that they will do what one wants (n. intimidation)
instill /ɪnˈstɪl/ v. to gradually but firmly establish (an idea or attitude) in a person's mind
disrupt /dɪsˈrʌpt/ v. to make it difficult for sth. to continue in the normal way
constructively /kənˈstrʌktɪvli/ adv. helpfully (adj. constructive)
bin Laden 本·拉登
indispensable /ˌɪndɪˈspensəbəl/ adj. essential; too important to be without

Better Know More

1. Noam Chomsky (1928–)

American linguist, writer, teacher, and political activist, Noam Chomsky is considered the founder of transformational-generative linguistic analysis, whose principal linguistic works include *Syntactic Structures* (1957), *Current Issues in Linguistic Theory* (1964), *Language and Mind* (1972), *Studies on Semantics in Generative Grammar* (1972), and *Knowledge of Language* (1986).

In addition, he has extensive political interests. He was an early and candid critic of U.S. involvement in the Vietnam War and has written widely on many political issues from a generally left-wing point of view. Chomsky's controversial bestseller *9-11* (2002) is an analysis of the World Trade Center attack that, while disapproving of the killing of the event, traces its origins to the actions and power of the United States, which he calls "a leading terrorist state."

2. George W. Bush (1946–)

George W. Bush, 43rd President of the United States (2001—2009). In one of the closest and most disputed elections in U.S. history, Bush, the Republican Party candidate, defeated Vice President Al Gore, the Democratic candidate, in a protracted contest that continued weeks after Election Day.

3. The September 11th Attack

The coordinated terrorist strike on the United States in 2001 that killed more than 3,000 people and shook the nation to its core. On the sunny morning of September 11, 2001, 19 terrorists, working in teams of 4 or 5, hijacked four commercial jetliners and turned them toward targets chosen for destruction. Two of the planes, loaded with fuel and passengers, were flown at full speed into the twin towers of the World Trade Center in the financial district of New York City. The buildings burst into flame and then collapsed, killing thousands. A third terrorist crew smashed their plane into the Pentagon, headquarters of the U.S. military in Arlington, Virginia. The hijackers of the fourth airliner apparently intended to hit another target in the Washington, D.C. area, but failed. This airplane crashed in a field in rural Pennsylvania. The terrorist attacks were the deadliest in United States history.

4. Donald Rumsfeld (1932–)

American politician and Secretary of Defense under President Gerald Ford from 1975 to 1977 and under President George W. Bush from January 20, 2001 to December 18, 2006. He was responsible for directing the actions of the Defense Department in response to the terrorist attacks on September 11, 2001. Rumsfeld held a variety of government positions in four different presidential administrations. When President Ford appointed him secretary of defense, he was the youngest person in U.S. history to serve in that position.

5. Reagan Ronald Wilson (1911–2004)

Reagan Ronald Wilson was the 40th President of the United States (1981—1989), who implemented policies that reversed trends toward greater government involvement in economic and social regulation. He also brought in a new style of presidential leadership, downgrading the role of the President as an administrator and increasing the importance of communication via national news media. He was the oldest person ever to serve as President.

6. Saddam Hussein (1937–2006)

President of Iraq from 1979 to 2003. Born to a poor farming family in Tikrit, a town north of Baghdad, Hussein was raised by his widowed mother and other relatives. He created an international crisis in 1990 when his army invaded Kuwait. The invasion was condemned by the United Nations (UN), which initiated a trade embargo and, later, a military campaign against Iraq. Saddam was overthrown in April 2003 by a United States-led invasion and was hanged on December 30, 2006 for crimes against humanity, a dramatic, violent end for a leader who ruled Iraq by fear for three decades before the U.S. invasion toppled him.

7. Kurds

Most Kurds are Sunnis Muslims, more than half of them live in southeastern Turkey. About 25 percent reside in northern Iran, and about 17 percent live in western Iraq. After the Kurds supported Iran in the 1980—1988 Iran-Iraq war, Saddam Hussein retaliated, razing villages and attacking peasants with chemical weapons. In July of 1982, several Shiite militants attempted to assassinate Saddam Hussein while he was riding through the area. Hussein responded by ordering the slaughter of some 148 residents, including dozens of children.

8. The War with Iran

Iran-Iraq War, armed conflict that began when Iraq invaded Iran in September 1980 and ended in August 1988 after both sides accepted a cease-fire sponsored by the United Nations (UN). The war was one of the longest and most destructive of the 20th century, with more than one million casualties. Despite the conflict's length and cost, neither Iran nor Iraq made significant territorial or political gains, and the fundamental issues dividing the countries remained unresolved at the end of the war.

9. **Osama bin Laden (1957–2011)**

Osama bin Laden, a wealthy Saudi exile, is believed to be responsible for the September 11 terrorist attacks on the United States, in which more than 3,000 people were killed. Fiercely opposed to U.S. influence in the Islamic world, bin Laden also allegedly financed and directed several earlier, smaller terrorist attacks on U.S. interests from his base in Afghanistan.

Check Your Understanding

Please answer the following questions based on what you have learnt in the text.

1. Do you think terrorist attacks around the world share common themes? If the answer is yes, what are they?
2. Who is the terrorist in the mirror?
3. What is state-directed international terrorism?
4. What was the purpose for the U.S. to establish close relations with Saddam Hussein and provide him with large-scale aid during the first stage of the War on Terror?
5. What is the most elementary moral principle?
6. Why would the principle of universality almost eliminate the discipline of "Just War" theory?
7. How do you define "terrorism"?
8. What is your understanding of the last sentence in the text?

A Sip of Word Formation

Adjective and Adverb Suffixes

1. As previously discussed, *-ly* is added to the end of a noun with the meaning of "having the qualities of" to form an adjective or adverb (e.g. *friendly*). *-ly* can also be added to the end of an adjective with the meaning of "in the way mentioned" to form an adverb (e.g. *happily, hardly, darkly*).
2. *-ward* is used to form an adjective or adverb with the meaning of "towards a specified direction in time or space" (e.g. *downward, leftward, eastward*).
3. The suffix *-wise* derives adverbs from nouns, with two distinguishable sub-groups:
   (1) manner/dimension adverbs, which have the meaning "in the manner of..., like..." (e.g. *lengthwise*);
   (2) and the smaller group of view-point adverbs, whose meaning can be rendered as "with respect to, in regard to, concerning..." (e.g. *food-wise, statuswise*).

4. *-fold* is added to the end of a cardinal numeral with the meaning of "multiplied; having the number of parts mentioned" to form an adjective (e.g. *fivefold, fiftyfold*).

Adjective Suffixes

-let, -ette, -ess, -ling, -y, and *-ie* are noun suffixes, representing diminution and femininity. The diminutive, the opposite of augmentative, conveys a slight degree of root meaning, smallness of the object named, intimacy and endearment.
1. *-let* is added to a noun meaning "small, not very important" (e.g. *filmlet, piglet*).
2. *-ette* is added to a noun meaning "diminutive or female" (e.g. *kitchenette, usherette*).
3. *-ess* is used to indicate "female" (e.g. *goddess, hostess*).
4. *-ling* is used to form a noun with the meaning of "small" (e.g. *birdling, duckling*).
5. *-y* or *-ie*, is added to a noun to refer to a pet name or familiar name (e.g. *piggy, doggie, daddy, sweetie*).

Build Your Vocabulary

A. For each of the following sentences, a word is provided in the brackets. Use the appropriate form of the word to fill in the blank in the sentence, so that the sentence is logical and grammatical.

1. The little boy's mother said _____ that she has never heard her son whine or complain about his illness. (emphasize)
2. He looked calm, but his shaking hands showed his _____ fear. (in)
3. The ice accumulation in Antarctica is less than it was 1,000 years ago and its _____ flow is not so voluminous as it once was. As a result there are patches of bare rock here and there along the coast and inland. (sea)
4. When something is moving _____, it is moving in a circle in the same direction as the hands on a clock. (clock)
5. All the photographs in this book are taken by Mr. Smith unless _____ stated. (other)
6. You'd better not complain any more for you're already where you want to be _____. Many people are not so blessed. (career)
7. Fiction is like a spider's web, attached ever so slightly perhaps, but still attached to life at all four corners. Often the attachment is _____ perceptible. (scarce)
8. Hyundai has reported a _____ increase in profits between October and December as government incentives helped to boost car sales. (four)

B. Read and decide which diminutive suffixes can be added to the following words to form new ones. Write down the new words and then give their Chinese meanings.

author _____   goose _____   disk _____
cigar _____   eye _____   dear _____
cat _____   pig _____   book _____
lion _____   sweet _____   leather _____

You'd Like to Be

📖 A Skilled Text Weaver

Fill in the blanks with the words you have learnt in this text, one word for each blank. You are advised to read the text carefully until you have become very familiar with it before starting to work on this task.

Five years after the attacks of September 11, 2001, the _____ against terrorism is still _____. The international community has achieved significant success in dismantling terrorist organizations and _____ their leadership. Working with _____ and partners across the world, the U.S. has also created a less permissive operating environment for terrorists and made progress in organizing regional responses to terrorists who operate in ungoverned spaces or across national _____. Despite this undeniable progress, major challenges remain. Al-Qaida and its affiliates have focused more attention and resources on their propaganda and misinformation efforts. They exploit and interpret the actions of numerous local, pseudo-independent actors, using them to mobilize supporters and sympathizers, and _____ opponents, and influence international opinion. There was increasing evidence of terrorists and _____ manipulating the grievances of alienated youth or immigrant populations and then cynically exploiting those grievances to subvert _____ authority and create unrest. Experience since 9/11 has shown that, to _____ the resurgent threat, all _____ of national power, including diplomatic, military, economic, and intelligence, must be integrated and _____ in a coordinated whole-of-government fashion.

📖 A Sharp Interpreter

Please paraphrase the following sentences. Change the sentence structure wherever necessary.

1. Facts matter, even if we do not like them.
2. The topic, however, is under a practical ban.
3. What happened is hardly obscure, but unacceptable, therefore protected from inspection.
4. Decent people apply to themselves the same standards that they apply to others, if not more severe ones.
5. It would wipe the record almost clean with regard to the War on Terror.
6. The principle of universality is rejected, for the most part tacitly, though sometimes clearly.
7. I purposely put them in a stark form to invite you to challenge them, and I hope you do.
8. Although the statements are somewhat overdrawn—purposely—they nevertheless are uncomfortably close to accurate and in fact very fully documented.

A Solid Sentence Constructor

The following is a list of words and expressions you have learnt in the text. Please make a sentence with each of them.

1. for the most part
2. to distinguish... from...
3. let alone
4. to investigate
5. to apply to
6. to instill

A Careful Writer

The following are two groups of words. You are required to study the words in each group carefully and then use them to write a paragraph of your own. Make sure that the paragraphs you have written are grammatical and coherent.

1. border   ban   commit   unanimous   legitimate

2. adherence   campaign   eliminate   stark   coercion   intimidate

A Superb Bilingualist

Please translate the following sentences into English using words or expressions provided in the brackets.

1. 他的话不是针对我说的,可我还是忍不住对他发了火。(direct to, repress)
2. 他坚持说公司的经营状况良好,但我们都觉得事实并非如此。(claim, conceal)
3. 没有几个人赞同他的方案,更不用说全体通过了。(let alone, unanimous)
4. 局势尚不明朗,官方暂未取消这一计划。(obscure, eliminate)

5. 政府取消农业税，目的就是要减轻农民负担。(alleviate, ban)
6. 新技术应用到了现代生活的方方面面。(apply to)
7. 网瘾像瘟疫一样在青少年中蔓延，甚至有报道说有些年轻人在网上实施犯罪。(cyber addiction, plague, commit)

Text B

I Express My Shame

By Gerhard Schröder
(Abridged and Edited)

(January 25, 2005)
Survivors of Auschwitz-Birkenau,
Ladies and gentlemen,

I would like to thank the International Auschwitz
5 Committee for the invitation to speak to you here today.

In my estimation an invitation of this kind is still not something that can be taken for granted. It would be fitting for us Germans to remain silent in the face of what was the greatest crime in the history of mankind.
10 Words by government leaders are inadequate when confronted with the absolute immorality and senselessness of the murder of millions.

We look for rational understanding of something that is beyond human comprehension. We seek definitive
15 answers, but in vain.

What is left is the testimony of those few who survived and their descendants.

What is left are the remains of the sites of these murders and the historical
20 record.

What is left also is the certainty that these extermination camps were a manifestation of absolute evil.

Evil is not a political or scientific
25 category. But, after Auschwitz, who could doubt that it exists, and that it manifested itself in the hate-driven murderer carried out by the Nazi regime? However, noting this fact does not permit us to avoid our
30 responsibility by blaming everything on a

Auschwitz /ˈaʊʃwɪts/ 奥斯维辛(集中营)
Birkenau /ˈbəkənaʊ/ 比克瑙，奥斯维辛的二号营地
inadequate /ɪnˈædɪkwɪt/ *adj.* lacking the quality or quantity required; insufficient for a purpose
confront /kənˈfrʌnt/ *v.* to make sb. face or deal with an unpleasant or a difficult person or situation
rational /ˈræʃənəl/ *adj.* (of behavior, ideas, etc.) based on reason rather than emotions
testimony /ˈtɛstəˌmoʊni/ *n.* a formal written or spoken statement saying what one knows to be true, usually in a court of law
descendant /dɪˈsɛndənt/ *n.* a person descended from a particular ancestor or race
exterminate /ɪkˈstɜːməˌneɪt/ *v.* to kill all the members of a group of people or animals (n. extermination)
manifestation /ˌmænəfɛˈsteɪʃən/ *n.* an indication of the existence, reality or presence of sth.
Nazi /ˈnɑːtsi/ 纳粹

demonic Hitler. The evil manifested in the Nazi ideology was not without its precursors. There was a tradition behind the rise of this brutal ideology and the accompanying loss of moral inhibition.
35 Above all, it needs to be said that the Nazi ideology was something that people supported at the time and that they took part in putting into effect.

Now, sixty years after the liberation of Auschwitz by the Red Army, I stand before you as
40 the representative of a democratic Germany. I express my shame for the deaths of those who were murdered and for the fact that you, the survivors, were forced to go through the hell of a concentration camp.

45 We bear this burden with sadness, but also with a serious sense of responsibility. Millions of men, women, and children were gassed, starved, or shot by German troops and their helpers.

Jews, gypsies, homosexuals, political prisoners, and resistance fighters from across Europe were exterminated with cold industrial perfection or were enslaved and worked to death.

50 Never before had there been a worse breakdown of thousands of years of European culture and civilization. After the war it took some time before the full extent of this breakdown was realized. We are aware of it, but I doubt that we will ever be able to understand it. The past cannot be "overcome." It is the past. But its traces and, above all, the lessons to be learned from it extend to the present.

55 There will never be anything that can make up for the horror, the suffering, and the agony that took place in the concentration camps. It is only possible to provide the families of those who died and the survivors a certain amount of compensation.

Germany has faced this responsibility for a long period of time now with its government policies and court decisions, supported by a sense of justice on the part of the
60 people.

The young men and women in the photo we see here were freed in the summer of 1945. Most survivors went in different directions after their liberation: to Israel, to North and South
65 America, to neighboring European countries, or back to their countries of origin.

However, some of them stayed in or returned to Germany, the country where the so-called "Final Solution" originated.

70 It was an extraordinarily difficult decision for them, and often enough it was not a voluntary decision, but rather the result of total desperation. However, hope did return to their disrupted lives, and many did remain in

---

demonic /dɪˈmɑnɪk/ *adj.* relating to or characteristic of demons or evil spirits

precursor /prɪˈkɔːsəʳ/ *n.* [formal] a person or a thing that comes before sb./ sth. similar and that leads to or influences its development

inhibition /ˌɪnhəˈbɪʃən/ *n.* a shy or nervous feeling that stops one from expressing his/her real thoughts or feelings

democratic /ˌdɛməˈkrætɪk/ *adj.* (of a country, state, system, etc.) controlled by representatives who are elected by the people of a country; connected with this system

enslave /ɛnˈsleɪv/ *v.* [formal] to make sb. a slave

agony /ˈægəni/ *n.* extreme physical or mental pain

originate /əˈrɪdʒəˌneɪt/ *v.* [formal] to have as a cause or beginning

desperation /ˌdɛspəˈreɪʃən/ *n.* the state of being desperate, hopeless

Germany, and we are grateful for that.

Today the Jewish community in Germany is the third-largest in Europe. It is full of energy and growing rapidly. The Jewish community is and will remain an irreplaceable part of our society and culture. Its brilliant as well as painful history will continue to be both an obligation and a promise for the future.

We will use the powers of government to protect it against the anti-Semitism of those who refuse to learn the lessons of the past. There is no denying that anti-Semitism continues to exist. It is the task of society as a whole to fight it. It must never again become possible for anti-Semites to attack and cause injury to Jewish citizens in our country or any other country and in doing so bring disgrace upon our nation.

Right-wing extremists, with their spray-painted slogans, have the special attention of our law enforcement and justice authorities. But the process of dealing politically with neo-Nazis and former Nazis is something we all need to do together.

It is the duty of all democrats to provide a strong response to neo-Nazi incitement and attempts on their part to play down the importance of the crimes perpetrated by the Nazi regime. For the enemies of democracy and tolerance there can be no tolerance.

The survivors of Auschwitz have called upon us to be on your guard, not to look away, and not to pretend we don't hear things. They have called upon us to acknowledge human rights violations and to do something about them. They are being heard, particularly by young people, for instance by those who are looking at the Auschwitz memorial today with their own eyes. They are speaking with former prisoners. They are helping to maintain and preserve the memorial. They will also help to inform future generations of the crimes committed by the Nazi regime.

The vast majority of the Germans living today bear no guilt for the Holocaust. But they do bear a special responsibility. Remembrance of the war and the murderer perpetrated by the Nazi regime has become part of our living constitution. For some this is a difficult burden to bear.

Nonetheless this remembrance is part of our national identity. Remembrance of the Nazi era and its crimes is a moral obligation. We owe it to the victims, we owe it to the survivors and their families, and we owe it to ourselves.

It is true, the temptation to forget is very great. But we will not surrender to this temptation.

The Holocaust memorial in the center of Berlin cannot restore the lives or the dignity of the victims. It can perhaps serve survivors and their descendants as a symbol of their suffering. It serves us all as a reminder of the past.

We know one thing for sure. There would be no freedom, no human dignity, and no justice if we were to forget what happened when freedom, justice, and human dignity were desecrated by government power. Excellent efforts are being undertaken in many German schools, in companies, in labor unions, and in the

---

extremist /ɪkˈstrɪmɪst/ *n.* one who holds extreme views or advocates extreme measures

enforcement /ɪnˈfɔːsmənt/ *n.* The act of enforcing, implementation of rule(s)

neo-Nazi /ˈniəʊˈnɑːtsi/ 新纳粹分子

incitement /ɪnˈsaɪtmənt/ *n.* the act of encouraging sb. to do sth. violent, illegal or unpleasant

Holocaust /ˈhɒləˈkɔːst/ *n.* mass killing of European Jews and others by the Nazis during World War II

era /ˈɪərə/ *n.* a period of time, usually in history, that is different from other periods because of particular characteristics of events

dignity /ˈdɪɡnɪti/ *n.* the act of being given honor and respect by people

desecrate /ˈdesɪˌkreɪt/ *v.* to damage a holy thing or place or treat it without respect

churches. Germany is facing up to its past.

From the Shoa and Nazi terror a certainty has arisen for us all that can best be expressed by the words "never again." We want to preserve this certainty. All Germans, but also all Europeans, and the entire international community need to continue to learn to live together with respect, humanity, and in peace.

> Shoa /ʃoː/ *n.* the Holocaust, named Ha-Shoah in Hebrew
>
> convention /kənˈvɛnʃən/ *n.* an agreement between states, sides, or military forces, especially an international agreement dealing with a specific subject, such as the treatment of prisoners of war
>
> genocide /ˈdʒɛnəˌsaɪd/ *n.* the systematic and planned killing of an entire national, racial, political, or ethnic group

The Convention on the Prevention and Punishment of the Crime of Genocide was a direct effect of the Holocaust on international law. It requires people of different cultural, religious, and racial origins to respect and protect life and human dignity throughout the world. You in the International Auschwitz Committee support this with the good work you are doing in the interest of all people.

Together with you I bow my head before the victims of the death camps. Even if one day the names of the victims should fade in the memory of mankind, their fate will not be forgotten. They will remain in the heart of history.

Notes

For some of the terms in the following, no explanation is provided. You are required to explain them by making use of the library, the Internet or whatever sources accessible.

1. Gerhard Schröder

_____
_____
_____
_____
_____
_____
_____
_____
_____
_____

2. Auschwitz

Auschwitz was established by Germans in 1940, in the suburbs of Oswiecim, due to the fact that mass arrests of Poles were increasing beyond the capacity of existing "local" prisons. Initially, Auschwitz was to be one more concentration camp of the type that the Nazis had been setting up since the early 1930s. It functioned as a place where the enemies of the Nazis were enslaved, starved, tortured and killed throughout its existence and it also became the largest of the death camps. Auschwitz has become a symbol of terror, genocide, and the Holocaust.

3. International Auschwitz Committee

4. Red Army

The Red Army refers to the Soviet Union's army created by the Communist government after the Bolshevik Revolution of 1917. The "Red Army" name represents, symbolically, the bloodshed by the working class in its struggle against capitalism, and the belief that all people are equal. The Red Army was renamed the Soviet Army in 1946.

5. Final Solution

6. Anti-Semitism

7. Right-wing extremists

Right-wing extremists are governed by the idea that ethnic affiliation to a nation or race is of the utmost importance for an individual. All other interests and values, including civil and human rights, are subordinate to it.

8. Holocaust

9. Genocide

Comprehension Questions

Please answer the following questions based on what you have learnt in the text.

1. Who delivered this speech?
2. Does he believe that words are enough when confronted with the murder of millions?
3. What should we do about the manifestation of absolute evil mentioned by Chancellor Schroder?
4. What does Chancellor Schroder say to the dead and the survivors?
5. What is the current state of the Jewish Community in Germany?
6. At the end of his speech, what does Schroder call on the whole society to do?

Writing Practice

  Most people believe war is inhuman and harmful while some other people hold the idea that war is not always wrong. There are situations when war can be justified, or even a smart thing to do.
  Now you are expected to write an essay to present your own view on wars. Specific reasons and examples are needed to support your view.

Further Study

  This is the end of Unit 10; but you can also gain more knowledge by accessing the following resources.

1. If possible, please read the book *9-11* by Noam Chomsky. In this book, Chomsky dissects the root causes of the September 11th disaster, the historic precedents for it, and the likely outcomes as the United States responds with its "new war on terrorism." You can also

find more information about this book by reading an interview scripts available at http://www.counterpunch.org/chomskyintv.html.
2. Film recommended: *World Trade Center*—A true story of two Port Authority police officers, Will Jimeno and John McLoughlin, who rushed into the World Trade Center on September 11th of 2001 to rescue people, but became trapped themselves when the tower collapsed. The two heroes will take us back to the scene of the catastrophic event.
3. Film recommended: *Fahrenheit 911*—It is a film that received the Palme d'Or at Cannes in 2004. In this film, Director Michael Moore turns his eyes to George W. Bush and his War on Terrorism agenda. Through facts, footage and interviews, Moore illustrates his contention of how Bush and his buddies have gotten America into worse trouble than ever before and why Americans should not stand for it.

Unit 11

Honesty

Unit Goals

Upon completing the texts in this unit, students should be able to:
- have a greater understanding of the importance of honesty as a human virtue;
- know what it means by positive dishonesty and when positive dishonesty is better than outright honesty;
- use noun suffixes correctly to form new words.

Before Reading

Hands-on Activities and Brainstorming

1. Honesty is one of the great virtues that people everywhere value very much. However, hardly can any of us claim that in our lives, we have never behaved dishonestly. What do you think is the reason for a person's dishonesty? Do you think that in whatever circumstances, people should stay honest? Whether your answer is "yes" or "no", give specific examples to support your view.
2. When people tell lies, cheat, steal or are dishonest in some other ways, they always try to justify themselves by inventing some excuses or rationalizations. How valid do you think the excuses and rationalizations are? Can you point out what is wrong with them?
3. Have a group discussion on the following:
   - Do you consider yourself an honest person? Why?
   - How do you define dishonesty?
   - What do you think of dishonest people?
   - In what way should we treat them?
4. Visit the website http://www.school-for-champions.com/character/honesty.htm and find out what honesty means.

A Glimpse at Words and Expressions

Please read the following sentences. Pay attention to the underlined part in each sentence and to how it is used in the sentence and then decide on its meaning. Write down the meaning in the brackets.

1. The legend <u>in the making</u> involve mad, all-night scrambles to launch a web site. (   )
2. While CenterBeam hasn't yet <u>gone public</u>, it has attracted ever-higher valuations from VCs and strategic investors. (   )
3. Their favorite stories <u>touch on</u> a theme that hardly ever takes center stage in Silicon Valley. (   )
4. Early on, for example, CenterBeam was on <u>a hiring spree</u>, trying to recruit enough people to carry out its rapid expansion plans. (   )
5. The point, says Mann, isn't that startups need to <u>let go of</u> their ambitious dreams. (   )
6. But they <u>came across</u> as very reliable, trustworthy people. (   )
7. That may make it a little harder to <u>wrap up</u> recruiting efforts in a hurry. (   )
8. But Mann's honesty usually <u>pays off</u> when tough times arise. (   )
9. ... —whether the deal <u>in question</u> involves a $40,000 supply contract or a $20 million marketing alliance. (   )
10. In the long run, argues Scott Sandell, 35, a partner at New Enterprise Associates, a Menlo Park-based venture-capital firm, a more even-handed approach may be the <u>best bet</u>, even in the fast-paced world of Internet negotiations. (   )

Text A

Honesty Is the Best Policy

By George Anders
(Abridged and edited)

It's always fascinating to step inside a Silicon Valley startup and ask the people there to share stories about what makes their company special. The anecdotes that rank-and-file employees tell a visitor tend to reflect the way that their company views its character and its culture.

> startup /ˈstɑːtˌʌp/ *n.* a company with a limited operating history
> rank-and-file *n.* the ordinary members of an organization

At some companies, the legends in the making involve mad, all-night scrambles to launch a web site or to release a new piece of software. At other companies, the best lore involves relentless efforts to line up customers. And if a company is attracting favor from venture capitalists or from public shareholders, it's a safe bet that at least one story will
10 involve the shock and delight of employees upon realizing how valuable the business has become.

Employees at CenterBeam Inc., based in Santa Clara, California, could tell variants of all of these stories. Since April 1999, CenterBeam's main service—taking charge of small companies' computer departments by installing networks of wireless, Internet-oriented
15 machines—has attracted hundreds of customers. While CenterBeam hasn't yet gone public, it has attracted ever-higher valuations from VCs and strategic investors. But those aren't the stories that CenterBeam's employees want to tell. Their favorite stories touch on a theme that hardly ever takes center stage in Silicon Valley: integrity—that is, the make-or-break importance of simply keeping your word.

20 Early on, for example, CenterBeam was on a hiring spree, trying to recruit enough people to carry out its rapid expansion plans. The company offered a job to one candidate, but before that person could accept, a résumé from an absolutely dazzling contender arrived. Could the first offer be rescinded, managers wanted to know, so that the company could hire this superstar instead? The answer from
25 Sheldon Laube, 49, CenterBeam's chairman and CEO: No way. "We made a promise to the first candidate," Laube recalls. "If we're going to be the kind of company that people trust, we've got to keep our promises."

30 Around that same time, CenterBeam executives ordered $500,000 worth of tape drives from a distributor. Those drives (vital equipment that the company uses to back up customer-data files) soon arrived at CenterBeam's
35 headquarters. But before engineers could unpack the merchandise, they learned that a rival distributor was offering comparable machines at a price that would save CenterBeam $93,000 a year. A few engineers wanted to refuse
40 delivery of the more-expensive machines. But CenterBeam executives treated the shipment as binding. Instead, they asked the distributor to take back the expensive system and then bought the cheaper system from the same
45 distributor—at a cost that was roughly $50,000 more than the rival distributor was charging.

What's the road to success for a startup? For many companies, it's whatever road leads them to the most business in the least amount
50 of time. The Internet economy worships at the

---

scramble /ˈskræmbəl/ n. a situation in which people push, fight or compete with each other in order to get or do sth.

launch /lɔntʃ/ v. to put sth./sb. into action; to set going

lore /lɔr/ n. knowledge and information related to a particular subject, especially when this is not written down; the stories and traditions of a particular group of people

line up to get sth. or sb. for a specific purpose

venture /ˈventʃə/ n. a business project or activity, especially one that involves taking risks

a safe bet n. (or a good bet) something that is likely to happen, to succeed to to be suitable

install /ɪnˈstɔl/ v. to fix equipment, furniture, etc. in position for use, especially by making the necessary connections with the supply of electricity, water, etc.

orient /ˈɔriənt/ v. [=orientate] to direct or aim sth. (at sb.)

make-or-break adj. to be the thing that makes sb./sth. either a success or a failure

spree /spri/ n. a short period of time that one spends doing one particular activity that he enjoys, but often too much of it

recruit /rɪˈkrut/ v. to find new people to work in a company, join an organization, do a job, etc.

contender /kənˈtendə/ n. a person who takes part in a competition or tries to win sth.

rescind /rɪˈsɪnd/ v. to officially state that a law, contract, decision, etc. is no longer valid

binding /ˈbaɪndɪŋ/ adj. that must be obeyed because it is accepted in law

altar of fast action, fast growth, and fast results. Plenty of companies (and the people who lead them) are prepared to cut a few ethical corners in order to move
55 faster: not gross violations, such as accounting manipulations or outright fraud, but day-to-day dilemmas—leadership moments in which you do either the right thing or the expedient thing. Are you
60 aboveboard with investors when you know that the next quarter may be disappointing? Will you say anything to recruit a great job candidate, or are you honest about the risks involved in an
65 assignment?

gross /gros/ adj. clearly wrong and unacceptable
accounting /əˈkaʊntɪŋ/ n. [=accountancy] the profession or work of keeping or checking financial accounts
manipulation /məˌnɪpjʊˈleɪʃən/ n. the act of making someone think and behave exactly as one wants him to, by skillfully deceiving or influencing him
outright /ˈaʊtraɪt/ adj. complete and total; open and direct
fraud /frɔd/ n. the crime of deceiving sb. in order to get money or goods illegally
dilemma /dɪˈlɛmə/ n. a situation in which one has to make a very difficult choice between things of equal importance
expedient /ɪkˈspidiənt/ adj. useful or necessary for a particular purpose, but not always fair or right
aboveboard /əˈbʌvˌbɔrd/ adj. (especially of a business transaction) honest and open
Sunday-school lesson a class held on Sundays in which especially Christian children are given religious teaching
triumph /ˈtraɪəmf/ v. to be successful or victorious
vanquish /ˈvæŋkwɪʃ/ v. to defeat sb. completely in a competition, war, etc.
entrepreneur /ˌɑntrəprəˈnɜ/ n. a person who makes money by starting or running businesses, especially when this involves taking financial risks
bluster /ˈblʌstə/ n. noisy but empty threats; vain and empty boasting
exaggeration /ɪɡˌzædʒəˈreɪʃən/ n. a statement or description that makes sth. seem larger, better, worse or more important than it really is
phase /feɪz/ n. any stage in a series of events or in a process of development
devious /ˈdiviəs/ adj. behaving in a dishonest or indirect way in order to get sth.
hubris /ˈhjubrɪs/ n. the fact of sb. being too proud
extravagant /ɪkˈstrævəɡənt/ adj. (of ideas, speech or behavior) very extreme or impressive but not reasonable or practical
stumble /ˈstʌmbəl/ v. to step awkwardly while walking or running and fall or begin to fall
credibility /ˌkrɛdəˈbɪlɪti/ n. the quality sb. has that makes people believe or trust him
ooze /uz/ v. to emit a particular essence or quality

If this were a Sunday-school lesson, the answers would be obvious. Virtue would triumph, and cheaters would be vanquished by truth tellers. But the startup business is not so simple. There's a widespread feeling among entrepreneurs and venture capitalists that if a new company doesn't display a bit of bluster and outright exaggeration in its launch phase, it won't
70 be taken seriously—and it won't get a chance to change the world. What fun is starting a company if you can't be a little devious?

Yet if hubris was a winning strategy in the past, its perils have recently become all too clear. Many of the Net companies that went public on the strength of extravagant promises have stumbled badly. In some cases, signs of a credibility gap are so severe that they ooze from companies' financial statements — and translate into plummeting stock prices.

"It's amazing how many employees have come up to me and said, 'It's great to work at a company that has integrity,'" says Laube. "Many employees tell me that at their old companies, 'people promised things that they just didn't deliver.'" Yolanda Gonzalez, 48, VP of human resources at CenterBeam, estimates that two-thirds of the company's new hires tell her that they were uncomfortable with the low ethical standards that prevailed at their former employers.

Some of the clearest thinking about integrity in the Internet economy comes from Darlene Mann, 39, a general partner at Onset Ventures, in Menlo Park, California. Her firm has bankrolled dozens of startups, and she has worked inside numerous high-tech companies. If executives want "integrity" to be more than just a buzzword in a mission statement, she says, they need to think hard about three issues: the growth goals that they promise to customers and investors, the career opportunities that they promise to employees, and the tone that they strike in day-to-day negotiations with business partners. In some cases, Mann acknowledges, keeping one's word carries extra short-term costs. But wiggling away from the truth can be disastrously expensive in the long run.

The point, says Mann, isn't that startups need to let go of their ambitious dreams. But they do need to ensure that promises made to the outside world are believable to their own people. Otherwise, they will be built on a foundation of cynicism and distrust.

What's more, in the current culture of hype, companies that undersell their strengths can win remarkable loyalty. Last year, when Carl Russo was CEO of Cerent Corp., an optical-networking company, he signed up Calico Commerce to build his company's web site. "Unlike everyone else, they were very subdued in what they promised us," recalls Russo, 44, now a VP and a general manager at Cisco Systems, which recently acquired Cerent. "But they came across as very reliable, trustworthy people." Russo had a good experience with Calico, and now he is one of that company's most valuable customer references.

As the Internet sector undergoes a shakeout of sorts, people are paying a lot of attention to the explicit or implicit promises that companies make to employees and managers. No one ever said that working for an Internet startup was a lifetime job. But some top executives and board members have done a good job of communicating, each step of the way, what could go right and what could go wrong—a practice that makes it easy to regroup when times change.

---

plummet /ˈplʌmɪt/ *v.* to decline suddenly and steeply
prevail /prɪˈveɪl/ *v.* to get control or influence
bankroll /ˈbæŋkˌroʊl/ *v.* to support sb./sth. financially
buzzword /ˈbʌzˌwɜːd/ *n.* a word or phrase connected with a particular subject, that has become fashionable and popular and is used a lot in newspapers, etc.
strike /straɪk/ *v.* to produce a musical note, sound, etc.
wiggle /ˈwɪɡəl/ *v.* to move from side to side or up and down in short quick movement
cynicism /ˈsɪnɪˌsɪzəm/ *n.* a scornful, bitterly mocking attitude or quality
hype /haɪp/ *n.* [informal, disapproving] advertisements and discussions on television, radio, etc. telling the public about a product and about how good or important it is
undersell /ˌʌndəˈsɛl/ *v.* to sell goods or services at a lower price than one's competitors
optical /ˈɑptɪkəl/ *adj.* connected with the sense of sight or the relationship between light and sight
subdue /səbˈdu/ *v.* to calm or control one's feelings
reference /ˈrɛfərəns/ *n.* a person willing to make a statement about another person's character or abilities
sector /ˈsɛktə/ *n.* a part or division, as of a national economy
shakeout /ˈʃɛkˌaʊt/ *n.* a situation in which people lose their jobs and less successful companies are forced to close because of competition and difficult economic conditions
explicit /ɪkˈsplɪsɪt/ *adj.* clearly and fully expressed

By contrast, other business leaders have opportunistically hired what they thought was a winning growth team, making grand promises without building the kind of stability that gets a company through hard times.

At Onset Ventures, Mann tells some executive recruits to work in their new job for a few months, and to make sure that it will work out, before relocating their families. She also preps candidates on the risks that come with taking a given job. That may make it a little harder to wrap up recruiting efforts in a hurry, but Mann's honesty usually pays off when tough times arise. A person who knows the risks of a job up front, says Mann, "is much more likely to be a good hire in a difficult situation."

Less dramatic, but every bit as challenging, is the issue of how high-tech startups treat their business partners. Perhaps the most common failing of a young, ambitious Internet executive is the tendency to squeeze every possible advantage out of negotiations with an outsider—whether the deal in question involves a $40,000 supply contract or a $20 million marketing alliance. That's just not wise, says Ram Shriram, 43, a former Amazon.com vice president who is now an angel investor. It leaves an undercurrent of bitterness—and a very small list of partners that will want to continue doing business with such a razor-sharp deal maker.

opportunistic /ˌɒpətjuˈnɪstɪk/ adj. taking immediate advantage, often unethically, of any circumstance of possible benefit [adv. opportunistically]
recruit /rɪˈkruːt/ n. someone who has recently joined an organization, group of people, etc.
prep /prɛp/ v. to prepare sb./sth.
alliance /əˈlaɪəns/ n. an agreement between countries, political parties, etc. to work together in order to achieve sth. that they all want
squeeze /skwiːz/ v. to obtain something, especially money or information, from someone using persuasion or force
undercurrent /ˈʌndəˌkʌrənt/ n. underlying feeling or influence or trend, especially one opposite to the apparent one
razor-sharp /ˈreɪzəʃɑːp/ adj. extremely sharp; showing that sb. is extremely intelligent
even-handed /ˌiːvənˈhændɪd/ adj. fair and impartial
swoop /swuːp/ v. (of a bird or plane) to fly quickly and suddenly downwards, especially to attack sb./sth.
stake /steɪk/ n. money, etc. invested by sb. in an enterprise so that he has an interest or share in it
unilateral /ˌjuːnɪˈlætərəl/ adj. done by or affecting one person, group, country, etc. and not another; one-sided [adv. unilaterally]
backer /ˈbækə/ n. a person who gives (especially financial) support to another person, undertaking, etc.

In the long run, argues Scott Sandell, 35, a partner at New Enterprise Associates, a Menlo Park-based venture-capital firm, a more even-handed approach may be the best bet—even in the fast-paced world of Internet negotiations. To illustrate his point, Sandell tells a story of the financing negotiations that got CenterBeam in business. New Enterprise had planned on being one of two firms that would bankroll the business. But at the last moment, a third firm, Accel Partners, swooped in.

That was good news for CenterBeam and for its CEO, Sheldon Laube—but potentially bad news for the earlier investors, who might have ended up getting a smaller stake in the company. Rather than unilaterally reworking CenterBeam's financing terms, Laube asked his early backers if they were willing to add Accel to the financing group. And he didn't revise the deal until they said yes.

According to Sandell, it's all too easy to think that because everything moves so fast in the Internet economy, there just isn't enough time to fuss over the fine points of integrity. In fact, he says, the urgency of Internet-based business means that "there is no time for lack of integrity. Without it, everything becomes more complicated, because you can't depend on people to do what they say they will do."

> fuss /fʌs/ v. to do things, or pay too much attention to things, that are not important or necessary
> hearten /'hɑrtn/ v. to make (sb.) feel cheerful and encouraged
> maverick /'mævərɪk/ n. a person who does not behave or think like everyone else, but has independent, unusual opinions

Sure, we live and work in a world where "the Internet changes everything." But it's heartening to see that some of the Web's smartest mavericks believe that honesty is still the best policy.

Better Know More

1. Silicon Valley

Located in southern part of the San Francisco Bay Area in Northern California, U.S., Silicon Valley is home to many of the world's largest technology corporations.

2. Venture capitalist

Venture capitalist, or VC, is an investor who provides capital, at a later time than angel investors (see Better Know More 13), to either start-up ventures or small companies who wish to expand but do not have access to public funding.

Venture capital, or risk capital, refers to money made available for investment in innovative enterprises or research, especially in high technology, in which both the risk of loss and the potential for profit may be considerable.

3. CenterBeam Inc.

An IT outsourcing company based in California, U.S., engaged exclusively in serving organizations of small and medium sizes. Its official website is http://www.centerbeam.com/.

4. Santa Clara

A city located in the center of Silicon Valley, in Santa Clara County, California, U.S. Founded in 1777 and incorporated in 1852, Santa Clara is home to the headquarters of many high-tech companies, including Intel, Applied Materials, Sun Microsystems, NVIDIA, Agilent Technologies, etc.

5. Onset Venture

A company focusing on early-stage investments in information, communication, and medical technology. Its official website is http://www.onset.com/.

6. Menlo Park

A city in San Mateo County, California, U.S.

7. Cerent Corp.

Used to be an optical equipment company based in Petaluma, California, U.S., Cerent Corp. was originally founded in 1937 and acquired by Cisco Systems in 1999.

8. Calico Commerce

Bankrupted in 2001, Calico Commerce used to be a provider of software and services that enabled customers to engage in e-business. Headquartered in San Jose, California, U.S., and with branches throughout America and Europe, the company sold complex products and services over the Internet.

9. Cisco Systems

The leading supplier of routers (路由器), hubs (集线器), Ethernet (以太网), LAN/ATM (局域网/异步传输模式) switches, dial-up access servers, software, and other networking equipment and network management for the Internet. Its official website is http://www.cisco.com/.

10. Angel investor

A firm or an individual who invests in startup companies which are unable to raise venture capital. Angels rarely get involved in the actual management of these companies, but they provide enough capital to bring a product to production stage.

11. New Enterprise Associates

One of the world's leading venture capital firms, engaged mainly in IT and healthcare investments. Its official website is http://www.nea.com/.

12. Accel Partners

A venture capital firm focusing on bankrolling entrepreneurs who possess unique insight to develop new categories and to build world-class technology companies. Its official website is http://www.accel.com/.

Check Your Understanding

Please answer the following questions based on what you have learnt in the text.

1. Among the rank-and-file employees of Silicon Valley startups, what are the most popular stories about what makes their company special?
2. What are CenterBeam's employees' favorite stories?

3. According to the author, what ethical dilemma does the Internet economy face?
4. How would a new company benefit from being honest in the long run?
5. What can we learn from the story of Calico Commerce executives treating their customers and investors?
6. Why do the executives of Onset Ventures keep their employees informed of the risks involved in a job?
7. How did the executives of CenterBeam Inc. help their business partners secure their interest?
8. In your opinion, what is the best policy to gain success for a new company? Why?

A Sip of Word Formation

Noun Suffixes

Nominal suffixes are often employed to derive abstract nouns from verbs, adjectives, and nouns. *-ful*, *-ion*, *-ment*, *-al*, *-age*, *-ness*, *-ith*, and *-ant* are nominal suffixes.

1. The nominal suffix *-ful* is employed to derive measure partitive nouns (度量单位名词) from nominal base words that can be construed as containers (e.g. *cupful*).
2. Derivatives ending in *-ion* denote events or results of processes. When attached to a verb ending in *-ify*, the verbal suffix and *-ion* are combined to form *-ification* (e.g. *personification*). When attached to a verb ending in *-ate*, we find the allomorph *-ation* (e.g. *starvation*). There is also a comparatively large number of forms, found primarily in scientific discourse with words denoting chemical or other substances as bases, where *-ation* is directly attached to nouns without any intervening verb ending in *-ate* (e.g. *sediment→sedimentation*).
3. The suffix *-ment* derives action nouns denoting processes or results, mainly from verbs, with a strong preference for monosyllables or disyllabic base words with stress on the last syllable (e.g. *assessment, endorsement*).
4. The suffix *-al* is used to mean a process or state (e.g. *survival, approval*).
5. The suffix *-age* derives nouns that express an activity or its result (e.g. *coverage*), and nouns denoting a collective entity or quantity (e.g. *acreage*). The meaning can be extended to include locations (e.g. *orphanage*).
6. The suffix *-ness* can attach to practically any adjective, as well as some nouns (e.g. *thingness*), pronouns (e.g. *us-ness*) and phrases (e.g. *over-the-top-ness, all-or-nothing-ness*).
7. Nouns ending in *-ity* denote qualities, states or properties usually derived from Latinate adjectives (e.g. *curiosity, productivity*).
8. The suffix *-ant* forms count nouns referring to persons (often in technical or legal discourse, e.g. *accountant*) or to substances involved in biological, chemical, or physical processes (e.g. *attractant, dispersant*).

Build Your Vocabulary

For each of the following sentences, a word is provided in the brackets. Use the appropriate form of the word to fill in the blank in the sentence, so that the sentence is logical and grammatical.

1. My best friend, a typical shopaholic, ended up penniless last month after buying a _____ of useless antique furniture online during the post-Christmas sales. (house)
2. The _____ who has displayed satisfactory skills during the interview should be given the job. (apply)
3. With a history of more than 2,000 years, Traditional Chinese Medicine (TCM) adopts a system entirely different from that of the Western Medicine for the diagnosis and _____ of diseases. (treat)
4. When travelling in the North, southerners find it difficult to adapt to the _____ of the air. (dry)
5. It is customary for the Brits, after receiving invitations to formal occasions with the letters RSVP printed on them, to write back indicating grateful acceptance or polite _____ . (refuse)
6. The U.S. government used armed forces to break the _____ organized by the Labor Union. (demonstrate)
7. Poor circulation and _____ of blood in the leg arteries (动脉) produces an aching, tiring, and sometimes burning pain in the legs. (block)
8. Kindergartens are required to send children to the hospital immediately if _____ of their body temperature, as well as other signs of infectious diseases, is detected. (normal)

You'd Like to Be

A Skilled Text Weaver

Fill in the blanks with the words you have learnt in this text, one word for each blank. You are advised to read the text carefully until you have become very familiar with it before starting to work on this task.

"Congratulations on getting the annual Best Director Award, Pete! This movie is absolutely _____. It is no _____ to say that even your _____, that is, the other candidates for the Award, love your work." I said. "Well, lately, many readers have been writing to us, eager to know what inspired you to _____ _____ the theme of honesty. Would you like to share the story with us?"

"Thank you very much. I'd love to." My interviewee replied with a smile. "In fact, it all started when I was looking for a financial _____ when I tried to _____ my first piece of work after I graduated ten years ago. I went to Mr. Stephen Watson, the most successful _____ in this city, because I was told that Mr. Watson, although mainly doing business in the Internet _____, often _____ young movie directors."

"How did you _____ _____ in the meeting with him? Did he like your movie?" I asked curiously.

"He was obviously interested in my proposal and seemed satisfied with my qualifications," answered Pete, "but after I showed my movie to him, he strongly insisted that I should _____ the ending."

"He did?"

"Yes. And when I asked him why, he told me he didn't like the last scene because it was too _____, by which he meant that the information was not clear enough."

"Did you take his advice?"

"Well, it was indeed a _____: if I said no, I might _____ _____ offending him and getting nothing that day, which meant that I was _____ _____ _____ a good opportunity; but if I agreed, which was clearly an _____ thing to do, that would mean that I must _____ _____ my true artistic feelings... Then I remembered something which helped me make the decision."

"What was it?"

"My dream. What I always wanted was not fame, nor _____ life style, but movies, movies that do not _____ away from my principles, movies that I would not hesitate to place on the _____ of art... So I apologized to him for not being able to change the ending, explained my reason, and prepared to leave."

"That was not the ending of YOUR story, was it?"

"Fortunately, no. Mr. Watson stopped me and asked me to stay. He said he was deeply impressed by my attitude, and asked me if I wanted to work for him in his newly _____ firm."

"Work for him?"

"Yes. What I didn't know at first was that he was starting a new movie-making company himself, and was _____ directors. He told me that I was the right kind of employee needed in his new company, where integrity was not merely a _____, but a guarantee for profit in the long run."

"Ah, so that was how you started your career as a professional director!"

"Exactly. And that was also how I got the inspiration for this movie: it was _____ to know that honesty would still _____ in modern time!"

A Sharp Interpreter

Please paraphrase the following sentences. Change the sentence structure wherever necessary.

1. The anecdotes that rank-and-file employees tell a visitor tend to reflect the way that their company views its character and its culture.
2. The Internet economy worships at the altar of fast action, fast growth, and fast results. Plenty of companies (and the people who lead them) are prepared to cut a few ethical corners in order to move faster...

3. In some cases, signs of a credibility gap are so severe that they ooze from companies' financial statements—and translate into plummeting stock prices.
4. In some cases, Mann acknowledges, keeping one's word carries extra short-term costs. But wiggling away from the truth can be disastrously expensive in the long run.
5. What's more, in the current culture of hype, companies that undersell their strengths can win remarkable loyalty.
6. By contrast, other business leaders have opportunistically hired what they thought was a winning growth team, making grand promises without building the kind of stability that gets a company through hard times.
7. Perhaps the most common failing of a young, ambitious Internet executive is the tendency to squeeze every possible advantage out of negotiations with an outsider.

A Solid Sentence Constructor

The following is a list of words and expressions you have learnt in the text. Please make a sentence with each of them.

1. to pay off
2. to rescind
3. to plummet
4. unilaterally
5. even-handed
6. make-or-break
7. rank-and-file

A Careful Writer

The following are three groups of words. You are required to study the words in each group carefully and then use them to write a paragraph of your own. Make sure that the paragraphs you have written are grammatical and coherent.

1. hubris   vanquish   alliance   stake   contender

2. dazzling   install   credibility   fraud   binding

3. peril   spree   lore   manipulation   relentless

📖 A Superb Bilingualist

Please translate the following sentences into English using words or expressions provided in the brackets.

1. 米歇尔自己生了孩子以后，才意识到对初为人母的人来说，整天为宝宝大惊小怪是很自然的。(fuss over)
2. 网络社会同样倡导诚实守信，这符合我们的传统价值观。(keep one's word)
3. 在高科技产业中，风险资本投入是企业能否成功的关键因素之一。(venture capital)
4. 要想从展览中尽可能多地获得知识，最好的办法就是参观博物馆之前先查阅相关资料。(the best bet)
5. 那位分销商总想靠说空话和邪门歪道获取利益，真是精明过头了。(distributor, bluster, devious, razor-sharp)
6. 随着人民币升值(appreciation)，中国大学里正在兴起出国留学的新浪潮。(in the making)
7. 按照计划，我们的会谈将在本周内结束。如果你有不同意见，请直接提出来。(wrap up, outright)

Text B

To Lie or Not to Lie?

Anonymous
(Abridged and Edited)

Some fibs benefit others, but Lilliputians teach lesson of societal responsibility.

Those who never lie or cheat can stop reading. Most likely, we all lie in some way or another. Completely honest individuals tell the truth at all times... even when it causes

> **fib** /fib/ *n.* a statement that is not true; a lie about sth. that is not important

discomfort. Honest people speak up when their silence could mislead others. They tell the grocery store checker about his mistake when the error is in their favor.

10   Yet, even extremely honest people might lie for the purpose of convenience—to simplify or speed up conversations. How often do you tell people, "I'm fine" when you're actually not doing so well? Is anyone completely
15 honest?

Dishonesty comes in varying complexities. Obvious forms of dishonesty include perjury and intentional deception. Some people make up stories for shock value. Some lie to hide
20 shameful or embarrassing secrets. They are afraid of what others will think, and the lies become so internalized that it's difficult to stop lying. Yet, blatant fabrication is detrimental to others, society and oneself.

25   Other forms of dishonesty are more subtle because they don't involve outright lies—but they still involve harmful deception:

"I didn't tell the checker he gave me extra change because it makes up for those
30 high prices" or "because I didn't want to cause a commotion and hold up the line." But didn't you hold up the line last week when you were shortchanged or overcharged? Let's face it: Selective honesty has its benefits.

35   However, is that falsely acquired $2 really a benefit? In retrospect, is a guilty conscience worth $2? Is a guilty conscience even worth that $500 you fudged when you did your taxes? Perhaps some of us don't pay attention
40 to our consciences, so guilt is not an issue.

"I have to cheat because this class is graded on a curve, and I know at least 10 people who have seen the exam." If you had the opportunity to view an exam before it is proctored, would you? Even though you may feel a twinge of guilt, would you cast aside
45 honesty and join your cheating classmates? Does academic survival justify dishonesty?

Further, if you decided not to cheat, would you tell the professor about the others? Should we go out of the way to snitch on dishonest individuals? Maybe not. The point is to be responsible for your own honesty and to encourage others to follow your example—not to act as some kind of honesty police officer on a mission.

perjury /ˈpɜːdʒəri/ n. [law] the crime of telling a lie in a court of law
internalize /ɪnˈtɜːnəlaɪz/ v. to make a feeling, an attitude, or a belief part of the way one thinks and behaves
blatant /ˈbleɪtnt/ adj. [disapproving] (of actions that are considered bad) done in an obvious and open way without caring if people object or are shocked
fabrication /ˌfæbrɪˈkeɪʃn/ n. a piece of information or story that someone has invented in order to deceive people
detrimental /ˌdetrɪˈmentl/ adj. harmful
commotion /kəˈməʊʃn/ n. sudden noisy confusion or excitement
retrospect /ˈretrəˌspekt/ n. thinking about a past event or situation, often with a different opinion from what one thought at the time
conscience /ˈkɒnʃəns/ n. the awareness of a moral or ethical aspect to one's conduct together with the urge to prefer right over wrong
fudge /fʌdʒ/ v. to avoid giving clear and accurate information, or a clear answer
curve /kɜːv/ n. line of which no part is straight and which changes direction without angles
proctor /ˈprɒktə/ v. [=invigilate] to watch people while they are taking an exam to make sure that they have everything they need, that they keep to the rules, etc.
twinge /twɪndʒ/ n. a sudden short feeling of pain; a sudden short feeling of an unpleasant emotion
justify /ˈdʒʌstɪˌfaɪ/ v. to demonstrate or prove to be just, right, or valid
snitch /snɪtʃ/ v. [informal, disapproving] to tell parent, teacher, etc. about sth. wrong that another child has done

"I knew the accident was my fault, but I wasn't going to admit it. You're supposed to let the insurance companies work it out." Here, dishonesty does include the withholding of truth because you are personally responsible.

These cases of subtle dishonesty weigh the truth-telling process against its outcome. Whether or not to lie or cheat becomes a question of how it will benefit us: We gain $2 or an A grade.

As dishonesty's boundaries become blurred, we assign value to honesty based on its outcome instead of its intrinsic worth. If the outcome of telling the truth is negative for us, we justify a lie: "It won't hurt anyone." "If I tell the truth, I'm in trouble." We want to protect ourselves from the negative consequences of speaking truth, such as punishment. But the ultimate goal should be to uphold honesty, whether the result suits our fancy, or not.

However, when it involves the feelings of others, honesty can be a brutal choice. In these cases, unlike in those of personal benefit or pain, the outcome can be taken into consideration when you decide to "break the truth." How do you tell your friend that you don't like her new haircut when she asks you? Sometimes there are ways to soften the truth, to deliver it gently and still avoid a lie.

Parents find themselves in this predicament when they want to encourage their children in a particular endeavor. It would be cruel to tell your child he was a disaster in the school play. You might scar him for life and shatter his dream. Parents recognize potential when they "lie" to their children, and this kind of lie is not considered deception. Parents have a nurturing role to fulfill, and a little positive dishonesty will not harm their kids, but rather build self-confidence.

So, there are exceptions to the famous maxim ("Honesty is the best policy"). However, selfish dishonesty is harmful to society. Instances of dishonesty are so pervasive we lose a clear understanding of what constitutes a lie. We change its name to white lie, fib or half-truth. In addition, because lies are second nature to most people, the concept of conscience loses its effect, and we fail to clearly discern our own dishonesty. We rationalize untruths with all sorts of "good reasons."

And the problem with all of this is that when deceit exists on so many planes, and when we, ourselves, partake in it, we question whether or not we can trust others. Trust builds personal, political, casual, business and family relationships. Society's lenient attitude toward dishonesty ultimately breaks down trust. Dishonesty is so commonplace; it is accepted as a normal part of life. In a perfect world, we would be certain that people were telling us the truth. Doubt would not exist. Lilliput, in Jonathan Swift's Gulliver's Travels, comes close to such a world.

The people of Lilliput, Gulliver relates, "look upon fraud as a greater crime than theft ... for they allege that care and vigilance, with a very common understanding, may

---

blur /blə/ *v.* to become less clear

intrinsic /ɪnˈtrɪnzɪk/ *adj.* belonging to or part of the real nature of sth./sb.

predicament /prɪˈdɪkəmənt/ *n.* a difficult or unpleasant situation, especially one where it is difficult to know what to do

scar /skɑr/ *v.* (of an unpleasant experience) to leave sb. with a feeling of sadness or mental pain

shatter /ˈʃætə/ *v.* to cause the destruction or ruin of; destroy

pervasive /pəˈvesɪv/ *adj.* present and perceived everywhere

discern /dɪˈsən/ *v.* to know, recognize or understand sth., especially sth. that is not obvious

partake /pɑrˈtek/ *v.* to take part in an activity

lenient /ˈliniənt/ *adj.* not as strict as expected when punishing sb. or when making sure that rules are obeyed

preserve a man's goods from thieves; but
95 honesty hath no fence against superior cunning."

Lilliputians see fraud, a form of dishonesty, as a far worse transgression against fellow humans than theft, because those who trust are completely vulnerable. They have no way of
100 securing themselves against deceit. To paraphrase Swift, trusting individuals expect that others use language to serve its purpose as a means of communication. Lying defeats language in that it hinders understanding.

105 Thus, honesty is immensely crucial in maintaining trust and communication. Society needs role models to set standards of behavior. Role models are people who remind us to practice honesty, people who aren't afraid to
110 speak up and challenge those who would lie or cheat, people who refuse to sneak into movie theaters—at the risk of exclusion from their friends. We can look for role models in the people we trust. Better yet, we can look to be role models ourselves.

> **allege** /əˈlɛdʒ/ v. to state sth. as a fact but without giving proof
> **vigilance** /ˈvɪdʒələns/ n. alert watchfulness
> **hath** /hæθ/ v. [old use] =has
> **cunning** /ˈkʌnɪŋ/ n. skill in deception
> **transgression** /trænsˈɡrɛʃən/ n. a violation of law, command, or duty
> **hinder** /ˈhɪndə/ v. to make it difficult for sb. to do sth. or sth. to happen

Notes

For some of the terms in the following, no explanation is provided. You are required to explain them by making use of the library, the Internet or whatever sources accessible.

1. Lilliputians and Gulliver's Travels

_____
_____
_____
_____

2. Shock value

The potential of an image, text, or other form of communication to provoke a reaction of disgust, shock, anger, fear, or similar negative emotion.

3. Jonathan Swift (1667–1745)

Anglo-Irish essayist, prose satirist, poet, political, pamphleteer, and cleric; works include *Gulliver's Travels, A Modest Proposal, A Journal to Stella, Drapier's Letters, The Battle of the Books, An Argument Against Abolishing Christianity,* and *A Tale of a Tub,* which were originally published under pseudonyms or anonymously.

Comprehension Questions

Please answer the following questions based on what you have learnt in the text.

1. Under what circumstances might extremely honest people lie?
2. According to the author, in what forms may dishonesty come?
3. What is the author's opinion on dishonesty for the purpose of survival?
4. On what occasions is dishonesty acceptable?
5. What is the significance of honesty for the society in general?
6. In your opinion, what part can "role models" play in promoting honesty?

Writing Practice

It is commonly agreed that, under certain circumstances, people have to tell white lies in order to avoid hurting other people's feelings, which the author of this article calls "exceptions to the famous maxim ('Honesty is the best policy')."

Do you think there is some way in which people can tell the truth while protecting others from its harmful consequences? Write an essay to illustrate how we can strike a balance between the two.

Further Study

This is the end of Unit 11; but you can also gain more knowledge by accessing the following resources.

Rrecommended film: *Jakob the Liar*—In 1944, Jakob, a Jewish shopkeeper in Poland, happened to overhear a German radio broadcast in ghetto headquarters about the movements of the Russian army. He shared this secret with a friend after he went back to the ghetto. One thing led to another, and rumors were created that there was a secret radio in the ghetto. Seizing this chance, Jakob, who was secretly protecting a little Jewish girl, pretended that the radio did exist, and continued to spread among ghetto inhabitants favorable information, in order to keep their hopes alive. The Germans, having learnt about the radio, began to search for the person who ran it. Finally, when Jakob told a German officer that he had only listened to the radio in the headquarters, and that there was no radio at all, he was requested to announce in public that everything was a lie. He was shot for his refusal to make the announcement.

Unit 12

Ambition

Unit Goals

Upon completing the texts in this unit, students should be able to:
- understand the importance of ambition to a person's success;
- know how to bring into full play our God-given gifts and potentials;
- use the noun suffixes correctly to form new words.

Before Reading

Hands-on Activities and Brainstorming

1. Go to the library or surf the Internet for information about such great people as Zhou Enlai, Madam Curie and about how they realized their ambitions. You are encouraged to develop into a presentation what you have found.
2. It's true that some people are more ambitious than others. It is also true that some ambitious people would do anything for the realization of their ambitions. What is your attitude toward ambitious people? Do you think ambition is an essential element to success?

A Glimpse at Words and Expressions

Please read the following sentences. Pay attention to the underlined part in each sentence and to how it is used in the sentence and then decide on its meaning. Write down the meaning in the brackets.

1. In the years since, the company has <u>outgrown</u> one building, then another and the brothers are about to move a third time.   (   )

2. Every buffalo you kill for your family is one less for somebody else's; every acre of land you occupy <u>elbow out</u> somebody else.   (   )

3. For every person consumed with the need to achieve, there's someone content to accept whatever life brings.   (   )

4. People with goals but no energy are the ones who wind up sitting on the couch saying "One day I'm going to build a better mousetrap."   (   )

5. Is the successful musician to whom melody comes naturally more driven than the unsuccessful one who sweats out every note?   (   )

6. Most troubling of all, what about when enough ambition becomes way too much?   (   )

7. They have by no means thrown the curtain all the way back, but they have begun to part it.   (   )

8. The phlegmatic child never really showed much go.   (   )

9. But if it's genes that run the show, what accounts for the Shipps, who didn't bestir themselves until the cusp of adulthood.   (   )

10. It's members of the upper middle class, reasonably safe economically but not so safe that a bad break couldn't spell catastrophe, who are most driven to improve their lot.   (   )

Text A

Ambition: Why Some People Are Most Likely to Succeed

By Jeffrey Kluger
(Abridged and Edited)

You don't get as successful as Gregg and Drew Shipp by accident. Shake hands with the 36-year-old fraternal twins who co-own the sprawling Hi Fi Personal Fitness club in Chicago, and it's clear you're in the presence of people who thrive on their drive. But that wasn't always the case. The twins' father founded the Jovan perfume company, a glamorous business that spun off the kinds of glamorous profits that made it possible for the

---

fraternal /frəˈtɜːnəl/ *adj.* connected with the relationship that exists between brothers
sprawling /ˈsprɔːlɪŋ/ *adj.* spreading in an untidy way
thrive on to enjoy sth. or be successful at sth., especially sth. that other people would not like
glamorous /ˈɡlæmərəs/ *adj.* especially attractive and exciting, and different from ordinary things or people
spin off to happen or to produce sth. as a new or unexpected result of sth. that already exists

Shipps to amble through high school, coast into college and never much worry about getting the rent paid or keeping the fridge filled. But before they graduated, their sense of drift began to trouble them. At about the same time, their father sold off the company, and with it went the cozy billets in adult life that had always served as an emotional backstop for the boys.

That did it. By the time they got out of school, both Shipps had entirely transformed themselves, changing from boys who might have grown up to live off the family's wealth to men consumed with going out and creating their own. "At this point," says Gregg, "I consider myself to be almost maniacally ambitious."

It shows. In 1998 the brothers went into the gym trade. They spotted a modest health club doing a modest business, bought out the owner and transformed the place into a luxury facility where private trainers could reserve space for top-dollar clients. In the years since, the company has outgrown one building, then another, and the brothers are about to move a third time. Gregg, a communications major at college, manages the club's clients, while Drew, a business major, oversees the more hardheaded chore of finance and expansion.

"We're not sitting still," Drew says. "Even now that we're doing twice the business we did at our old place, there's a thirst that needs to be quenched."

Why is that? Why are some people born with a fire in the belly, while others—like the Shipps—need something to get their pilot light lit? And why do others never get the flame of ambition going? Is there a family anywhere that doesn't have its overachievers and underachievers—its Jimmy Carters and Billy Carters, its Jeb Bushes and Neil Bushes—and find itself wondering how they all could have come splashing out of exactly the same gene pool?

Of all the impulses in humanity's behavioral portfolio, ambition—that needs to grab an ever bigger piece of the resource pie before someone else gets it—ought to be one of the most democratically distributed. Nature is a zero-sum game, after all. Every buffalo you kill for your family is one less for somebody else's; every acre of land you occupy elbows out somebody

amble /'æmbəl/ v. to walk at a slow relaxed speed
coast /kost/ v. to be successful at sth. without having to try hard
backstop /'bækstɒp/ n. sb. or sth. providing additional support or protection in case sb. or sth. else fails
consume /kən'sum/ v. to fill somebody's mind or attention fully [often passive]
maniacally /mə'naɪəkəlli/ adv. wildly or violently
hardheaded /'hɑrd'hɛdɪd/ adj. determined and not allowing one's emotions to affect his decisions
quench /kwɛntʃ/ v. to drink so that one no longer feels thirsty
pilot light n. a small flame that burns all the time, for example on a gas boiler, and lights a larger flame when the gas is turned on
gene /dʒin/ n. a unit inside a cell which controls a particular quality in a living thing that has been passed on from its parents
portfolio /pɔrt'foli,o/ n. a thin flat case used for carrying documents, drawings, etc.
zero-sum game n. a situation in which what is gained by one person or group is lost by another person or group
buffalo /'bʌfə,lo/ n. a large animal of the cow family 水牛

else. Given that, the need to get ahqead ought to be hard-wired into all of us equally.

And yet it's not. For every person consumed with the need to achieve, there's someone content to accept whatever life brings. For everyone who chooses the 80-hour workweek, there's someone punching out at 5.

Men and women—so it's said—express ambition differently; so do Americans and Europeans, baby boomers and Gen Xers, the middle class and the well-to-do. Even among the manifestly motivated, there are degrees of ambition.

Not only do we struggle to understand why some people seem to have more ambition than others, but we can't even agree on just what ambition is. "Ambition is an evolutionary product," says anthropologist Edward Lowe at Soka University of America, in Aliso Viejo, Calif. "No matter how social status is defined, there are certain people in every community who aggressively pursue it and others who aren't so aggressive."

Dean Simonton, a psychologist at the University of California, Davis, who studies genius, creativity and eccentricity, believes it's more complicated than that. "Ambition is energy and determination," he says. "But it calls for goals too. People with goals but no energy are the ones who wind up sitting on the couch saying 'One day I'm going to build a better mousetrap.' People with energy but no clear goals just dissipate themselves in one desultory project after the next."

Assuming you've got drive, dreams and skill, is all ambition equal? Is the overworked lawyer on the partner track any more ambitious than the overworked parent on the mommy track? Is the successful musician to whom melody comes naturally more driven than the unsuccessful one who sweats out every note? We may listen to Mozart, but should we applaud Salieri?

Most troubling of all, what about when enough ambition becomes way too much? Grand dreams unmoored from morals are the stuff of tyrants—or at least of Enron. The 16-hour workday filled with high stress and at-the-desk meals is the stuff of burnout and heart attacks. Even among kids, too much ambition quickly starts to do real harm. In a just completed study, anthropologist Peter Demerath of Ohio State University surveyed 600 students at a high-achieving high school where most of the kids are triple-booked with

punch out to record the time one leaves work by putting a card into a special machine
manifestly /ˈmænəˌfestli/ adv. easily seen or understood
anthropologist /ˌænθrəˈpɑlədʒɪst/ n. a person who studies anthropology
eccentricity /ˌɛksɛnˈtrɪsɪti/ n. behavior that one thinks strange or unusual; the quality of being unusual and different from other people
mousetrap /ˈmaʊsˌtræp/ n. a trap with a powerful spring that is used, for example in a house, for catching mice
dissipate /ˈdɪsəˌpet/ v. to waste sth., such as time or money, especially by not planning the best way of using it
desultory /ˈdɛsəlˌtɔri/ adj. going from one thing to another, without a definite plan and without enthusiasm
melody /ˈmɛlədi/ n. a tune, especially the main tune in a piece of music written for several instruments or voices
moor /mʊr/ v. to attach a boat, ship, etc. to a fixed object or to the land with a rope, or to anchor it
burnout /ˈbɜːnˌaʊt/ n. the state of being extremely tired or ill, either physically or mentally, because one has worked too much

advanced-placement courses, sports and after-school jobs. About 70% of them reported that they were starting to feel stress some or all of the time.

Anthropologists, psychologists and others have begun looking more closely at these issues, seeking the roots of ambition in family, culture, gender, genes and more. They have by no means thrown the curtain all the way back, but they have begun to part it. "It's fundamentally human to be prestige conscious," says Soka's Lowe. "It's not enough just to be fed and housed. People want more."

If humans are an ambitious species, it's clear we're not the only one. Many animals are known to signal their ambitious tendencies almost from birth. Even before wolf pups are weaned, they begin sorting themselves out into alphas and all the others. The alphas are quicker, more curious, greedier for space, milk, Mom—and they stay that way for life. Alpha wolves wander widely, breed annually and may live to a geriatric 10 or 11 years old. Lower-ranking wolves enjoy none of these benefits—staying close to home, breeding rarely and usually dying before they're 4.

Humans often report the same kind of temperamental determinism. Families are full of stories of the inexhaustible infant who grew up to be an entrepreneur, the phlegmatic child who never really showed much go. But if it's genes that run the show, what accounts for the Shipps, who didn't bestir themselves until the cusp of adulthood? And what, more tellingly, explains identical twins—precise genetic templates of each other who ought to be temperamentally identical but often exhibit profound differences in the octane of their ambition?

Ongoing studies of identical twins have measured achievement motivation—lab language for ambition—in identical siblings separated at birth, and found that each twin's profile overlaps 30% to 50% of the other's. In genetic terms, that's an awful lot. But that still leaves a great deal that can be determined by experiences in infancy, subsequent upbringing and countless other imponderables.

But even if something as primal as the reproductive impulse wires you one way, it's possible for other things to rewire you completely. Two of the biggest influences on your level of ambition are the family that produced you and the culture that produced

placement /ˈpleɪsmənt/ n. a job often as part of course of study, where one gets some experience of a particular kind of work
pup /pʌp/ n. a young animal of various species
wean /wiːn/ v. to gradually stop feeding a baby or young animal with its mother's milk and start feeding it with solid food
alpha wolf a top-ranking wolf; the leader of a wolf pack
geriatric /ˌdʒeriˈætrɪk/ adj. of or relating to geriatrics or to elderly people
temperamental /ˌtemprəˈmentl/ adj. connected with one's nature and personality
phlegmatic /flegˈmætɪk/ adj. not easily made angry or upset
bestir /bɪˈstɜː/ v. to start doing things after a period during which one has been doing nothing
cusp /kʌsp/ n. a point of transition (as from one historical period to the next)
template /ˈtemplɪt/ n. a thing that is used as a model for producing other similar examples
octane /ˈɒkˌteɪn/ n. same as octane number, a measure of the quality of a petrol
imponderable /ɪmˈpɒndərəbəl/ n. a factor that is difficult or impossible to estimate or assess
primal /ˈpraɪməl/ adj. connected with the earliest origins of life; very basic
wire /waɪə/ v. to control a function in the body by means of a neurological or physiological structure or process

your family.

When measuring ambition, anthropologists divide families into four categories: poor, struggling but getting by, upper middle class, and rich. For members of the first two groups, who are fighting just to keep the electricity on and the phone bill paid, ambition is often a luxury. For the rich, it's often unnecessary. Its members of the upper middle class, reasonably safe economically but not so safe that a bad break couldn't spell catastrophe, who are most driven to improve their lot.

But some societies make you more anxious than others. The U.S. has always been a me-first culture, as befits a nation that grew from a scattering of people on a fat saddle of continent where land was often given away. That have-it-all ethos persists today, even though the resource freebies are long since gone. Other countries came of age differently, with the need to cooperate getting etched into the cultural DNA. The American model has produced wealth, but it has come at a price—with ambition sometimes turning back on the ambitious and consuming them whole.

Ultimately, it's that very flexibility—that multiplicity of possible rewards—that makes dreaming big dreams and pursuing big goals worth all the bother. Ambition is an expensive impulse, one that requires an enormous investment of emotional capital. Like any investment, it can pay off in countless different kinds of coin. The trick, as any good speculator will tell you, is recognizing the riches when they come your way.

| spell /spɛl/ v. to have sth., usually sth. bad, as a result; to mean sth., usually sth. bad |
| catastrophe /kəˈtæstrəfi/ n. an event that causes one person or a group of people personal suffering, or that makes difficulties |
| befit bɪˈfɪt/ v. to be suitable and good enough for sb./sth. |
| ethos /ˈiːˌθɑs/ n. the moral ideas and attitudes that belong to a particular group or society |
| freebie /ˈfriːbi/ n. something that is given to sb. without payment, usually by a company |
| etch /ɛtʃ/ v. to engrave |
| impulse /ˈɪmˌpʌls/ n. something that causes something else to happen or happen more quickly; an impetus |

Better Know More

1. Jeffrey Kluger

Jeffrey Kluger is a senior writer for *TIME*. He was a staff writer for Discover magazine, writing the humor column Light Elements. He also worked as a writer and editor for the *New York Times Business World Magazine*, the *Family Circle* magazine, and *Science Digest*. Kluger joined *TIME* as a contributor in 1996, and was named a senior writer in 1998. He has written a number of cover stories, including reports on the connection between sex and health, the Mars Pathfinder landing, the loss of the shuttle Columbia and the collision aboard the Mir space station. Kluger

was awarded the Whitman Bassow Award by the Overseas Press Club of America in 2002, an award he shared with two other colleagues. The award was given for Best Reporting in any Medium on the international issues of global warming.

2. Jimmy Carter and Billy Carter

Jimmy Carter, born in 1924, was the 39th president of the United States (1977—1981) and was the recipient of the 2002 Nobel Peace Prize, the only U.S. President to have received the Prize after leaving office.

Billy Carter was the younger brother of President Jimmy Carter. With a thirteen-year age difference, Billy spent much of his life in the shadow of his older brother Jimmy. Carter worked for the family business and gradually took over the responsibilities from his older brother as Jimmy began to pursue a career in politics. Carter was known for his outlandish public behavior. For example, he once urinated on an airport runway in full view of the press and dignitaries. After Jimmy took office in 1977, Billy was happy to capitalize on his notoriety as the president's brother. He launched his own beer company that same year, selling what he called Billy Beer, though it was eventually a failed venture. In 1978 and in 1979, Carter visited the country of Libya and received a $220,000 loan from the Libyan government for an oil business deal. Some thought that he was abusing his position as the president's brother and Billy's actions became the subject of a Senate

investigation. The timing of the investigation was incredibly damaging to Jimmy Carter's re-election bid, even though he was never involved in his brother's activities. The whole incident had cast a dark cloud over Jimmy Carter's campaign and may have contributed to his eventual defeat by Ronald Reagan in 1980 election.

3. Jeb Bush and Neil Bush

John Ellis "Jeb" Bush, born on February 11th, 1953, in Midland, Texas, was the 43rd Governor of Florida, as well as the first Republican to be re-elected to that office. Jeb Bush is son of the 41st president of the United States, George Bush, and brother of the 43rd president, George W. Bush.

Neil Mallon Bush, born January 22nd, 1955, is the younger brother of President George W. Bush and Governor Jeb Bush. He worked on his brother George's failed 1978 congressional campaign and helped out with each of his father's campaigns. He was on the board of directors of Silverado Savings and Loan during the 1980s and was a focal point of publicity stemming from the savings and loan crisis (The failure of Silverado cost the federal taxpayers $1 billion). No criminal charges were presented against Bush and a civil action brought against him and the other Silverado directors by the Federal Deposit Insurance Corporation was settled. Bush was fined $50,000 and restricted from future banking activity.

4. Gen Xers

A Gen Xer refers to someone of Generation X, commonly abbreviated to Gen X, the generation born after the Western post-World War II baby boom ended. The term generally includes people born in the 1960s and 70s, ending in the late 1970s to early 80s, usually not later than 1982. The term had also been used in different times and places for various different subcultures or countercultures since the 1950s.

5. Soka University of America (SUA)

It is a private four-year liberal arts college and graduate school located in Aliso Viejo, Orange County, California. Soka is a sister school of the much larger and older Soka University of Japan located in Hachioji, Tokyo. SUA offers undergraduate, graduate and international study abroad programs as part of the tuition. It is also host to the Pacific Basin Research Center and the academic journal *Annals of Scholarship*.

6. Aliso Viejo, Calif

Aliso Viejo is a city in Orange County, California, United States.

7. Enron

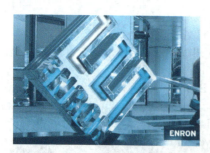

Enron Corporation was an American energy, commodities, and services company based in Houston, Texas. Billed by *Fortune* magazine as "America's Most Innovative Company" for six straight years from 1996 to 2001, the Enron Corporation was one of the world's leading electricity, natural gas, communications, and pulp and paper companies, with claimed revenues of nearly $101 billion in 2000. At the end of 2001, it was revealed that its reported financial condition was sustained substantially by institutionalized, systematic, and creatively planned accounting fraud, known as the "Enron scandal." Enron has since become a popular symbol of willful corporate fraud and corruption.

8. Mozart

Wolfgang Amadeus Mozart (1756—1791), Austrian composer, is considered one of the most brilliant and versatile composers ever. From the age of five, Mozart toured Europe and became widely regarded as a miracle of nature because of his musical gifts as a performer of piano, harpsichord, and organ and as a composer of instrumental and vocal music. He worked in all musical genres of his era, wrote inspired works in each genre, and produced an extraordinary number of compositions, especially considering his short life. By the time Mozart died at age 35, he had completed 41 symphonies, 27 piano concertos, 23 string quartets, 17 piano sonatas, 7 major operas, and numerous works for voice and other instruments. Mozart is among the most enduring popular of European composers and many of his works are part of the standard concert repertoire.

9. Salieri

Italian composer Antonio Salieri (1750—1825) was highly admired in his time. Although Salieri is remembered chiefly for his rivalry with Wolfgang Amadeus Mozart, there is little evidence of any animosity between the two composers. Born in Legnago, Austria, he studied with the Austrian composers Florian Gassmann and Christoph Willibald Gluck and became a court composer in Vienna. His works are primarily operas, church music, and cantatas; his students included the Hungarian Franz Liszt and the Austrian Franz Schubert.

Check Your Understanding

Please answer the following questions based on what you have just learnt in the text.

1. Why do you think the author says "you don't get as successful as Gregg and Drew Shipp by accident" in the first paragraph?
2. What did the brothers do in 1998? How did their career develop after 1998?
3. Why does the author say "nature is a zero-sum game"?
4. What does the author try to convey by quoting "ambition is an evolutionary product" from the anthropologist Edward Lowe?
5. What are the findings of the studies on the achievement motivation of identical siblings separated at birth?
6. What are two of the biggest influences on one's level of ambition?
7. According to the author, what kind of people is most driven to improve their lot?
8. What is the price paid for wealth produced by the American model?
9. Why does the author say that ambition is "like investment"?

A Sip of Word Formation

Noun Suffixes

-*er* (-*or*), -*eer*, -*ist*, and -*ant* are person noun forming suffixes.

1. The suffix -*er* can be seen as closely related to -*ee*, as its derivatives frequently signify entities that are active or volitional participants in an event (e.g. *driver, fighter*). This is, however, only a sub-class of -*er* derivatives, and there is a wide range of forms with quite heterogeneous meanings.

    (1) -*er* (-*or*) frequently signifies entities that are active or volitional participants in an event. That is performers of actions (e.g. *teacher, singer, writer*);

    (2) -*er* (-*or*) signifies instrument nouns (e.g. *blender, mixer, steamer, toaster*);

    (3) -*er* (-*or*) can be used to denote entities associated with an activity (e.g. *diner, lounger, trainer*);

    (4) -*er* is used to create person nouns indicating place of origin or residence (e.g. *Londoner, New Yorker, Highlander, New Englander*);

    (5) the orthographic variant -*or* occurs mainly with Latinate bases ending in /s/ or /t/ (e.g. *conductor, oscillator, compressor*).

2. -*eer* is another person noun forming suffix, whose meaning can be paraphrased as "person who deals in, is concerned with, or has to do with X", as evidenced in forms such as *auctioneer, budgeter, cameleer, mountaineer, pamphleteer*. Many words have a depreciative tinge. The suffix -*eer* is autostressed and attaches almost exclusively to bases ending in a stressed syllable followed by an unstressed syllable.

3. This suffix -*ist* derives nouns denoting persons, mostly from nominal and adjectival bases (e.g. *balloonist, careerist, fantasist, minimalist*). All nouns in -*ism* which denote attitudes, beliefs or theories have potential counterparts in -*ist*. The semantics of -*ist* can be considered underspecified "person having to do with X", with the exact meaning of the derivative being a function of the meaning of the base and further inferencing. Thus, a *balloonist* is someone who ascends in a balloon, a *careerist* is someone who is chiefly interested in her/his career, while a *fundamentalist* is a supporter or follower of fundamentalism.

4. -*ant* forms count nouns referring to persons (often in technical or legal discourse, cf. *applicant, defendant, disclaimant*) or to substances involved in biological, chemical, or physical processes (*attractant, dispersant, etchant, suppressant*). Most bases are verbs of Latinate origin.

Build Your Vocabulary

For each of the following sentences, a word is provided in the brackets. Use the appropriate form of the word to fill in the blank in the sentence, so that the sentence is logical and grammatical.

1. The Taliban are a _____ Islamic group, primarily consisting of Sunni Muslims, who

want to impose a strict Muslim code of behavior on the region. (fundamental)
2. When most people hear the word _____, they think of a confident, fast-talking person standing behind a podium, gavel in hand, chanting "going once, going twice, and sold!" (auction)
3. The board may at any time decide to mandate an independent _____ to evaluate the executive schemes, undertake any research necessary and report to the directors. (consult)
4. After more than a decade of involvement in programs for seriously violent _____, we decided to reassess the empirical evidence underpinning violence rehabilitation in adult. (offend)
5. Prosecutors arrested a _____ yesterday who was said to be at the heart of Reserve Bank of Australia bribery scandal. (racket)
6. The programmers of this online game created a series of tools for the player who wants to log in and role-play as an _____ or just chat with friends while hanging out in a social environment. (entertain)
7. A _____ is a historical term for someone who creates or distributes pamphlets in order to get people to vote for their favorite politician or to articulate a particular political ideology. (pamphlet)
8. Over the last 30 years Slash has cemented himself as one of the most iconic _____ in the history of Rock'N'Roll. His signature sound and unmistakable riffs have helped power some of this generation's most popular rock anthems. (guitar)
9. Social work _____ support social workers in carrying out their duties within the community, hospitals, and other settings such as hostels and residential care homes. (assist)
10. Chemical _____ may be supplied ready to use or may need accurate dilution to provide an appropriate solution. (disinfect)

You'd Like to Be

A Skilled Text Weaver

Fill in the blanks with the words you have learnt in this text, one word for each blank. You are advised to read the text carefully until you have become very familiar with it before starting to work on this task.

FDNY (New York City Fire Department) is a team of _____ comrades whose duty is, as stated in its mission, to protect the lives and property of New York City residents and visitors against a _____ of situations such as fires, public safety and medical emergencies, disasters and terrorist acts. Though _____ and brave even in the face of _____ fire, the firefighters can't stop feeling empty at the _____ loss of their colleagues in lower Manhattan on September 11, 2001. The tragic event has been _____ in everyone's memory. Years later, some firemen are still _____ with grief and sorrow. Luckily, many more have rediscovered their faith and courage. Unlike other people _____ in at 9 and out at 5, the firefighters still have calls to answer, 24/7. But now they do the job with more caution. In recent months, firefighters have attended terrorist-awareness classes. There, they have learned how to respond to nuclear, chemical, and biological threats. "Without proper training, such situation may _____ catastrophe. That is a _____ lesson we learn from 9/11," says 40-year-old John Napolitano of Company Engine 5. FDNY never lacks _____ to continue its unwavering call to protect and serve. The firefighters are once again redefining their _____ of service, bravery, dedication and preparedness.

A Sharp Interpreter

Please paraphrase the following sentences. Change the sentence structure wherever necessary.

1. You don't get as successful as Gregg and Drew Shipp by accident.
2. By the time they got out of school, both Shipps had entirely transformed themselves.
3. Of all the impulses in humanity's behavioral portfolio, ambition—that need to grab an ever bigger piece of the resource pie before someone else gets it—ought to be one of the most democratically distributed.
4. And what, more tellingly, explains identical twins—precise genetic templates of each other who ought to be temperamentally identical but often exhibit profound differences in the octane of their ambition?
5. But even if something as primal as the reproductive impulse wires you one way, it's possible for other things to rewire you completely.
6. The U.S. has always been a me-first culture, as befits a nation that grew from a scattering of people on a fat saddle of continent where land was often given away.

A Solid Sentence Constructor

The following is a list of words and expressions you have learnt in the text. Please make a sentence with each of them.

1. in the presence of
2. impulse
3. to sell off
4. zero-sum game
5. prestige
6. glamorous
7. to spin off
8. profile

A Careful Writer

The following are three groups of words. You are required to study the words in each group carefully and then use them to write a paragraph of your own. Make sure that the paragraphs you have written are grammatical and coherent.

1. pilot light   desultory   coast   be consumed with   catastrophe

2. punch in   glamorous   amble   melody   befit

3. freebie   ambitious   template   sprawling   status quo

A Superb Bilingualist

Please translate the following sentences into English using words or expressions provided in the brackets.

1. 疯牛病(Mad Cow Disease)已经在几个郡蔓延开来,市政府召集了来自各个领域的专家共同研究对策。(a portfolio of)
2. 接下来的一周,阴雨天气将会笼罩整个华北地区,各地防汛形势会进一步吃紧。(dissipate)
3. 朝韩之间的边界冲突极大地改变了两国及其各自盟国间的现状,也使得东亚局势紧张起来。(status quo)
4. 20世纪70年代英国在北海发现石油之后,逐步摆脱了对外国石油的依赖。(wean off)
5. 危机中上任的新董事会成员是一群精明能干的企业家,他们明白必须尽快完成公司的改革与重组才能避免破产的命运。(hard-headed)

6. 有一些人是天生的完美主义者，永远要尽一切可能把事情做得尽善尽美。(temperamental)
7. 演唱会进行到一半时天降大雨，但是雨水无法浇灭乐队和歌迷的热情。(quench)
8. 在全球衰退和国内不稳定的经济状况下，新兴IT企业仍能呈现出持续发展的态势。(thrive)

Text B

The Roots of My Ambition

By Russell Baker
(Abridged and Edited)

My mother, dead now to this world but still roaming free in my mind, wakes me some mornings before daybreak. "If there's one thing I can't stand, it's a quitter."

5   I have heard her say that all my life. Now, lying in bed, coming awake in the dark, I feel the fury of her energy fighting the good-for-nothing idler within me who wants to go back to sleep instead of tackling the
10 brave new day.

Silently I protest: I am not a child anymore I have made something of myself. I am entitled to sleep late.

"Russell, you've got no more initiative
15 than a bump on a log."

She has hounded me with these battle cries since I was a boy in short pants.

"Make something of yourself!"

"Don't be a quitter!"
20 "Have a little ambition."

The civilized man of the world within me scoffs at materialism and strives after success: He has read the philosophers and social critics. He thinks it is vulgar and unworthy to spend
25 one's life pursuing money, power, fame, and...

"Sometimes you act like you're not worth the powder and shot it would take to blow you up with."

Life had been hard for my mother ever since her father died, leaving nothing but debts. The family house was lost, the children scattered. My mother's mother, fatally ill with

quitter /ˈkwɪtə/ n. [often disapproving] a person who gives up easily and does not finish a task he has started

fury /ˈfjʊri/ n. extreme anger that often includes violent behavior

tackle /ˈtækəl/ v. to make a determined effort to deal with a difficult problem or situation

a bump on a log [American informal] not reacting in a useful or helpful way to the activities happening around

hound /haʊnd/ v. to keep following sb. and not leave them alone, especially in order to get sth. from them or ask them questions

scoff /skɒf/ v. to talk about sb./sth. in a way that makes it clear that one thinks they are stupid or ridiculous

vulgar /ˈvʌlgə/ adj. not having or showing good taste; not polite, elegant or well behaved

tubercular /tʊˈbɜːkjələ/ adj. relating to, or covered with tubercles; tuberculate

tubercular infection, fell into a suicidal depression and was institutionalized. My mother, who had just started college, had to quit and look for work.

Then, after five years of marriage and three babies, her husband died in 1930, leaving my mother so poor that she had to give up her baby Audrey for adoption. Maybe the bravest thing she did was give up Audrey, only ten months old, to my Uncle Tom and Aunt Goldie. Uncle Tom, one of my father's brothers, had a good job with the railroad and could give Audrey a comfortable life.

My mother headed off to New Jersey with my other sister and me to take shelter with her brother Allen, poor relatives dependent on his goodness. She eventually found work patching grocers' smocks at ten dollars a week in a laundry.

Mother would have like it better if I could have grown up to be President or a rich businessman, but much as she loved me, she did not deceive herself. Before I was out of primary school, she could see I lacked the gifts for either making millions or winning the love of crowds. After that she began nudging me toward working with words.

Words ran in her family. There seemed to be a word gene that passed down from her maternal grandfather. He was a school-teacher, his daughter Lulie wrote poetry, and his son Charlie became New York correspondent for the Baltimore, Maryland, *Herald*. In the turn-of-the-century American South, still impoverished by the Civil War, words were a way out.

The most spectacular proof was my mother's first cousin Edwin. He was managing editor of the *New York Times*. He had traveled all over Europe, proving that words could take you to places so glorious and so far from the place you came from that your own kin could only gape in wonder and envy. My mother used Edwin as an example of how far a man could go without much talent.

"Edwin James was no smarter than anybody else, and look where he is today," my mother said, and said, and said again, so that I finally grew up thinking Edwin James was a dull clod who had a lucky break. Maybe she felt that way about him, but she was saying something deeper. She was telling me I didn't have to be brilliant to get where Edwin had got to, that the way to get to the top was to work, work, work.

When my mother saw that I might have the word gift, she started trying to make it grow. Though desperately poor, she signed up for a deal that supplied one volume of "World's Greatest Literature" every month at 39 cents a book.

I respected those great writers, but what I read with joy were newspapers. I lapped up every word about monstrous crimes, dreadful accidents and hideous butcheries committed in

---

infection /ɪnˈfɛkʃən/ *n.* the act or process of causing or getting a disease
suicidal /ˌsuːɪˈsaɪdl/ *adj.* people who are suicidal feel that they want to kill themselves
institutionalize /ˌɪnstɪˈtuːʃənəˌlaɪz/ *v.* to send sb. who is not capable of living independently to live in a special house (an institution) especially when it is for a long period of time
patch /pætʃ/ *v.* to cover a hole or a worn place, especially in clothes, with a piece of cloth or other material
smock /smɑk/ *n.* a long loose piece of clothing worn over other clothes to protect them from dirt, etc.
impoverish /ɪmˈpɑvərɪʃ/ *v.* to make sb. poor
kin /kɪn/ *n.* one's family or relatives
gape /ɡep/ *v.* to stare at sb./sth. with one's mouth open because one is shocked or surprised
clod /klɑd/ *n.* [informal] a stupid person
lap up to accept or receive sth. with great enjoyment, without thinking about whether it is good, true or sincere
monstrous /ˈmɑnstrəs/ *adj.* considered to be shocking and unacceptable because it is morally wrong or unfair
dreadful /ˈdrɛdfəl/ *adj.* causing fear or suffering
hideous /ˈhɪdiəs/ *adj.* very ugly or unpleasant
butchery /ˈbʊtʃəri/ *n.* cruel, violent and unnecessary killing

faraway wars. Accounts of murderers dying in the electric chair fascinated me, and I kept close track of last meals ordered by condemned men.

In 1947 I graduated from Johns Hopkins University in Baltimore and learned that the Baltimore Sun needed a police reporter. Two or three classmates at Hopkins also applied for the job. Why I was picked was a mystery. It paid $30 a week. When I complained that was insulting for a college man, my mother refused to sympathize.

"If you work hard at this job," she said, "maybe you can make something of it. Then they'll have to give you a raise."

Seven years later I was assigned by the Sun to cover the White House. For most reporters, being White House correspondent was as close to heaven as you could get. I was 29 years old and puffed up with pride. I went to see my mother's delight while telling her about it. I should have known better.

"Well, Russ," she said, "if you work hard at this White House job, you might be able to make something of yourself."

Onward and upward was the course she set. Small progress was no excuse for feeling satisfied with yourself. People who stopped to pat themselves on the back didn't last long. Even if you got to the top, you'd better not take it easy. "The bigger they come, the harder they fall" was one of her favorite maxims.

During my early years in the newspaper business, I began to entertain childish fantasies of revenge against Cousin Edwin. Wouldn't it be delightful if I became such an outstanding reporter that the Times hired me

---

sympathize /ˈsɪmpəˌθaɪz/ *v.* to feel sorry for sb.; to show that one understands and feels sorry about others' problems

be puffed up with pride to be too full of pride

maxim /ˈmæksɪm/ *n.* a well-known phrase that expresses sth. that is usually true or that people think is a rule for sensible behavior

entertain /ˌentəˈteɪn/ *v.* [formal] to consider or allow oneself to think about an idea, a hope, a feeling, etc.

vengeance /ˈvendʒəns/ *n.* [formal] the act of punishing or harming sb. in return for what they have done to one, one's family or friends

gaudy /ˈɡɔːdi/ *adj.* too brightly colored in a way that lacks taste

burlesque /bɜːˈlesk/ *n.* a performance or piece of writing which tries to make sth. look ridiculous by representing it in a humorous way

size sb. up to form a judgment or an opinion about sb.

---

without knowing I was related to the great Edwin? Wouldn't it be delicious if Edwin himself invited me into his huge office and said, "Tell me something about yourself, young man?" What exquisite vengeance to reply, "I am the only son of your poor cousin Lucy Elizabeth Robinson."

What would one day happen was right out of my wildest childhood fantasy. The Times did come knocking at my door, though Cousin Edwin had departed by the time I arrived. Eventually I would be offered one of the gaudiest prizes in American journalism: a column in the New York Times.

It was not a column meant to convey news, but a writer's column commenting on the news by using different literary forms: essay devices, satire, burlesque, sometimes even fiction. It was proof that my mother had been absolutely right when she sized me up early in life and steered me toward literature.

The column won its share of medals, including a Pulitzer Prize for journalism in 1979. My mother never knew about that. The circuitry of her brain had collapsed the year before, and she was in a nursing home, out of touch with life forevermore.

I can only guess how she'd have responded to news of the Pulitzer. I'm pretty sure she would have said, "That's nice, Buddy. It shows if you buckle down and work hard, you'll be able to make something of yourself one of these days."

In time there would be an attack on the values my mother preached and I have lived by. In the 1960s and 70s, people who admitted to wanting to amount to something were put down as materialists idiotically wasting their lives in the "rat race."

I tried at first to roll with the new age. I decided not to drive my children, as my mother had driven me, with those corrupt old demands that they amount to something.

The new age exalted love, self-gratification and passive Asian philosophies that aimed at helping people resign themselves to the status quo. Much of this seemed preposterous to me, but I conceded that my mother might have turned me into a coarse materialist (one defect in her code was its emphasis on money and position), so I kept my heretical suspicions to myself.

And then, realizing I had failed to fire my own children with ambition, I broke. One evening at dinner, I heard myself shouting, "Don't you want to amount to something?"

The children looked blank. Amount to something? What a strange expression. I could see their thoughts: That isn't Dad yelling. That's those martinis he had before dinner.

It wasn't the gin that was shouting. It was my mother. The gin only gave me the courage to announce to them that yes, by God, I had always believed in success, had always believed that without hard work and self-discipline you could never amount to anything, and didn't deserve to.

It would turn out that the children's bleak school reports did not forebode failure, but a refusal to march to the drumbeat of the

---

circuitry /ˈsəkɪtri/ n. a system of electrical circuits or the equipment that forms this
collapse /kəˈlæps/ v. to fail suddenly or completely
buckle down [informal] to start to do sth. seriously
idiotic /ˌɪdiˈɑtɪk/ adj. very stupid
rat race /ræt res/ [disapproving] the way of life of people living and working in a large city where everyone competes in an aggressive way with each other in order to be more successful, earn more money, etc.
corrupt /kəˈrʌpt/ adj. containing changes or faults, and no longer in the original state
exalt /ɪgˈzɔlt/ v. to praise sb./sth. very much
gratification /ˌɡrætəfɪˈkeʃən/ n. the state of feeling pleasure when sth. goes well for one or when one's desires are satisfied
resign oneself to to accept sth. unpleasant that cannot be changed or avoided
status quo n. the situation as it is now, or as it was before a recent change
preposterous /prɪˈpɑstərəs/ adj. completely unreasonable, especially in a way that is shocking or annoying
concede /kənˈsid/ v. to admit that sth. is true, logical, etc.
coarse /kɔrs,kors/ adj. rude and offensive
defect /ˈdiˌfɛkt/ n. a fault in sth. or in the way it has been made which means that it is not perfect
heretical /həˈrɛtɪkəl/ adj. characterized by, revealing, or approaching departure from established beliefs or standards
amount to sth. v. to be the same as sth., or to have the same effect as sth.
martini /mɑrˈtini/ n. a cocktail made of gin or vodka with vermouth
gin /dʒɪn/ n. an alcoholic drink made from grain flavored with juniper berries
bleak /blik/ adj. (of a situation) not hopeful or encouraging
forebode /fɔrˈbod/ v. to indicate the likelihood of; to portend
drumbeat /ˈdrʌmˌbit/ n. the sound that a beat on a drum makes

ordinary, which should have made me proud. Now they are grown people with children of their own, and we like one another and have good times when we are together.

So it is with a family. We carry the dead generations within us and pass them on to the future aboard our children. This keeps the people of the past alive long after we have taken them to the graveyard.

"If there's one thing I can't stand, Russell, it's a quitter."

Lord, I can hear her still.

Notes

For some of the terms in the following, no explanation is provided. You are required to explain them by making use of the library, the Internet or whatever sources accessible.

1. Russell Baker

Russell Wayne Baker (born August 14th, 1925) is an American Pulitzer Prize-winning writer known for his satirical commentary and self-critical prose, as well as for his autobiography, *Growing Up*. During his long career, Baker was a regular contributor to national periodicals such as *The New York Times Magazine, Sports Illustrated, Saturday Evening Post*, and *McCalls*. As a two-time Pulitzer Prize winner, Baker was the author of the nationally syndicated "Observer" column for the *New York Times* from 1962 to 1998. In addition, the noted journalist, humorist, essayist, and biographer has written or edited seventeen books. In this article, he talks about his old days and the background of his successful career.

2. Baltimore Herald

Baltimore Herald was a monthly newspaper first published in February 1873 by Tom Wash. Smith in Baltimore, Maryland.

3. Johns Hopkins University

_____
_____
_____
_____

4. White House correspondent

A White House correspondent is a journalist or reporter assigned to cover news about President and his administration and other topics concerning US politics.

5. The Baltimore Sun

_____
_____
_____
_____

Comprehension Questions

Please answer the following questions based on what you have learnt in the text.

1. What do you think of the author's mother when she says "if there's one thing I can't stand, it's a quitter"?
2. What was the life of the author's mother like after the death of her father?
3. What does the author mean by "working with words"?
4. Who is Edwin? What is his job? What can his traveling all over Europe prove?
5. After graduation from John Hopkins University, what kind of job did the author begin to do?
6. How did other reporters regard the job of White House correspondent?
7. What kind of column in the *New York Times* was the author offered?
8. What values did Baker's mother preach?
9. Why did the author at first decide to roll with the new age, but then become very angry at his children?
10. What did the children's bleak school reports forebode?

Writing Practice

Study the following essay carefully and write a summary in about 80 words.

  We continue to share with our remotest ancestors the most tangled and evasive attitudes about death, despite the great distance we have come in understanding some of the profound aspects of biology. We have as much distaste for talking about personal death as for thinking about it; it is an indelicacy, like talking in mixed company about venereal disease or abortion in the old days. Death on a grand scale does not bother us in the same special way: we can sit around a dinner table and discuss war, involving 60 million volatilized human deaths, as though we were talking about bad weather; we can watch abrupt bloody death every day, in color, on films and television, without blinking back a tear. It is when the numbers of dead are very small, and very close, that we begin to think in scurrying circles. At the very center of the problem is the naked cold deadness of one's own self, the only reality in nature of which we can have absolute certainty, and it is unmentionable, unthinkable. We may be even less willing to face the issue at first hand than our predecessors because of a secret new hope that maybe it will go away. We like to think, hiding the thought, that with all the marvelous ways in which we seem now to lead nature around by the nose, perhaps we can avoid the central problem if we just become, next year, say, a bit smarter. (excerpt from *The Lives of a Cell*)

Further Study

This is the end of Unit 12; but you can also gain more knowledge by accessing the following resources.

1. Ambition is very important in our life, and it can inspire people to achieve our goals. Visit http://www.about-personal-growth.com/ambition.html for more information about the realization of one's dream. After reading Text B, compare it with Text A to see the similarities and differences between the two articles.

2. Recommended film: *The Emperor's Club*— A dedicated teacher learned some important lessons about himself years after he retired from the classroom in this drama. William Hundert was an instructor at St. Benedict's School for Boys, an exclusive private academy on the East Coast where Hundert drilled his charges on the moral lessons to be learned through the study of Greek and Roman philosophers. Hundert was fond of telling his students, "A man's character is his fate," and he strived to impress upon them the importance of the ordered and examined life. In 1976, however, Hundert found himself with an especially challenging group of students—party-minded Fred Masoudi, introverted Martin Blythe, bright but mischievous Deepak Mehta, and most notably, openly rebellious Sedgewick Bell. Bell, the son of a powerful politician, pointedly run against the current of Hundert's example, questioning the importance of the material, flouting the school's rules, talking out of turn in class, and devoting as much time to his interest in girls as in his studies. However, Hundert saw the possibility of great things in Bell, and encouraged him to take part in the school's annual academic competition for the title of Mr. Julius Caesar. Hundert even went so far as to bend the rules in scoring to favor Bell at the early stages of the contest, but his faith was betrayed when Bell was discovered cheating during the contest finals. Years later, Hundert was reunited with his students, where he learned that the years had taught his students all a great deal about their virtues and weaknesses.

Vocabulary

生词总表

A

a bump on a log		12—B	
a safe bet	n.	11—A	
abode	n.	3—A	
aboveboard	adj.	11—A	
absenteeism	n.	3—B	
absurdity	n.	5—B	
access	n.	8—B	
acclaim	n.	5—A	
accountability	n.	4—B	
accounting	n.	11—A	
accreditation	n.	7—B	
adage	n.	3—B	
adherence	n.	10—A	
adultery	n.	5—B	
adverse	adj.	4—B	
advocate	v.	4—A	
Aeschylus	n.	9—A	
affiliate	n.	4—B	
afflict	v.	1—A	
affluent	adj.	4—B	
agency	n.	4—A	
agenda	n.	8—A	
aggregation	n.	8—B	
agony	n.	10—B	
airstrip	n.	5—B	
albeit	conj.	6—A	
algebra	n.	4—B	
alienate	v.	2—B	
allege	v.	11—B	
allegory	n.	5—B	
alliance	n.	11—A	
ally	n.	10—A	
alpha wolf		12—A	
alternate	v.	3—B	
alternative	n.	6—A	
amble	v.	12—A	
amendment	n.	4—B	
amount to sth.	v.	12—B	
amplify	v.	3—A	
anathema	n.	2—B	
anecdotal	adj.	4—B	
animated	adj.	2—A	
anthropologist	n.	12—A	
anticipate	v.	3—A	
antiquity	n.	9—A	
Apollo	n.	9—A	
appetite	n.	4—A	
apprehend	v.	1—A	
approachable	adj.	7—A	
appropriate	adj.	10—A	
aptitude	n.	5—A	
archbishop	n.	7—A	
assemble	v.	8—B	
assent	v.	1—A	
assessment	n.	8—A	
associated	adj.	7—A	
astride	prep.	1—B	
asunder	adv.	9—B	
Athenian	adj.	9—A	
Auschwitz		10—B	

B

backer	n.	11—A	
backflip	n	2—A	
backstop	n.	12—A	
Baghdad		10—A	
bakery	n.	5—B	
ban	n.	10—A	
bankroll	v.	11—A	
barrier	n.	8—B	
bash	n.	6—B	
be puffed up with pride		12—B	
bedchamber	n.	1—A	
befit	v.	12—A	
behold	v.	1—A	
beneficent	adj.	7—B	
beseech	v.	1—A	
beset	v.	4—A	
besiege	v.	9—A	
bestir	v.	12—A	
bid	v.	1—A	

197

bin Laden		10—A	Cithaeron	n.	9—A
binding	adj.	11—A	civic	adj.	3—B
Birkenau		10—B	clarity	n.	10—A
blasted	adj.	1—B	claustrophobic	adj.	2—B
blatant	adj.	11—B	cleric	n.	7—B
bleak	adj.	12—B	clod	n.	12—B
blossom	v.	5—A	clot	n.	7—B
blue ribbon		7—B	clumsy	adj.	5—B
blur	v.	11—B	coagulation	n.	7—B
blush	v.	1—A	coalition	n.	4—B
bluster	n.	11—A	coarse	adj.	12—B
bombardier	n.	5—B	coast	v.	12—A
bond	v.	6—A	coercion	n.	7—B
bonnet	n.	1—B	cohort	n.	3—A
boost	v.	4—A	coin	v.	7—B
border	n.	10—A	coincidence		8—A
borough	n.	2—B	collage	n.	2—B
boundary	n.	7—B	collapse	v.	12—B
breezy	adj.	2—B	collegiate system		7—A
buckle down		12—B	commit	v.	5—A
buddy	n.	6—A	commotion	n.	11—B
budget	v.	6—A	compelling	adj.	4—B
buffalo	n.	12—A	compensation	n.	7—B
buffer	v.	3—B	competent	adj.	4—A
bureaucracy	n.	4—A	complaisant	adj.	6—B
burlesque		12—B	complemented	adj.	8—B
burnout	n.	12—A	component	n.	10—A
butchery	n.	12—B	comprise	v.	7—B
buzzword	n.	11—A	compromise	v.	9—B
			conceal	v.	10—A
			concede	v.	12—B

C

			conception	n.	8—B
capacity	n.	8—B	concordance	n.	8—B
carom	v.	2—B	concrete	adj.	7—B
cartwheel	n.	2—A	condition	v.	3—A
cast	n.	5—B	confer	v.	3—B
catastrophe	n.	12—A	confidant	n.	2—B
catcall	n.	1—B	confiscate	v.	4—B
chair	v.	7—B	confront	v.	10—B
charm	n.	1—A	confrontation	n.	2—B
chart	v.	3—A	conman	n.	5—B
check sb. out		9—B	conscience	n.	11—B
chew the fat		6—A	consent	v.	1—A
chirp	v.	1—B	conspire	v.	9—B
choke sth. off		9—A	constantly	adv.	2—B
choreograph	n.	2—A	constrain	v.	2—B
chronological	adj.	5—B	constructively	adv.	10—A
circuit	n.	2—A	consume	v.	12—A
circuitous	adj.	9—A	consumption	n.	8—B
circuitry	n.	12—B	contagious	a.	6—A

198

Vocabulary

contemplate	v.	6—A	Delphi	n.	9—A	
contemporary	adj.	7—A	democratic	adj.	10—B	
contend	v.	4—A	demonic	adj.	10—B	
contender	n.	11—A	depict	v.	5—B	
contract	v.	5—A	descendant	n.	10—B	
contrast with		7—A	desecrate	v.	10—B	
convalescence	n.	5—A	desert	v.	5—B	
convention	n.	10—B	designer	n.	3—A	
converge	v.	9—A	desperation	n.	10—B	
coo	v.	2—A	destitute	adj.	3—A	
co-ordination	n.	7—B	desultory	adj.	12—A	
Corinth	n.	9—A	deterioration	n.	8—A	
corporation	n.	7—A	detrimental	adj.	11—B	
correspondence course		7—B	devious	adj.	11—A	
correspondent	n.	5—A	devour	v.	1—A	
corrupt	adj.	12—B	devout	adj.	5—A	
counsel	n.	7—B	dicumarol	n.	7—B	
county	n.	7—A	dignity	n.	10—B	
cover	v.	5—A	dilemma	n.	11—A	
credibility	n.	11—A	dimension	n.	8—B	
Creon	n.	9—A	Dionysus	n.	9—A	
crooked	adj.	1—B	dip	n.	2—B	
crumble	v.	2—A	dire	adj.	9—B	
cue	n.	3—B	discern	v.	11—B	
culprit	n.	9—A	discharge	n.	5—B	
cunning	n.	11—B	disciplined	adj.	5—A	
cup	v.	2—A	disgrace	n.	9—B	
curve	n.	11—B	disillusioned	adj.	6—A	
cushion	v.	6—A	disrupt	v.	10—A	
cusp	n.	12—A	dissipate	v.	12—A	
cynically	adv.	5—B	distort	v.	8—A	
cynicism	n.	11—A	distressed	adj.	6—A	
			distribute	v.	4—A	
D			domestic service	n.	8—A	
			dominate	v.	7—A	
dairy	n.	7—B	doom	v.	6—B	
daring	adj.	6—B	dread	v.	1—A	
Daulia		9—B	dreadful	adj.	12—B	
dazzling	adj.	5—B	drift	v.	4—A	
dazzlingly	adv.	2—B	driveway	n.	2—A	
dead ad	v.	6—A	drop-out	n.	8—A	
debilitating	adj.	3—A	drumbeat	n.	12—B	
decapitation	n.	5—B	dubious	adj.	4—A	
decent	adj.	3—A				
decoration	n.	5—A	**E**			
decouple	v.	3—A				
decry	v.	5—A	eccentricity	n.	12—A	
defect	n.	12—B	ecology	n.	7—B	
deformity	n.	1—A	edict	n.	4—A	
deity	n.	9—A	effects	n.	1—A	

199

elevated	adj.	3—A	feature	v.	5—A
eliminate	v.	10—A	federal	adj.	4—A
emergence	n.	7—A	fellow	adj.	6—A
encompass	v.	9—A	ferocious	adj.	2—A
enforcement	n.	10—B	fib	n.	11—B
enslave	v.	10—B	fictitious	adj.	5—A
entail	v.	6—A	fix	v.	6—A
entertain	v.	12—B	fixated	adj.	3—A
entitle	v.	4—A	flamboyant	adj.	5—A
entrepreneur	n.	11—A	flap	v.	2—B
ephemeral	adj.	3—B	flatter(oneself)	v.	1—A
epicure	n.	3—B	flexibility	n.	4—B
epigraph	n.	5—A	flick	n.	2—B
equalize	v.	4—A	fling	v.	2—B
equivalent	n.	1—B	flushed	adj.	1—B
era	n.	10—B	fodder	n.	9—A
eradicate	v.	6—A	folder	n.	5—B
esteem	v.	1—A	forebode	v.	12—B
etch	v.	12—A	forefront	n.	7—A
ethnicity	n.	8—B	forlorn	adj.	9—A
ethos	n.	12—A	foster	v.	5—A
etiquette	n.	2—B	foyer	n.	5—B
even-handed	adj.	11—A	fragmented	adj.	5—B
ever-present	adj.	8—A	fraternal	adj.	12—A
evict	v.	5—B	fratricide	n.	5—B
evident	adj.	6—A	fraud	n.	11—A
evocation	n.	5—B	freckle	n.	2—A
exaggeration	n.	11—A	freebie	n.	12—A
exalt	v.	12—B	fret	v.	1—A
exasperate	v.	2—A	friction	n.	7—A
exasperated	adj.	9—B	fudge	v.	11—B
excel	v.	2—A	furry	adj.	1—B
execute	v.	7—A	furtively	adv.	2—B
expatriate	adj.	5—A	fury	n.	12—B
expedient	adj.	11—A	fuss	v.	11—A
expendability	n.	2—B			
expiation	n.	9—A	**G**		
explicit	adj.	11—A			
explode	v.	6—A	gaffer	n.	9—A
exploitation	n.	8—A	gait	n.	6—A
exquisite	adj.	7—A	gallant	adj.	1—B
exterminate	v.	10—B	gallop	v.	1—B
exterminator	n.	2—B	gape	v.	12—B
extravagant	adj.	11—A	gaudy	adj.	12—A
extremist	n.	10—B	gender	n.	4—B
F			gene	n.	12—A
			geneticist	n.	3—B
fabrication	n.	11—B	genocide	n.	10—B
faculty	n.	7—B	geriatric	adj.	12—A
fatten	v.	4—A	gin	n.	12—B

glamorous	adj.	12—A	
gleefully	adv.	2—A	
gourmet	n.	2—B	
governance	n.	8—B	
gown	n.	1—A	
gownsman	n.	7—A	
graciously	adv.	6—A	
graduate	n.	7—A	
grandeur	n.	7—A	
gratification	n.	12—B	
grazing	n.	9—B	
Greco-		5—A	
gross	adj.	11—A	
gruesome	adj.	9—A	
grunt	v.	1—B	
guarantee	n.	6—B	
gulp	v.	1—B	

H

hag	n.	1—B	
hail	v.	5—B	
hall of residence		7—A	
handsome	adj.	1—A	
hapless	adj.	9—A	
harbinger	n.	3—B	
hardheaded	adj.	12—A	
hardwired	adj.	3—B	
hasten	v.	1—A	
hath	v.	11—B	
have a point		3—A	
hearten	v.	11—A	
Helios		9—B	
herald	v.	9—A	
heretical	adj.	12—B	
hideous	adj.	12—B	
hinder	v.	11—B	
holocaust	n.	10—B	
hoof	n.	1—B	
hop	v.	1—B	
horrendous	adj.	9—A	
hospitalize	v.	5—A	
hostile	adj.	5—B	
hound	v.	12—B	
hubris	n.	11—A	
hulk	n.	2—B	
hype	n.	11—A	
hypertension	n.	5—A	

I

identify	v.	8—B	
ideological	adj.	10—A	
idiotic	adj.	12—B	
illustrate	v.	8—B	
immortalize	v.	5—A	
immune	adj.	3—B	
impart	v.	4—A	
impede	v.	4—A	
impediment	n.	3—A	
implore	v.	4—A	
imponderable	n.	12—A	
impoverish	v.	12—B	
impulse	n.	12—A	
inadequate	adj.	10—B	
inane	adj.	2—A	
incentive	n.	4—A	
incest	n.	5—B	
incidence	n.	3—A	
incitement	n.	10—B	
index	n.	8—B	
indicator	n.	8—B	
indispensable	adj.	10—A	
infanticide	n.	5—B	
infantry	n.	5—A	
infection	n.	12—B	
infidelity	n.	2—B	
inflation	n.	3—A	
influential	adj.	7—A	
infrastructure	n.	8—A	
ingeniously	adv.	9—A	
inhabit	v.	5—A	
inherent	adj.	4—A	
inherit	v.	3—B	
inhibition	n.	10—B	
initially	adv.	8—A	
initiate	v.	3—B	
innumerable	adj.	4—A	
insane	adj.	5—B	
insomnia	n.	5—B	
install	v.	11—A	
instigate	v.	2—A	
instill	v.	10—A	
institute	n.	7—A	
institutionalize	v.	12—B	
integrate	v.	8—B	
intellectual	n.	5—A	
intensify	v.	6—A	

interloper	n.	2—B	malaria	n.	8—B
internalize	v.	11—B	maniacally	adv.	12—A
interweave	v.	1—A	manifestation	n.	10—B
intimidate	v.	10—A	manifestly	adv.	12—A
intriguing	adj.	3—B	manipulation	n.	11—B
intrinsic	adj.	11—B	martini	n.	12—B
invidious	adj.	2—B	marvelous	adj.	6—B
irrational	adj.	5—B	masochist	n.	2—B
			maternal	adj.	8—B
			maverick	n.	11—A
			maxim	n.	12—B

J

jangle	v.	3—A	meagre	adj.	8—A
Jocasta	n.	9—A	mechanism	n.	8—B
judicial	adj.	8—A	median	n.	3—A
justify	v.	11—B	mega	adj.	3—A
			melody	n.	12—B

K

kin	n.	12—B	mentor	n.	10—B
kit	n.	4—B	Merope	n.	9—A
			mess	n.	5—B
			militarism	n.	5—B
			millennium	n.	8—B
			minimize	v.	3—B
			minimum	n.	8—B

L

Laius	n.	9—A	mistress	n.	1—A
lanky	adj.	2—A	mobilize	v.	8—A
lap up		12—B	monotonous	adj.	5—B
launch	v.	11—A	monstrosity	n.	4—A
legislation	n.	8—A	monstrous	adj.	12—B
legislative	adj.	7—B	moor	v.	12—A
legitimate	adj.	10—A	more often than not		6—B
lengthy	adj.	4—A	morph	v.	2—B
lenient	adj.	11—B	mortality	n.	8—B
licensed	adj.	3—A	mortgage	n.	6—A
lieutenant	n.	5—B	motivate	v.	2—A
light bulb		6—B	mount	v.	5—B
liken	v.	5—A	mousetrap	n.	12—A
linchpin	n.	9—A	musical	adj.	5—A
line up		11—A			
live high on the hog		3—A			
live through		3—A			

N

lockstep	n.	3—A	Nazi		10—B
lodging	n.	7—A	negativity	n.	6—A
longhand	n.	5—B	neo-Nazi		10—B
lore	n.	11—A	neurobiology	n.	3—B
lot	n.	3—A	neurologist	n.	3—B
lurch	v.	9—A	neurosis	n.	2—B
			Nigeria		8—A
			norm	n.	7—A
			norm	n.	8—B

M

make-or-break	adj.	11—A	notable	adj.	7—A

O

numerical	adj.		8—B
nut	n.		1—B
oasis	n.		6—A
obligatory	adj.		4—A
obscure	adj.		10—A
octane	n.		12—A
Oedipus	n.		9—A
offset	v.		6—A
oncology	n.		7—B
ooze	v.		11—A
opportunistic	adj.		11—A
optical	adj.		11—A
oracle	n.		9—A
orient	v.		11—A
originate	v.		10—B
outlook	n.		6—A
outrage	v.		5—B
outreach	n.		7—B
outright	adj.		11—A
outweigh	v.		6—B
overarching	adj.		4—A

P

pad	v.		2—B
parade ground			5—B
paradoxically	adv.		3—A
parochial	adj.		4—B
partake	v.		11—B
participatory	adj.		8—B
pass sb. off as			9—A
patch	v.		12—B
pathetic	adj.		4—A
patio	n.		6—A
patricide	n.		5—B
patriotism	n.		5—A
pedagogical	adj.		4—A
perceive	v.		3—B
perfect	v.		2—A
peril	n.		4—B
perjury	n.		11—B
perpetrate	v.		10—B
perpetuate	v.		4—B
persecution	n.		7—A
persimmon	n.		3—B
persist	v.		8—B
pervasive	adj.		11—B
pestilence	n.		9—B
petite	adj.		2—A
petty	adj.		8—A
phase	n.		11—A
phlegmatic	adj.		12—A
Phocis			9—B
physician	n.		5—A
pilot light	n.		12—A
pine	v.		1—A
pioneering	adj.		7—B
piranha-like	adj.		4—A
placement	n.		12—A
plantation	n.		8—A
plasticity	n.		3—B
playwright	n.		9—A
plot	v.		9—B
plummet	v.		11—A
Polybus	n.		9—A
portent	n.		9—A
portfolio	n.		12—A
posthumous	adj.		5—A
precise	adj.		10—A
precursor	n.		10—B
predicament	n.		11—B
predictor	n.		3—A
preexisting	adj.		2—B
preliminary	adj.		3—B
prep	v.		11—A
preposterous	adj.		12—B
prestige	n.		3—A
prevail	v.		11—A
primal	adj.		12—A
primary	adj.		7—A
primordial	adj.		9—A
priority	n.		2—B
privilege	n.		7—A
proclaim	v.		7—B
proctor	v.		11—B
prolong	v.		6—A
prom	n.		2—A
prop	v.		4—A
prophetic	adj.		5—B
prosperous	adj.		4—A
prostitution	n.		8—A
protagonist	n.		5—A
prune	v.		6—A
pseudonym	n.		5—B
psychotherapist	n.		3—B
pull one's weight			6—A
pun	n.		5—B

203

punch out		12—A
pup	n.	12—A

Q

quadruple	n.	1—B
quantifiable	adj.	8—B
quench	v.	12—A
questionable	adj.	4—A
quitter	n.	12—B
quote	n.	6—B

R

rambunctious	adj.	2—A
rank-and-file	n.	11—A
rat race		12—B
rational	adj.	10—B
razor-sharp	adj.	11—A
realistic	adj.	7—A
reassurance	n.	2—B
rebel	n.	5—A
rebelliousness	n.	5—B
recipe	n.	4—A
reclaim	v.	2—A
recount	v.	5—B
recruit	v.	11—A
recruit	n.	11—A
recuperation	n.	5—B
reference	n.	11—A
regicide	n.	5—B
regime	n.	4—A
regularity	n.	6—B
regulation	n.	5—B
relentless	adj.	3—A
relieve	v.	5—B
remembrance	n.	2—A
render	v.	3—A
renowned	adj.	7—A
repetitious	adj.	5—B
replicate	v.	3—A
representation	n.	8—B
representative	n.	10—A
rescind	v.	11—A
resemble	v.	1—A
resign oneself to		12—B
resort	v.	7—B
resources	n.	6—A
respite	n.	1—A
retention	n.	4—B

retrospect	n.	11—B
retrovirus	n.	7—B
revelation	n.	9—A
revenue	n.	4—A
rewarding	adj.	6—B
riot	v.	7—A
ritzy	adj.	4—A

S

Saddam Hussein	n.	10—A
safari	n.	5—A
sanctuary	n.	6—A
sanity	n.	5—B
satirical	adj.	5—B
Saudi Arabia		10—A
scant	adj.	3—B
scar	v.	11—B
scattered	adj.	7—A
scheme	n.	3—A
schemer	n.	9—A
scoff	v.	12—B
scramble	v.	9—A
scramble	n.	11—A
sector	n.	11—A
seer	n.	9—B
seminar	n.	7—A
sensitivity	n.	4—A
sequel	n.	5—B
shack	n.	1—B
shakeout	n.	11—A
shatter	v.	11—B
Shoa	n.	10—B
shoestring	adj.	4—A
shortchange	v.	4—B
shot	n.	4—A
shrink	n.	2—B
shrub	n.	6—A
sidestep	v.	9—A
siege	n.	9—A
sigh	v.	6—A
singe	v.	9—A
site	n.	8—A
size sb. up		12—B
sketch	n.	5—A
slay	v.	1—A
slum	n.	8—A
smack	v.	1—B
smock	n.	12—B
snitch	v.	11—B

societal	adj.	8—B	supplant	v.	2—B
Sophocles	n.	9—A	surreal	adj.	5—B
sore	n.	1—B	sustainability	n.	8—B
spark	n.	6—A	swamp	n.	4—A
spectrum	n.	2—B	sweeping	adj.	10—A
spell	v.	12—A	sweet clover		7—B
Sphinx	n.	9—A	swingset	n.	2—A
spike	v.	9—A	swoop	v.	11—A
spin	v.	3—B	sympathize	v.	12—B
spin off		12—A	synthesize	v.	7—B
spire	n.	7—A			
spotter	n.	5—A	**T**		
spouse	n.	2—B			
sprawling	adj.	12—A	tacit	adj.	10—A
spree	n.	11—A	tackle	v.	12—B
spur	n.	2—B	Tanzania		8—A
squabble	n.	9—B	taxonomist	n.	2—B
squadron	n.	5—B	Teiresias	n.	9—A
squeeze	v.	11—A	telling	adj.	3—A
stake	n.	11—A	temperamental	adj.	12—A
standpoint	n.	6—A	template	n.	12—A
stark	adj.	3—A	temptation	n.	2—B
startup	n.	11—A	tendency	n.	6—A
statistical	adj.	3—A	tenet	n.	5—A
status quo	n.	12—B	testimony	n.	10—B
statute	n.	7—A	Thebes	n.	9—A
steed	n.	1—B	thinner	n.	7—B
stem cell		7—B	thrive on		12—A
stereotype	n.	4—B	torrent	n.	5—A
stimulate	v.	7—A	toss	v.	5—B
stimulation	n.	2—B	traffick	v.	8—A
stint	n.	5—A	transgression	n.	11—B
stoicism	n.	5—A	transmit	v.	8—A
strain	n.	7—B	treacherous	adj.	1—A
strain	n.	7—A	triumph	v.	11—A
strike	v.	11—A	trough	n.	4—A
stroke	n.	3—B	truism	n.	10—A
stumble	v.	11—A	tubercular	adj.	12—B
stylishly	adv.	2—A	tuck	v.	2—A
stylistic	adj.	5—A	tuition	n	6—A
subdivision	n.	2—A	tutorial system		7—A
subdue	v.	11—A	twinge	n.	11—B
submarine	n.	5—A	tyrannical	adj.	4—A
submissive	adj.	8—A			
subsequent	adj.	5—B	**U**		
suburban	adj.	5—A			
succeed	v.	7—A	unanimous	adj.	10—A
suicidal	adj.	12—B	unappealing	adj.	4—A
Sunday-school lesson		11—A	uncertified	adj.	4—A
superintendent	n.	4—B	undercurrent	n.	11—A

undergraduate	n.	7—A	walking time bomb		6—A
undersell	v.	11—A	Warfarin	n.	7—B
underway	adj.	10—A	wart	n.	1—B
uneasy	adj.	6—A	wean	v.	12—A
uneven	adj.	8—B	weary	adj.	1—A
unilateral	adj.	11—A	well-being	n.	8—B
urge	n.	6—A	whip sb./sth. up		2—B
			whirl	n.	2—B
V			wiggle	v.	11—A
			wire	v.	12—A
vanquish	v.	11—A	Wisconsin		7—B
vantage	n.	9—A	workaholism	n.	2—B
variant	n.	7—B			
vengeance	n.	12—B	**Y**		
vent	v.	6—B			
venture	n.	11—A	yak	n.	1—B
verdict	n.	9—A			
vigilance	n.	11—B	**Z**		
violate	v.	4—B			
vocational	adj.	8—A	zenith	n.	5—A
vulgar	adj.	12—B	zero-sum game	n.	12—A
vulnerability	n.	8—B	Zimbabwe		8—A
W					
wage	v.	10—A			

《英语综合教程》(修订版)第二册

尊敬的老师：

您好！

为了方便您更好地使用本教材，获得最佳教学效果，我们特向使用该书作为教材的教师赠送本教材配套参考资料。如有需要，请完整填写"教师联系表"并加盖所在单位系(院)公章，免费向出版社索取。

北京大学出版社

教 师 联 系

教材名称	《英语综合教程》(修订版)第二册			
姓名：	性别：	职务：		职称：
E-mail：		联系电话：		邮政编码：
供职学校：			所在院系：	(章)
学校地址：				
教学科目与年级：			班级人数：	
通信地址：				

填写完毕后，请将此表邮寄给我们，我们将为您免费寄送本教材配套资料，谢谢！

北京市海淀区成府路205号
北京大学出版社外语编辑部　孙　莹
邮政编码：100871
电子邮箱：sunying_najia@hotmail.com

邮 购 部 电 话：010-62534449
市场营销部电话：010-62750672
外语编辑部电话：010-62754382